Learning
Windows 8

Other Titles by the Same Authors

- Learning PageMaker 7
- Learning 3D Max
- Learning Computer Fundamentals
- Learning Java 7
- Learning Internet & E-mail
- Learning HTML 5
- Learning JavaScript with HTML 5
- Learning Visual Basic 6
- Learning SQL
- Learning Web Designing
- Learning Multimedia
- Learning Networking
- Learning PC Hardware
- Learning Desk Top Publishing
- Learning C
- Learning C++
- Learning Windows XP
- Learning Windows Vista
- Learning Windows 7
- Learning Windows XP, Vista, Office 2007 & Internet & E-mail
- Learning MS Office XP
- Learning MS Access 2003
- Learning MS Excel 2003
- Learning MS Word 2003
- Learning MS Office 2003
- Learning MS Access 2007
- Learning MS Excel 2007
- Learning MS Word 2007
- Learning MS Office 2007
- Learning Tally 9.0
- Learning Dreamweaver CS4
- Learning CorelDRAW X4
- Learning Photoshop CS4
- Learning Flash CS4
- Learning Illustrator CS4
- Learning Microsoft Access 2010
- Learning Microsoft Excel 2010
- Learning Microsoft Word 2010
- Learning Microsoft Office 2010
- Learning AutoCAD 2010
- Learning Dreamweaver CS5
- Learning CorelDraw X5
- Learning Flash CS5
- Learning Illustrator CS5
- Learning Photoshop CS5
- Learning ASP.Net 4.0
- Learning C# 4.0
- Learning ASP.Net and C#.Net
- Learning Tally 9.0 (Hindi)
- Learning Internet & E-mail (Hindi)
- Learning Desk Top Publishing (Hindi)

Learning
Windows 8

Ramesh Bangia
B.Sc., Comp. Sc. (IIT- Delhi)
Formerly Managing Editor, Software Today
Formerly Incharge Computer Centre, Hindustan Copper Ltd., New Delhi

KHANNA BOOK PUBLISHING CO. (P) LTD.

::: *Publisher of Engineering and Computer Books* :::

Head Office : 4C/4344, Ansari Road, Darya Ganj, New Delhi-110002
Phone : 011-23244447/48 **Fax :** 011-23244447
Regd. Office : 1694-95, Nai Sarak, Delhi-110006
Phone : 011-23283211 **Fax :** 011-23256658
E-Mail : contact@khannabooks.com
Website : www.khannabooks.com, www.khannapublishers.com

LEARNING WINDOWS 8
RAMESH BANGIA

ISBN : 978-93-82609-18-6
First Edition : 2013
Reprint : 2014

Published by:
KHANNA BOOK PUBLISHING CO. (P) LTD.
Head Off.: 4C/4344, Ansari Road, Darya Ganj, New Delhi-110 002
Phone: 011-23244447-48 **Fax:** 011-23244447
E-mail: contact@khannabooks.com
Website: www.khannabooks.com, www.khannapublishers.com

Regd. Off: 1694-95, 1st Floor, Nai Sarak, Delhi-110006 (India)
Phone: 011-23283211 **Telefax:** 011-23256658

Printed in India by:
India Book Printers & Binders, Delhi

PREFACE

Learning of a software is both easy and difficult. It depends upto what level you are planning to learn. If you are learning only for the working use, then it is very easy. But, when you try to go deep into it, then you realise how difficult it is to master it.

This book has been written in mind to make you aware of the options available in the software and how they can be used. It is like telling the child about the steps and stairs. You are the one who is to climb the stair. This book will just guide you how to use the stairs.

I am indeed debited to my publishers Khanna Book Publishing Co. Pvt. Ltd. for their suggestions and encouragement given in producing this book.

Suggestions for improvement of the book are indeed welcome.

Author

CONTENTS

CHAPTER 1

Exploring Windows 8

In this chapter you will read about:

- What is Windows 8?
- Online Features of Windows 8.
- Windows 8 Features.
- Upgrading to Windows 8.
- Windows 8 Requirements

What is Windows 8?

Windows 8 is the most recent operating system designed by Microsoft. It introduces a lot of new changes, so if you're thinking of upgrading from a previous version of Windows, you should carefully look at these changes to decide whether upgrading is a good idea.

There have been many different versions of Windows over the years, including Windows 7 (released in 2009) Windows Vista (2006) and Windows XP (2001). While previous versions of Windows mainly ran on desktop and laptop computers, Windows 8 is also designed to run on tablets. Because of this, the interface has been simplified so that it will work with touchscreens.

An operating system manages all of the hardware and software on a computer. Without it, the computer would be useless. To learn more about how operating systems work, check out Understanding Operating Systems and Getting to Know the OS in our Computer Basics tutorial.

How is Windows 8 Different From Earlier Versions?

There are many new features and changes in Windows 8, both small and large. These changes include a redesigned interface, online features, improved security, and more.

Interface Changes

The first thing that you'll notice about Windows 8 is that it looks totally different from previous versions of Windows. The all-new interface includes features like the Start screen, live tiles, and hot corners.

- **Start screen:** The main screen that you'll use is called the Start screen, and it displays all of your apps as tiles. You can personalize your Start screen by changing the color scheme, choosing a background image, and rearranging your tiles.
- **Live tiles:** Some apps use live tiles, which let you see information without even clicking on the app. For example, the Weather app displays the current weather on its tile, and you can click on it to see more details.
- **Hot corners:** You'll navigate through Windows 8 by using hot corners. To use a hot corner, just hover the mouse in the corner of the screen, and it will open a toolbar or tile that you can click. For example, to switch to another open app, you can hover the mouse in the top-left corner and then click. If you're using a tablet, you'll swipe from the left or right instead of using hot corners.
- **Charms bar:** Many of your computer's settings are now found in a toolbar called the Charms bar. You can access it by hovering in the top-right or bottom-right corner of the screen. If you're using a tablet, you can swipe from the right to open the Charms bar.

Online Features in Windows 8

Many people are starting to save their files and other information online (also known as the cloud). One way to do this is with Microsoft's SkyDrive service. Windows 8 is designed to connect seamlessly to SkyDrive, as well as other online services like Facebook and Twitter.

- **Sign in with Microsoft account:** Instead of creating an account on your computer, you can sign in with your free Microsoft account. This will bring all of your SkyDrive files, contacts, and more into your Start screen. You can even sign in to a different computer that has Windows 8, and all of your important files will be there.
- **Social networking features:** You can connect your Facebook, Twitter, and Flickr accounts to Windows 8, allowing you to see your friends' updates directly from your Start screen or from the built-in People app.

Apps on the Start screen

Live tiles

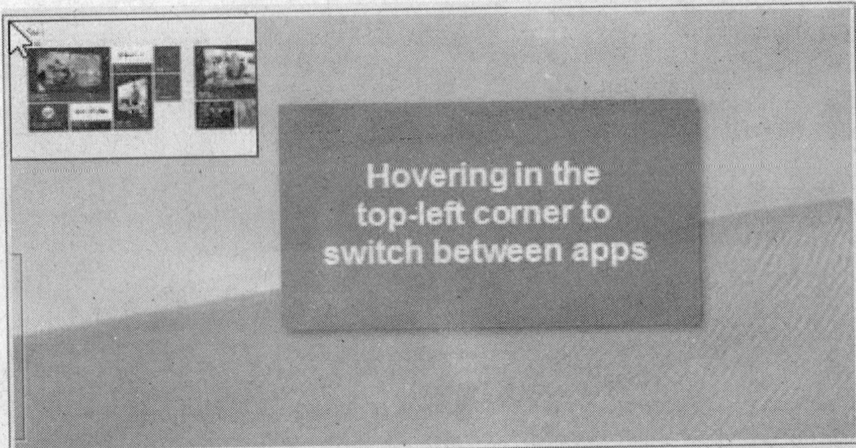

Hot corners

The Charms bar

Other Windows 8 Features

- **Simplified Desktop for increased speed:** Microsoft hasn't removed the Desktop, and you can still use it to manage your files or open many of your existing programs. However, it has removed some of the transparency effects that often caused Windows 7 and Vista to run slowly. The new Desktop should run more smoothly on most computers.

Signing in with a Microsoft account

- **No Start button:** The biggest change to the Desktop is that there is no Start button. In previous versions, the Start button was a very common place to go to launch apps, access settings, or search the computer. Although these features are now accessible from the Start screen, many people may find it disorienting to use Windows without the Start button.

The Desktop no longer has a Start button

- **Improved security:** Windows 8 has a built-in antivirus program called Windows Defender, which can also protect you from other types of malware such as spyware. The built-in Windows Store also helps to keep you and your computer safe by showing you what information each app will have access to. For example, some apps have access to your location, so if you're uncomfortable sharing your location you can decide not to download those apps.

How Will You Use Windows 8?

Since Windows 8 is so different, it will probably change the way you use your computer. This may take a while to get used to, but keep in mind that these changes are designed to make your computing experience easier and smoother.

For example, if you've used previous versions of Windows, you may be accustomed to launching programs by clicking on the Start button.

In Windows 8, you'll use the Start screen instead. On the other hand, you'll still be able to use the Desktop view to organize your files and folders, and to open older programs.

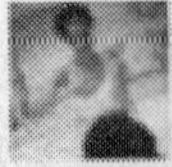

The People app

Most people will have to use both the Start screen and the Desktop, depending on the task. You'll probably have to switch back and forth, which may be disorienting at first.

However, if you mainly use your computer to browse the web, you may spend almost all of your time in the Start screen.

Should You Upgrade to Windows 8?

As you can see, Windows 8 is a big change from previous versions of Windows. It's not just a new version with new features — in many ways, it's a different operating system.

This app has permission to use:
Your location
Your Internet connection

An app that has access to your location and internet connection

If you don't like the idea of changing the way you use your computer, you may prefer to stick with your current version, or upgrade to Windows 7. But if you like the new features that you've seen so far, then you may find that Windows 8 offers an easier and more enjoyable experience.

In the next lesson, we'll cover some of the information you'll need to know before you upgrade, including different editions of Windows 8 and the hardware requirements.

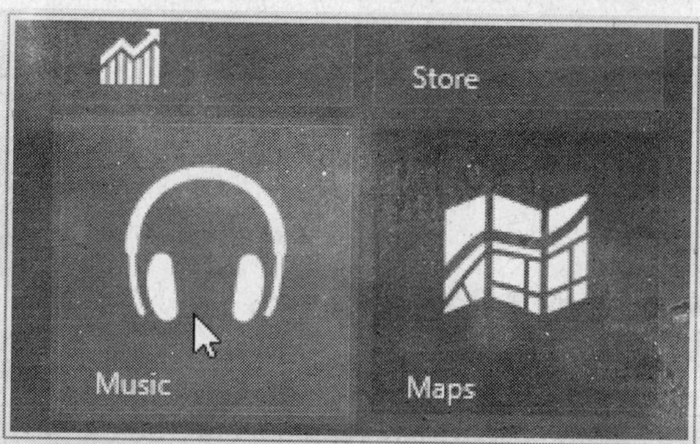

Launching an app from the Start screen

Upgrading to Windows 8

Now that you've seen some of the new features that Windows 8 has to offer, you'll need to decide whether you should upgrade an existing computer, or buy a new computer or tablet that has Windows 8 pre-installed.

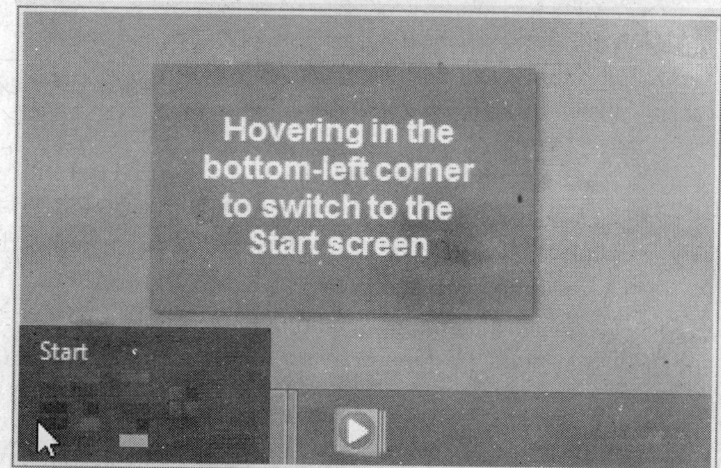

Switching from the Desktop to the Start screen

Windows 8 Editions and Pricing

There are three main editions of Windows 8:

- **Windows 8:** This is the standard edition, and it will run on desktops, laptops, and some tablets.
- **Windows 8 Pro:** This gives you all of the features of Windows 8, as well as some extra features intended for advanced users and businesses. For example, people who need more security can use BitLocker to encrypt their files.
- **Windows RT:** This is the edition that most tablets will have. It may also be used by some budget laptops and netbooks. Windows RT comes pre-installed with a version of Microsoft Office that is optimized for touchscreens.

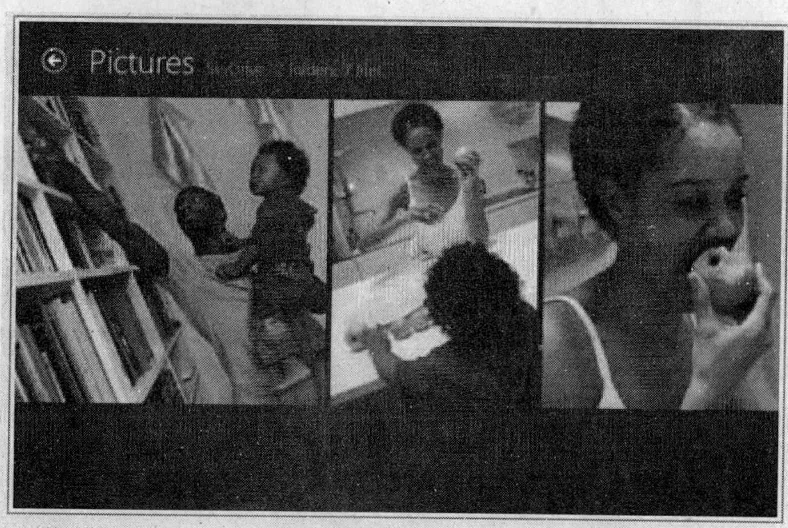

Windows 8

Windows 8 Tablets

If you want to use Windows 8 on a tablet, you'll need to buy a tablet that has Windows 8 pre-installed, such as the Microsoft Surface. The Surface comes in two versions: A cheaper version that runs Windows RT, and a more powerful version that runs Windows 8 Pro. Other companies are expected to release Windows 8 tablets over the next few months.

Microsoft Surface

Windows 8 Requirements

Before you upgrade to Windows 8, it's important to make sure your computer meets the minimum hardware requirements. Below are the requirements that Microsoft has given:

- 1 GHz (gigahertz) processor or faster. Your processor will either be 32 bits or 64 bits, and 64-bit processors will have stricter hardware requirements (see below).
- 1 GB (gigabyte) RAM (32-bit), or 2 GB RAM (64-bit).
- 16 GB available hard disk space (32-bit) or 20 GB (64-bit).
- DirectX 9 graphics device with WDDM 1.0 or higher driver.
- A screen resolution of at least 1024x768 pixels.

Note that these are the minimum requirements. If you use your computer for gaming or other demanding apps, you may need a faster processor, more RAM, or a more powerful graphics card.

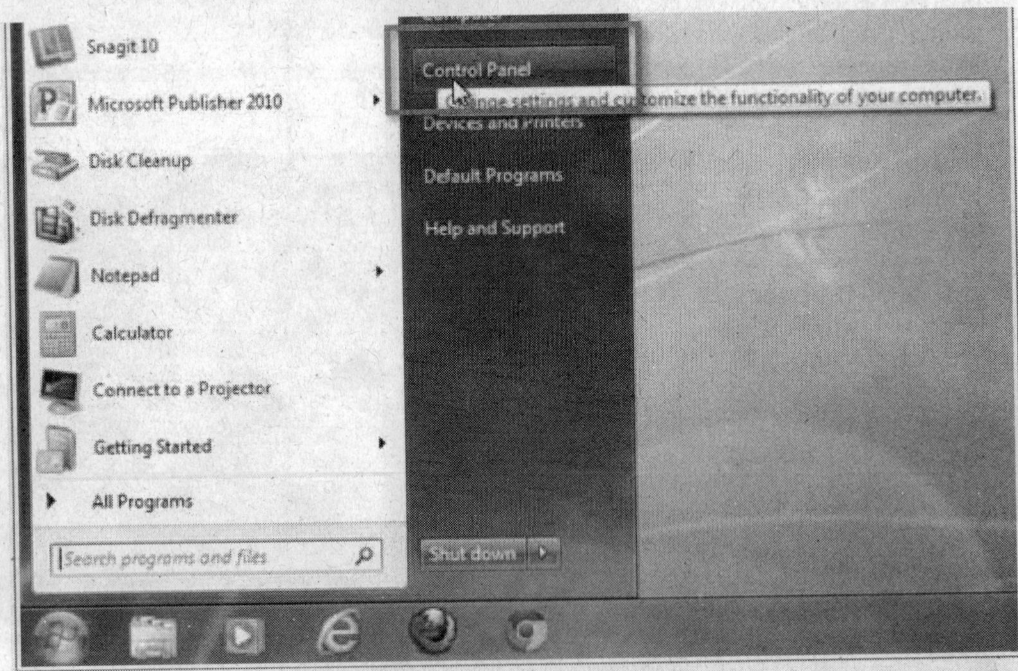

Opening the Control Panel in Windows 7

The good news is that Windows 8 has the same requirements as Windows 7, so if you're upgrading from Windows 7, you'll probably have no problems with Windows 8. On the other hand, if you want to upgrade from Vista or XP, you should check your computer's system information to see if it meets the requirements.

To View Information About Your Computer:

To see if your computer meets the requirements for Windows 8, you can view information about your computer by going to the Control Panel.

- Click on the Start button and select Control Panel.
- Click System and Security.
- Click System.
- You will now be able to see information about your computer's processor, RAM, and more.

Software Compatibility

In order for software to work, it has to be compatible with the operating system. Therefore, you may not be able to use all of your existing software if you switch to a different operating system. Before you upgrade to Windows 8, ask yourself if there is any software on your computer that you can't do without - and then do some research to find out if it is compatible.

If you are upgrading from Windows 7 or Vista, most of your apps should still work. However, if you're using an older version like Windows XP, there's a good chance some of your apps will not be compatible with Windows 8. A simple Google search will often be enough to tell if an app will be compatible in Windows 8.

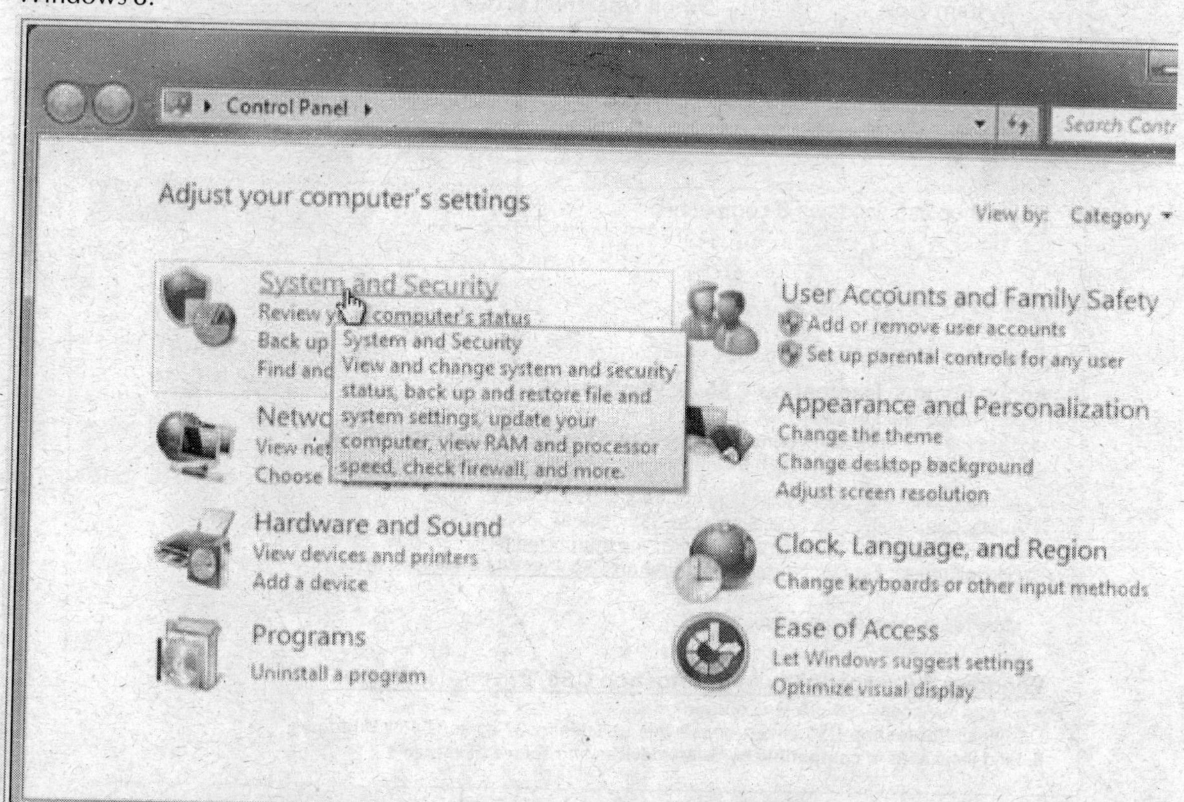

Clicking System and Security

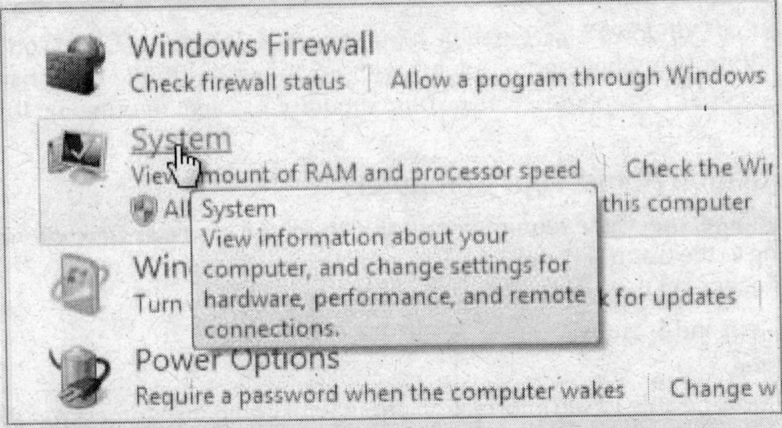

Clicking System

System

Rating:	5.4 Windows Experience Index
Processor:	Intel(R) Core(TM) i5-2400 CPU @ 3.10GHz 3.10 GHz
Installed memory (RAM):	2.00 GB
System type:	32-bit Operating System
Pen and Touch:	No Pen or Touch Input is available for this Display

Viewing system info

photoshop cs5 windows 8 compatible

About 54,700,000 results (0.29 seconds)

Adobe Forums: **Photoshop CS5** on **Windows 8**
forums.adobe.com/thread/973006
Mar 8, 2012 – I just installed **Windows 8**, and while it was very confusing I accidently deleted all of my programmes (I got confused with what the Reset Tab ...

Adobe Community: Do CS6 files run in **CS5**/5.5 - Sep 7, 2012
Adobe Community: CS6 beta along side **CS5** - Mar 26, 2012
Adobe Community: Which Graphics Cards are **supported** for ... - Mar 25, 2012
Adobe Forums: For Fun I Installed **Photoshop CS5**.1 on **Windows 8** - Sep 15, 2011
More results from forums.adobe.com »

Windows 8 Compatibility for **Photoshop CS5**: Drivers, Updates ...
www.microsoft.com/.../**windows**/**compatibility**/.../...
Download **Photoshop CS5** drivers or software updates for 32-bit and 64-bit **Windows 8**. Find thousands of **compatible** hardware devices and software programs.

Searching the web for compatibility info

CHAPTER 2

Getting Started with Windows 8

In this chapter you will read about:

- What is Windows 8?
- Online Features of Windows 8.
- Windows 8 Features.
- Upgrading to Windows 8.
- Windows 8 Requirements

Introduction

Windows 8 can be confusing at first, since the interface has changed so much. You'll need to know how to navigate the Start screen as well as the Desktop. Although the Desktop looks very similar to previous versions of Windows, it has one major change: The Start menu has been removed.

To Sign In to Windows 8:

When you're setting up Windows 8, it will require you to create an account name and password that you will use to sign in. You can also create additional accounts, and you'll have the option of associating each one with a Microsoft account.

- Click anywhere on the lock screen to unlock the computer.
- Your user account name and picture will appear. Type your password and then press Enter to sign in. Alternatively, you can press the back arrow to select a different user.
- The Start screen will appear.

Clicking the lock screen

Navigating Windows 8

There are several ways to navigate through Windows 8, including hot corners, keyboard shortcuts, and gestures if you're using a tablet.

Using Hot Corners

Whether you're in the Start screen or the Desktop, you can navigate through Windows 8 by using hot

The sign-in screen

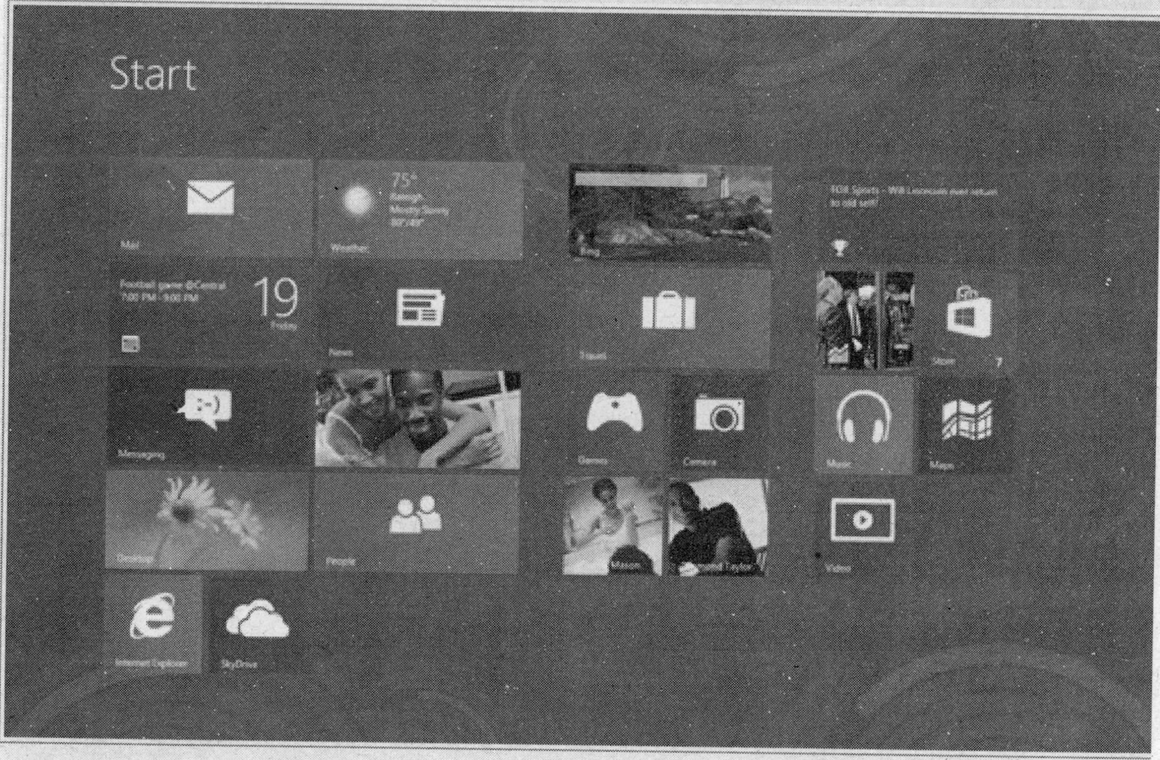

The Start screen

corners. To use a hot corner, just hover the mouse in the corner of the screen, and it will open a toolbar or tile that you can click. Each corner performs a different task:

- Lower left: When you're using an app, you can click in the lower-left corner to switch back to the Start screen.

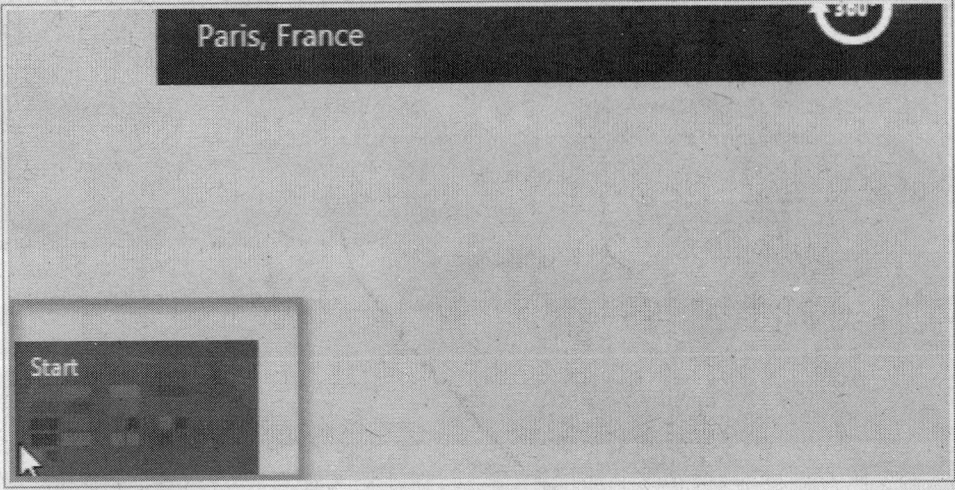

Clicking in the lower-left corner

- Upper left: If you click in the upper-left corner, it will switch to the previous app that you were using.

Clicking in the upper-left corner

- Upper right or lower right: You can hover the mouse in the upper-right or lower-right corner to open the Charms bar, which you'll use to adjust your computer's settings, manage printers, and more.

If you have several apps open, you can switch between them by hovering the mouse in the upper-left corner and then moving the mouse down. This displays a list of all of your open apps, and you can click the desired app to switch to it.

Navigating on a Tablet

If you have a Windows 8 tablet, you can navigate by using swipe gestures instead of hot corners:

- Swipe in from left edge lets you switch to a different open app.
- Swipe in from right edge opens the Charms bar.

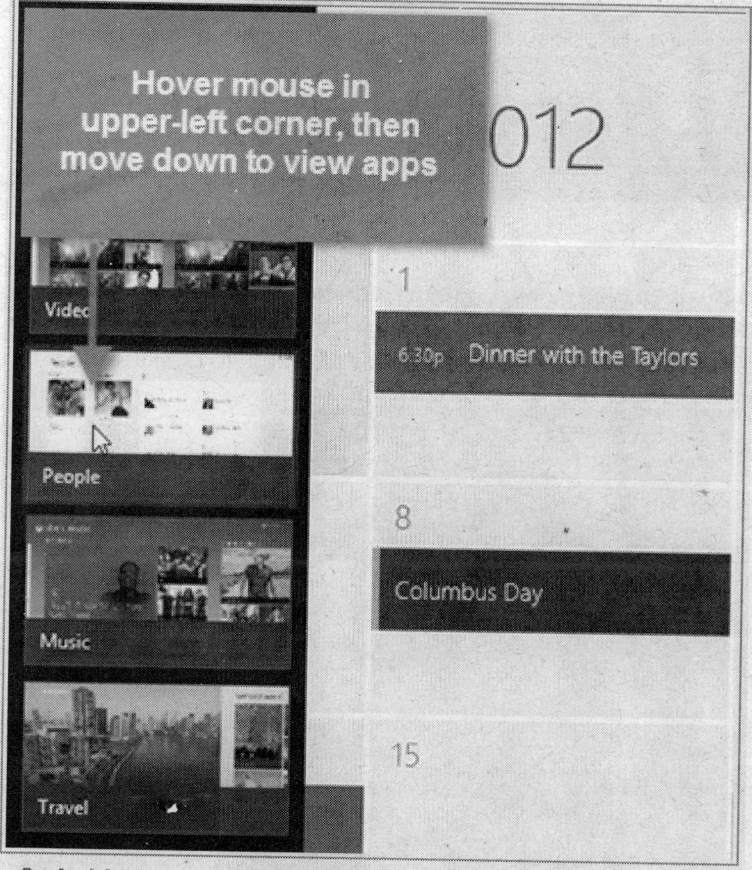

Switching to a different app

Hovering in the lower-right corner

Using Keyboard Shortcuts to Navigate

Windows 8 has several keyboard shortcuts that you can use to navigate more easily:

- **Alt + Tab:** You can hold down the Alt key and then press Tab one or more times to switch between your open apps. This feature is called Flip, and it works in both Desktop view and the Start screen.

Alt+Tab

- **Windows:** When you have an app open, you can press the Windows key to switch to the Start screen. This shortcut also lets you switch back to the Start screen when you are in Desktop view.
- **Windows + D:** You can hold down the Windows key and press D to switch to Desktop view.

Windows key

The Charms Bar

The Charms bar is a toolbar that lets you access your computer's settings, along with other options. You can access the Charms bar by hovering the mouse in the top-right or bottom-right corner.

Windows+D

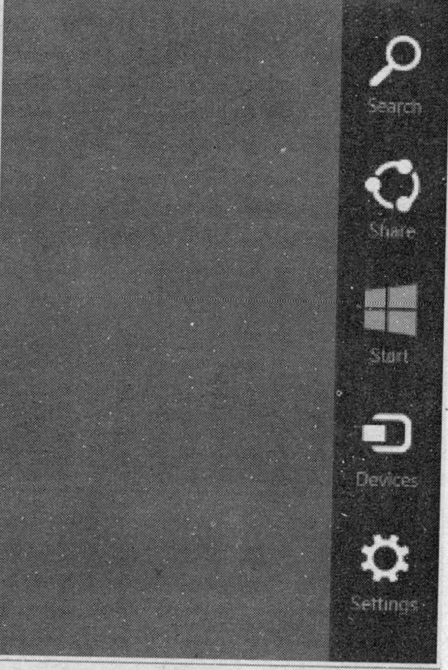

The Charms bar

Charms

The Charms bar contains several icons, which are called charms, and each one contains different options:

- **Search charm Search:** The Search charm lets you find apps, files, or settings on your computer. However, a simpler way to search is to go to the Start screen and type the name of the file or app that you're looking for.
- **Search charm Share:** The Share charm is basically a copy and paste feature that is designed to be as convenient as possible. It allows you to "copy" information (such as a photo or web address) and "paste" it into another app. For example, if you're viewing a photo in the Photos app, you can share it with the SkyDrive app, which will upload the photo to your SkyDrive. If you're reading an article online, you can share the address with the Email app, which lets you email the article to a friend.

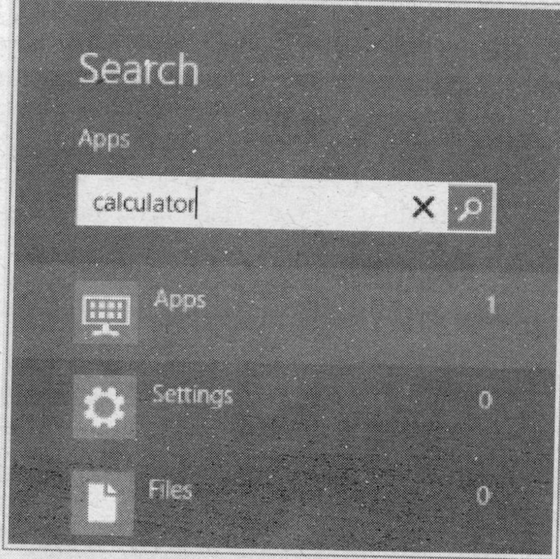

Searching for an app

- **Search charm Start:** This switches to the Start screen. If you're already on the Start screen, it will open the most recent app.
- **Search charm Devices:** This shows any hardware devices that are connected to your computer, such as printers or monitors.
- **Search charm Settings:** This lets you access general settings for your computer, as well as settings for the app you're currently viewing. For example, if you're in Internet Explorer, you can go to the Settings charm to access your Internet Options.

Using the Share charm to upload a photo to SkyDrive

Coping Without the Start Menu

One of the biggest complaints about Windows 8 is that it doesn't have a Start menu. The Start menu was a very important feature in previous versions of Windows, as it was used to launch apps, search for files, open the Control Panel, and shut down the computer. You can still do all of these things in Windows 8, but they're now found in different places.

To Launch an App:

There are several ways to open an app in Windows 8:

- Click the app icon on the taskbar.
- Double-click the app shortcut on the Desktop.
- Click the app tile in the Start screen.

To view all of your apps, right-click the Start screen background and select All apps.

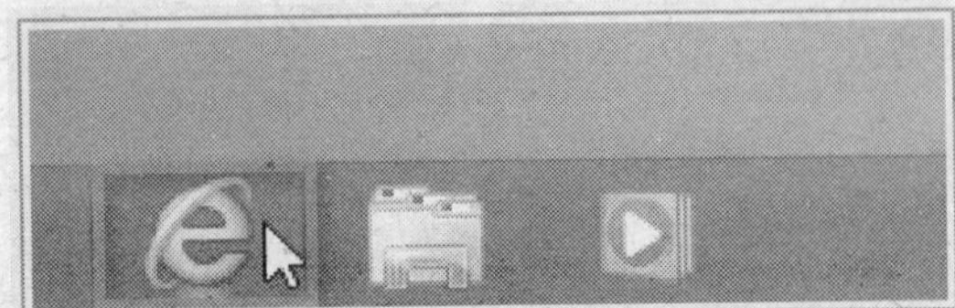

Opening an app from the taskbar

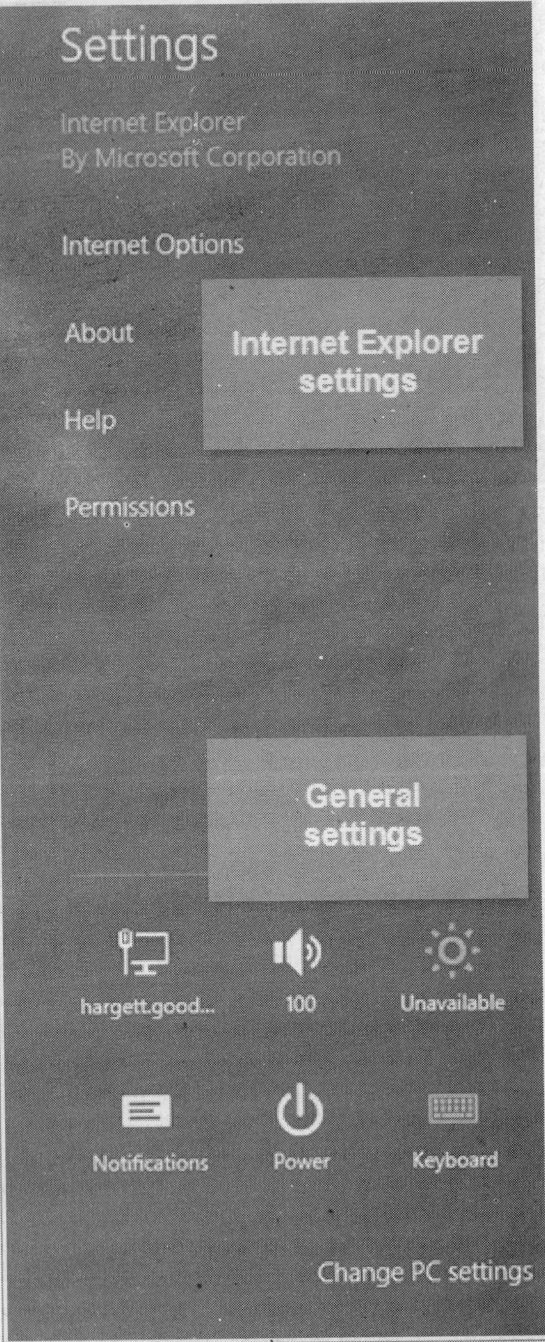

Viewing settings in Internet Explorer

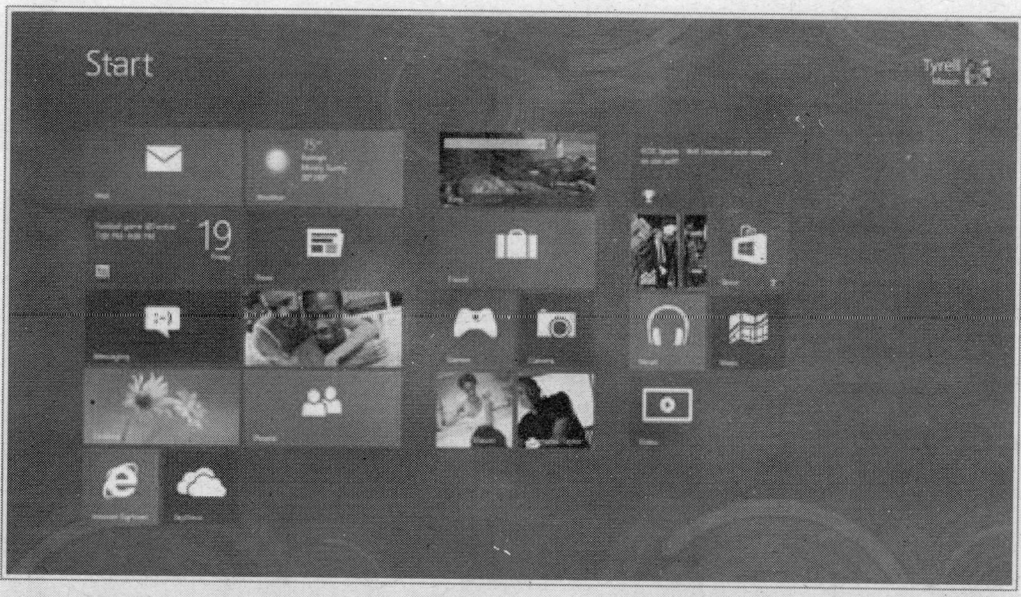

The Start screen

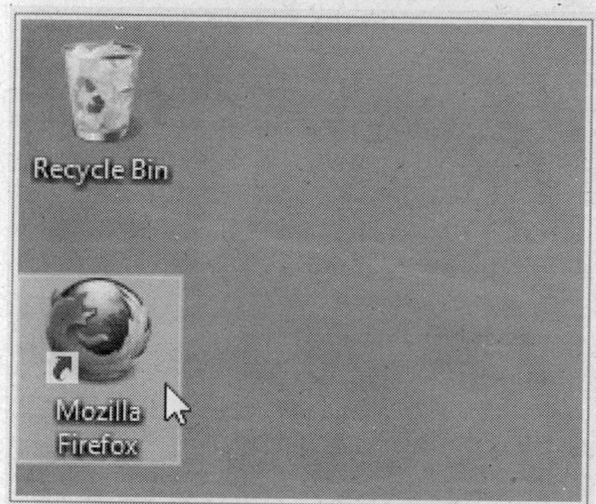

Opening an app from a shortcut

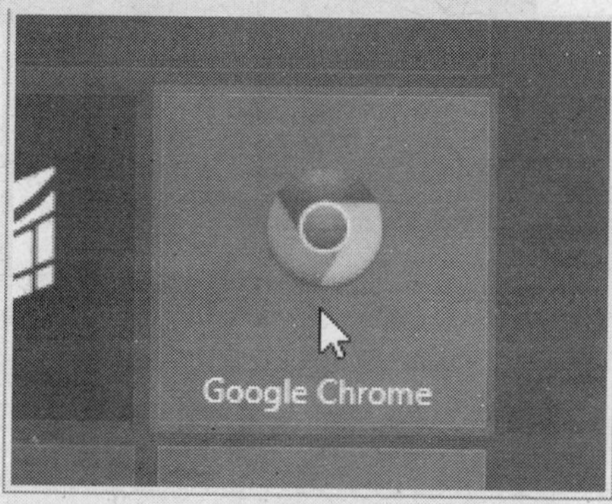

Opening an app from the Start scre

Clicking the All apps button

To Search for a File or App:

- Press the Windows key to switch to the Start screen, and then type what you're looking for. Your search results will instantly appear on the left side of the screen, and search options will appear on the right.

To Open the Control Panel:

- From the Desktop view, hover the mouse in the lower-right corner to access the Charms bar, then select Settings.
- Locate and select Control Panel from the Settings Pane.

Searching for the Calculator app

- The Control Panel will appear. You can then select the desired setting to change it.

To Shut Down Your Computer:

- Hover the mouse in the lower-right corner to access the Charms bar, then select Settings.
- Click Power and select Shut down.

Working with Start Screen Apps

Start screen apps are different from the "classic" Windows apps you may be used to. Apps fill the entire screen instead of opening in a window. However, you can still multitask by opening two apps side-by-side.

To Open an App:

- On the Start screen, locate and click the app that you want to open.
- The app will open and fill the entire screen.

The Settings charm

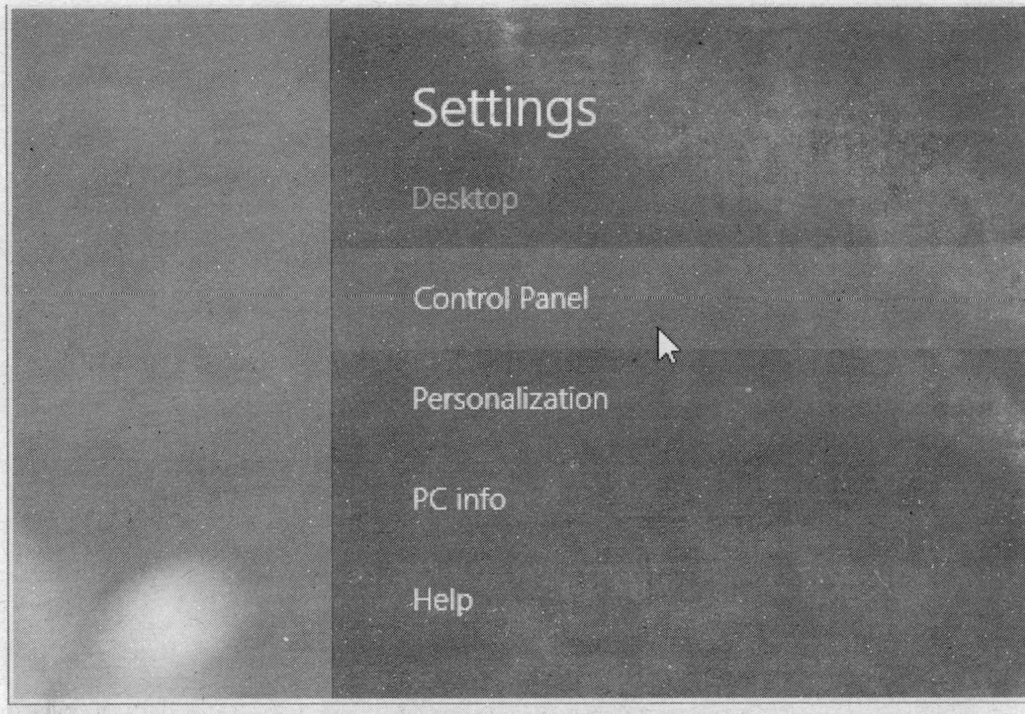

Clicking Control Panel

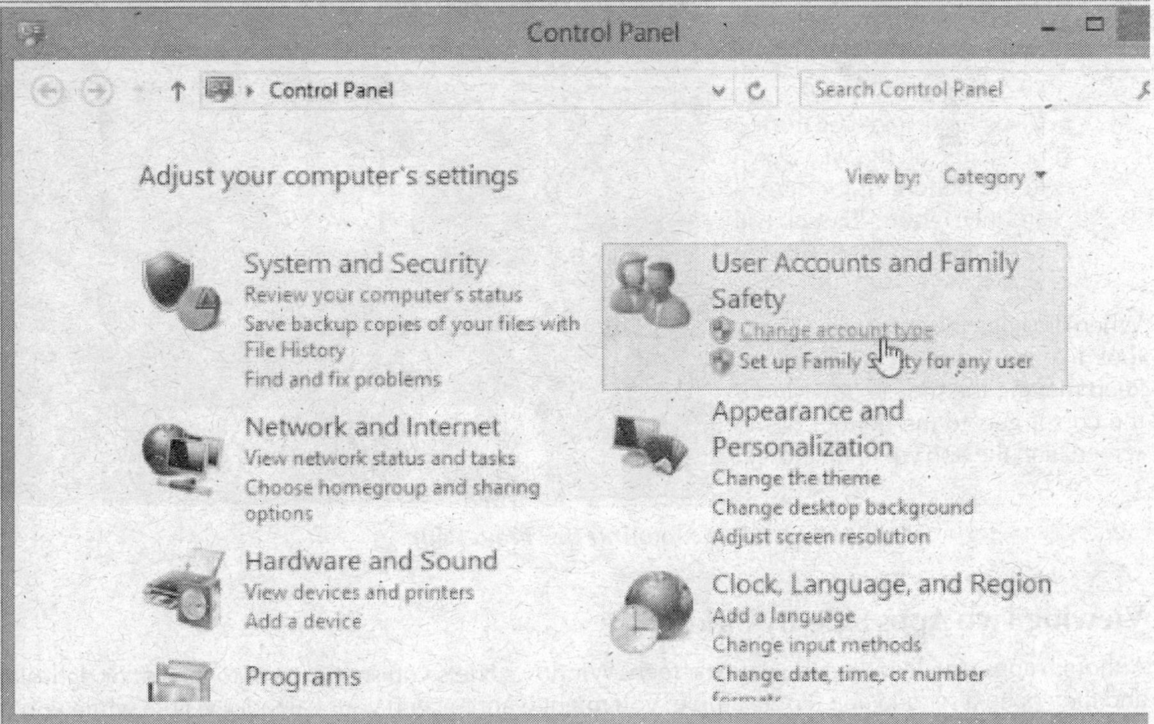

The Control Panel

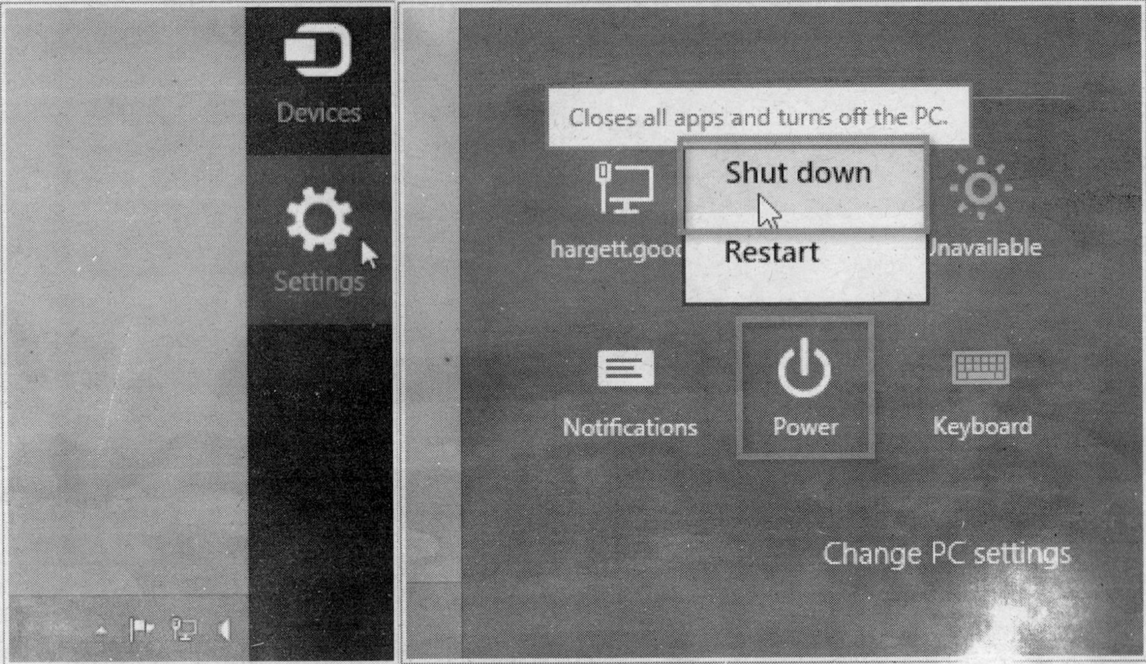

The Settings charm *Shutting down the computer*

To Close an App:

- Hover the mouse at the top of the app. The cursor will change to a hand icon.
- Click, hold, and drag the top of the app all the way down to the bottom of the screen and then release. The app will close, and you'll return to the Start screen.

When dragging the app down, it may look like it's "stuck." However, just keep moving the mouse down until the cursor gets to the bottom of the screen, and the app will then close.

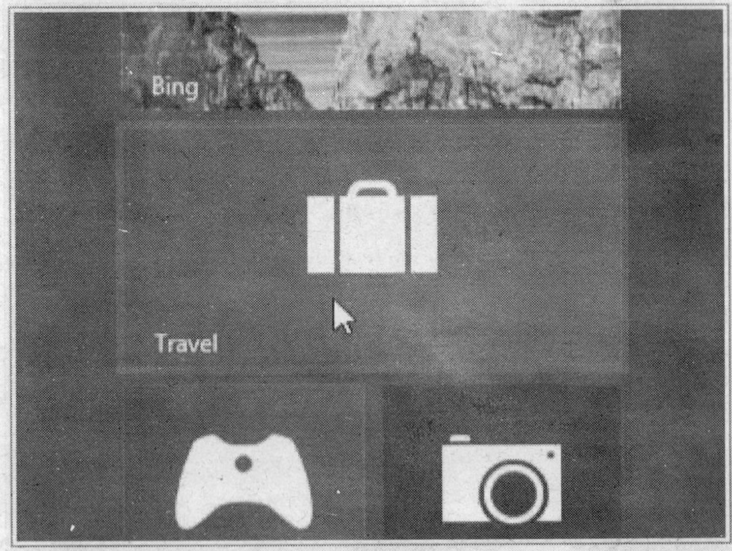

Opening the Travel app

Viewing Two Apps Side-By-Side

Although apps usually fill up the entire screen, Windows 8 lets you snap an app to the left or right side and then open a second app. For example, you might want to keep your calendar visible while you're using another app.

The Travel app

The hand icon

To View Two Apps Side-By-Side:

- From the Start screen, click on the first app to open it.
- Click, hold, and drag the top of the app all the way to the right or left side of the screen.

Closing an app

- Release the mouse, and the app will snap to the side of the screen. You cannot change the size of the snapped app.
- Click anywhere in the empty part of the screen to return to the Start screen.
- Click the second app to open it
- Both apps will now appear side-by-side.

Opening the Calendar app

Snapping is designed to work with wide-screen monitors. You will need a screen resolution of at least 1366x768 pixels to use this feature.

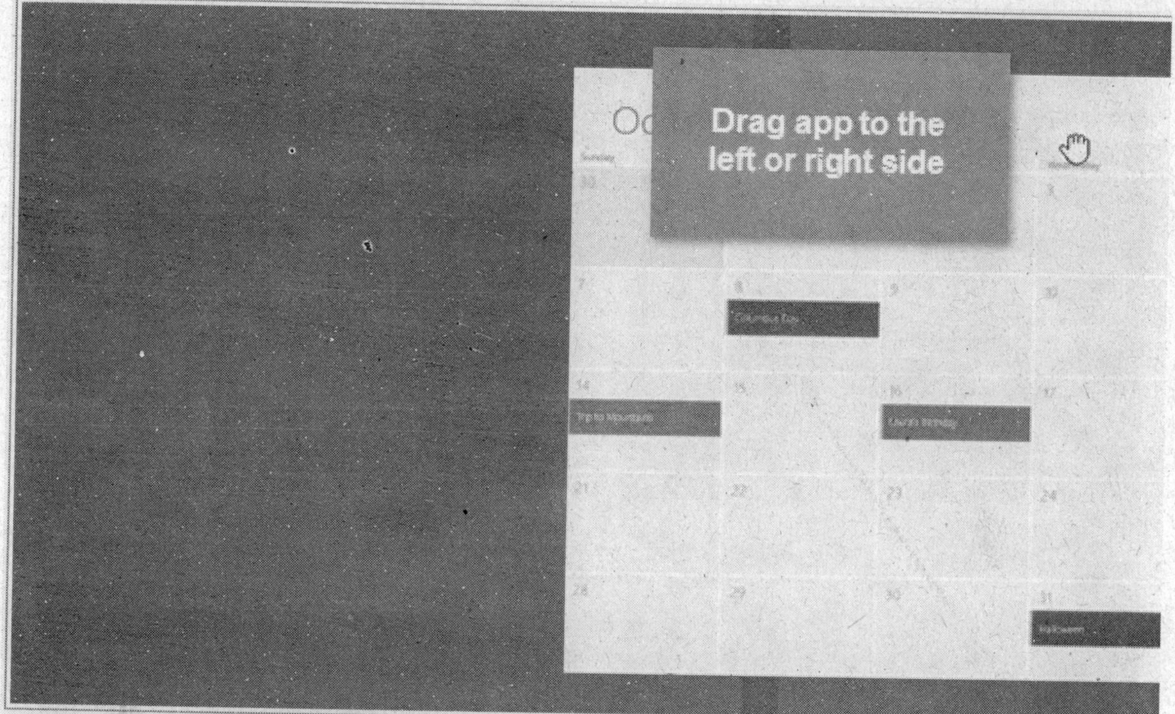

Snapping to the right side of the screen

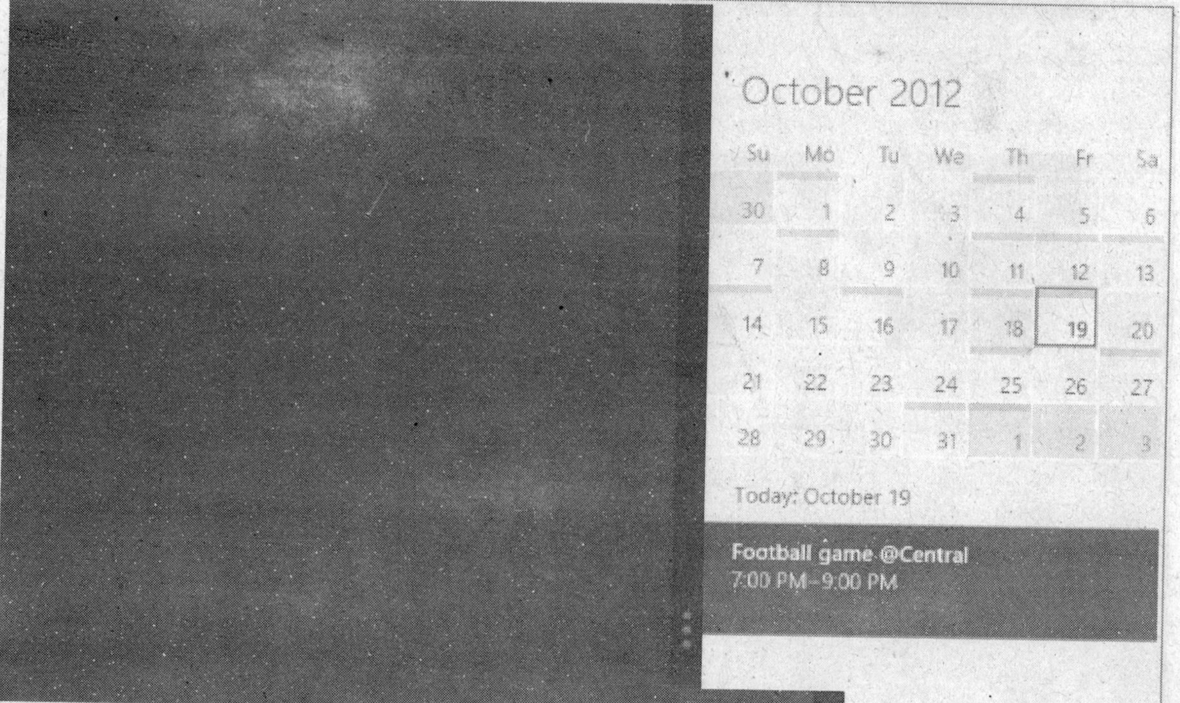

The snapped app

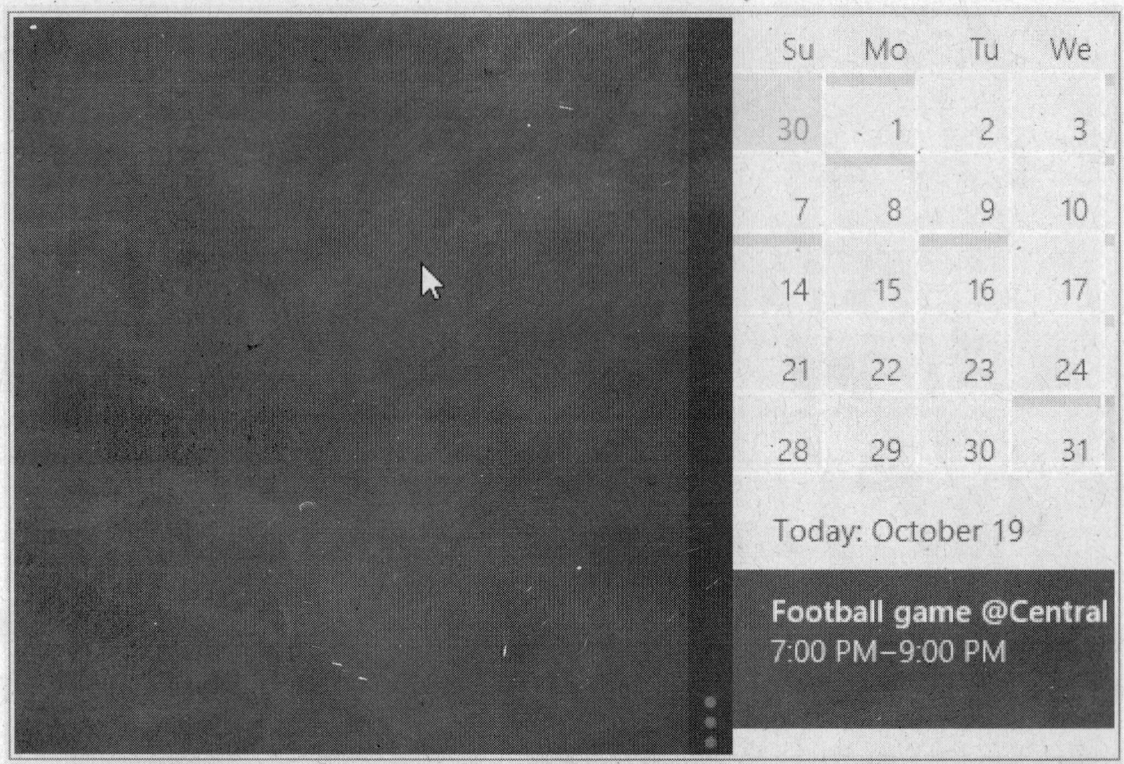

Su	Mo	Tu	We
30	1	2	3
7	8	9	10
14	15	16	17
21	22	23	24
28	29	30	31

Today: October 19

Football game @Central
7:00 PM–9:00 PM

Clicking in the empty part of the screen

People

Social

Me

Favorites

Olenna Mason

View
Notifications

What's new
Facebook

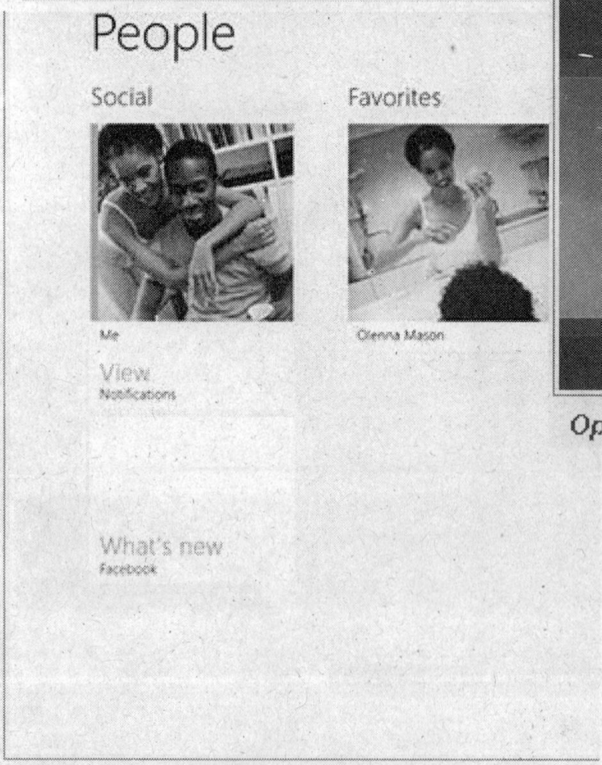

Two apps side-by-side

Opening the People app

CHAPTER 3

Using SkyDrive with Windows 8

In this chapter you will read about:

- Introduction to SkyDrive.
- Uploading Files to SkyDrive.
- Access SkyDrive in a Web Browser.
- Installing the SkyDrive Desktop App.

Introduction

One of the biggest changes in Windows 8 is that it is closely integrated with SkyDrive, Microsoft's online storage service. If you have files stored in your SkyDrive, you'll be able to access them easily with Windows 8. In this lesson, we'll show you how to manage your SkyDrive files, and also how to install the SkyDrive Desktop app.

Why Use SkyDrive?

If you've used previous versions of Windows, you're probably used to working with folders and files on your computer. But people are now more mobile than ever, and it's nice to have your files with you wherever you go. The cloud is generally the most convenient way to do this.

If you store your files online, then all you need is an internet connection, and you'll be able to access your files — whether you're at work, at home, or at a friend's house.

SkyDrive gives you 7 gigabytes of online storage space for free, and you can purchase more space if you need it.

You can decide whether you want to store all of your files online, or just the most important ones. When you log in to Windows with your Microsoft account, it automatically connects to your SkyDrive, allowing you to access your files from the built-in SkyDrive app or the Photos app.

To Upload Files to SkyDrive:

Some apps, such as Microsoft Office 2013, save files to SkyDrive by default. However, you may already have files on your computer that you would like to add to your SkyDrive.

1. Click the SkyDrive app in the Start screen.
2. Right-click anywhere on the screen. A menu will appear at the bottom of the screen.
3. Click the Upload button.
4. You will see a list of the folders and files in your Documents library.
5. To view your other files, click the Files drop-down arrow and select a different location (for example, Desktop).
6. When you've found the file you want to upload, select it and then click Add to SkyDrive. If you want, you can select multiple files.
7. The file(s) will be added to your SkyDrive.

The Photos app lets you access your SkyDrive photos

Opening the SkyDrive app

Opening the SkyDrive menu

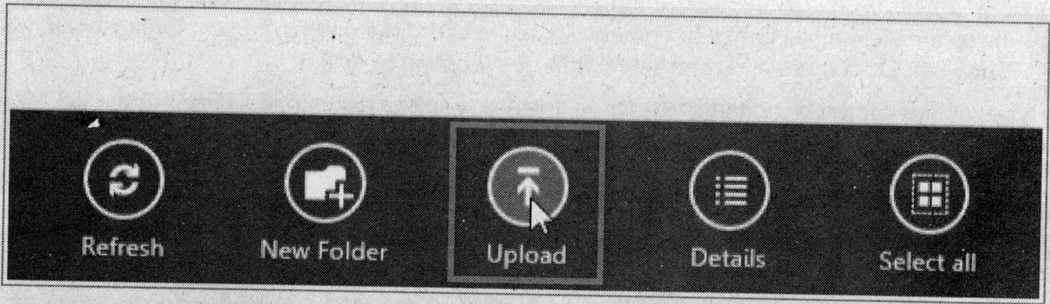

Clicking the Upload button

To Access SkyDrive in a Web Browser:

Now that you have files in your SkyDrive, you can access them from any computer that has an internet connection — even if the computer doesn't have Windows 8.

1. Go to www.skydrive.com and sign in with your Microsoft account.

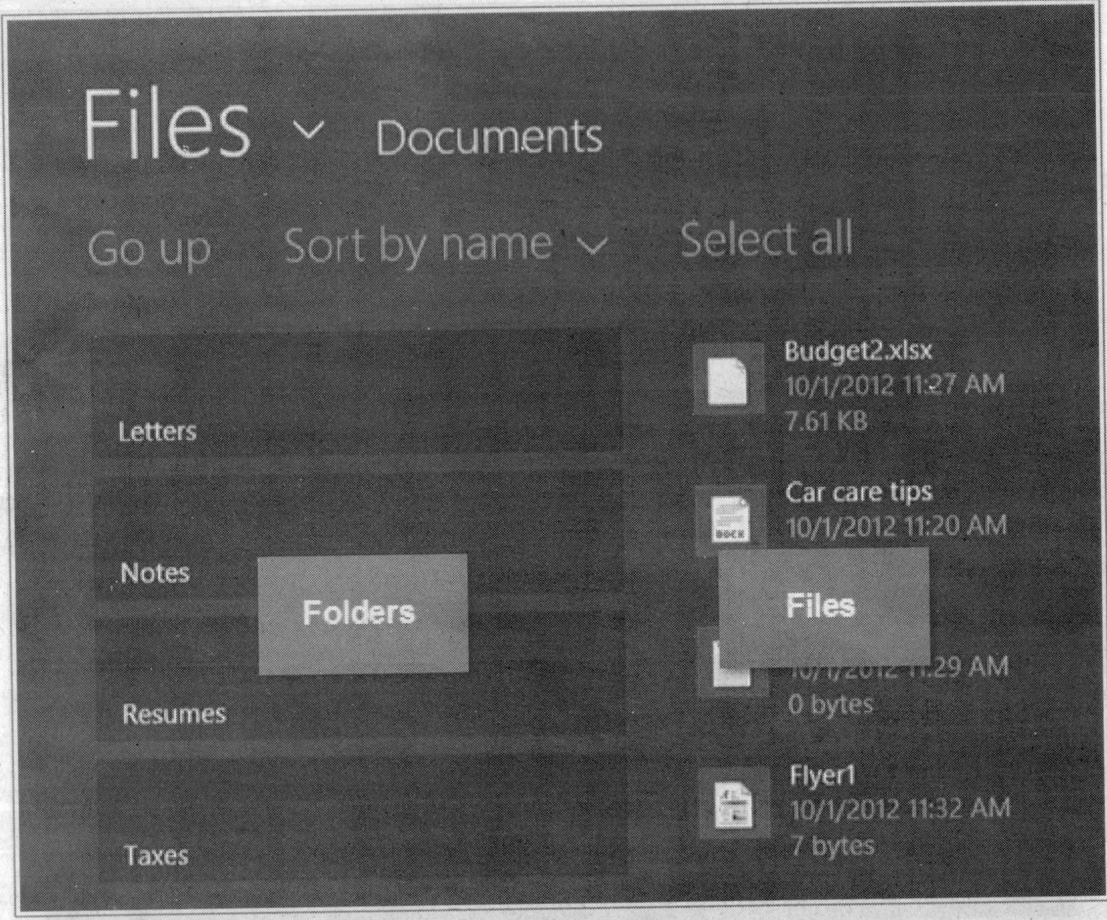

Folders and files in the Documents library

2. All of your folders and files will appear. Click on the desired folder or file to open it.
3. If you are viewing an Office document (such as a Word document or Excel spreadsheet), you can click Edit Document and then select Edit in Web App to edit it.

Some types of files cannot be edited in SkyDrive. Instead, you can download a file by right-clicking it and selecting Download. You can then open the downloaded file to edit it.

Installing the SkyDrive Desktop App

If you prefer working in the Desktop, you can download the SkyDrive Desktop app. This will add a SkyDrive folder to your File Explorer. When you move files into this folder, they will automatically be uploaded to SkyDrive, and you can access them anywhere you go. You'll even be able to access any files stored on your computer remotely, even if you haven't uploaded the files to SkyDrive.

To Install the SkyDrive Desktop App:

- Navigate to the Download SkyDrive page. Locate and select Download SkyDrive for Windows.
- Once the file is downloaded, click Run to open the SkyDrive Installer.
- The SkyDrive Installer will open. Click Get Started to continue.

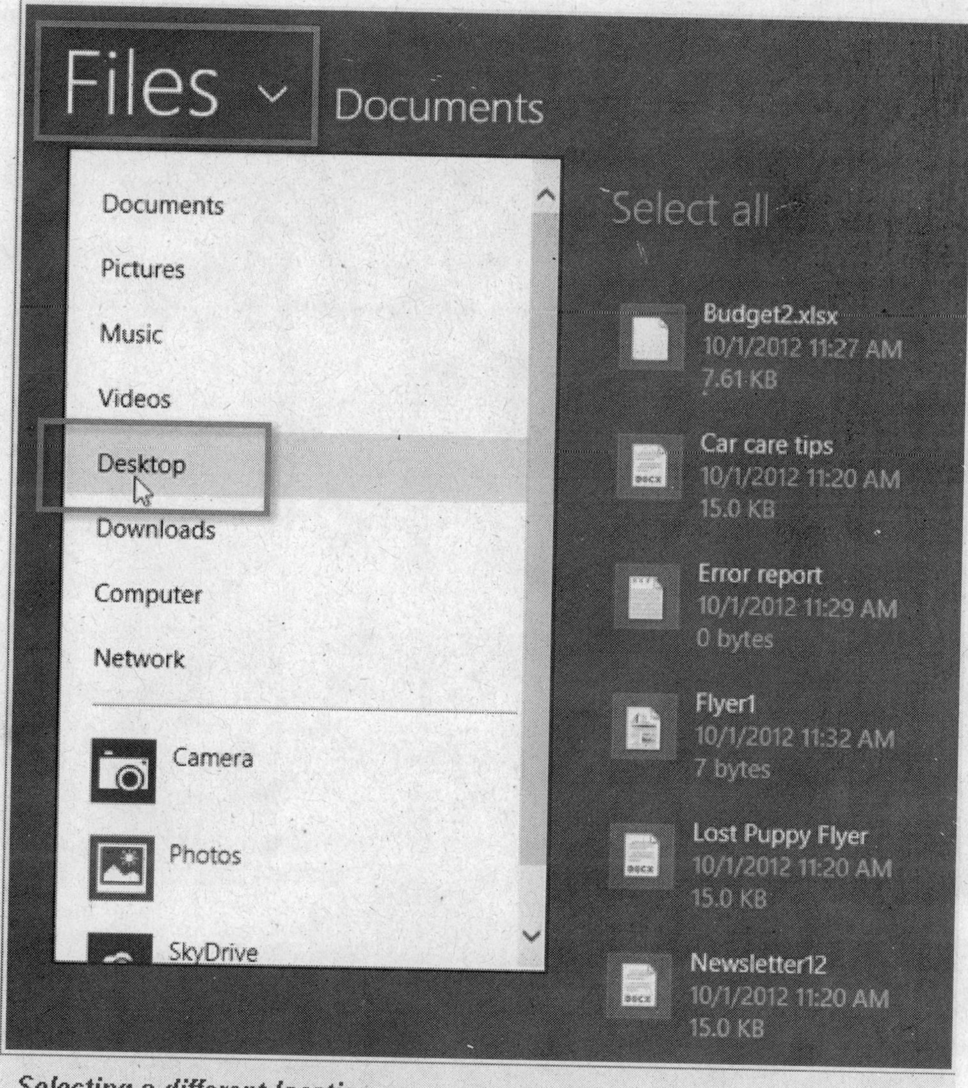

Selecting a different location

- The SkyDrive Folder window will appear, which explains how the SkyDrive folder works with your computer. Click Next to continue.
- Click Done to complete the installation. If you want to be able to access files on this computer remotely, leave the checkbox checked.
- The SkyDrive Desktop app is now installed on your computer. A SkyDrive folder will be added to your File Explorer, and any files you add to this folder will be uploaded to your SkyDrive.

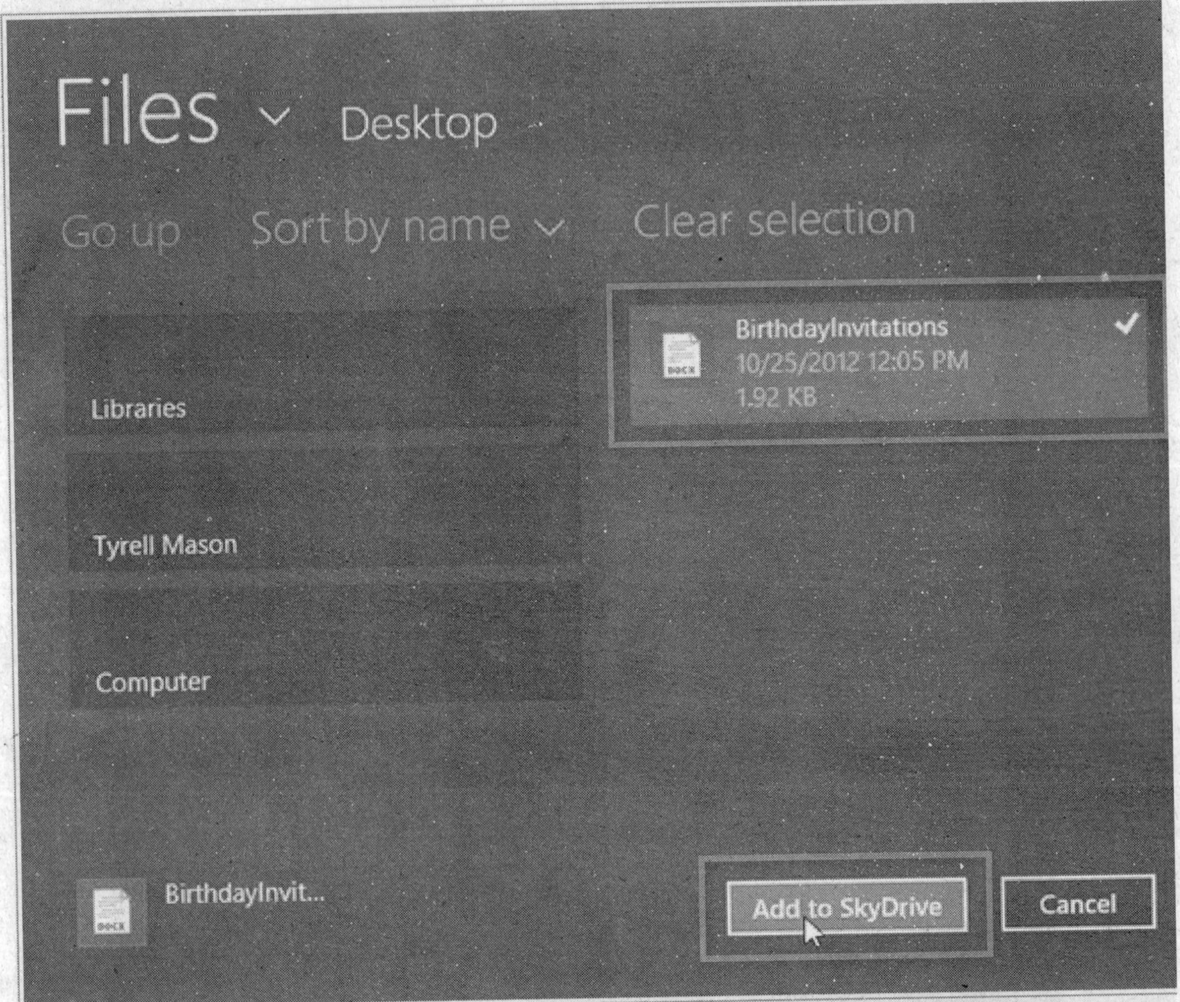

Adding a file to SkyDrive

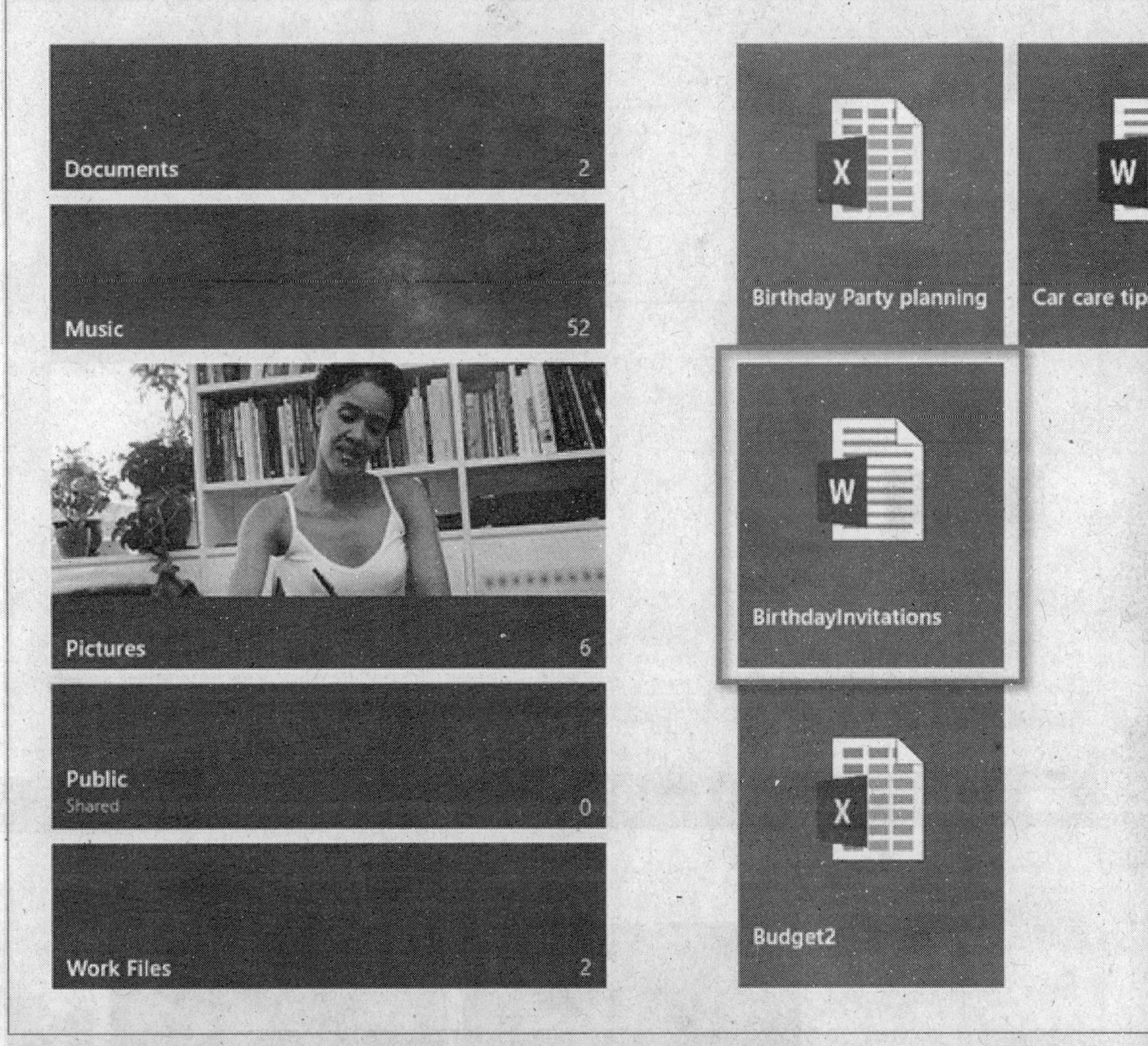

The uploaded file

SkyDrive

Microsoft account What's this?

tyrellmason30@gmail.com

••••••

Keep me signed in

Sign in

Can't access your account?

Sign in with a single-use code

Signing in to SkyDrive

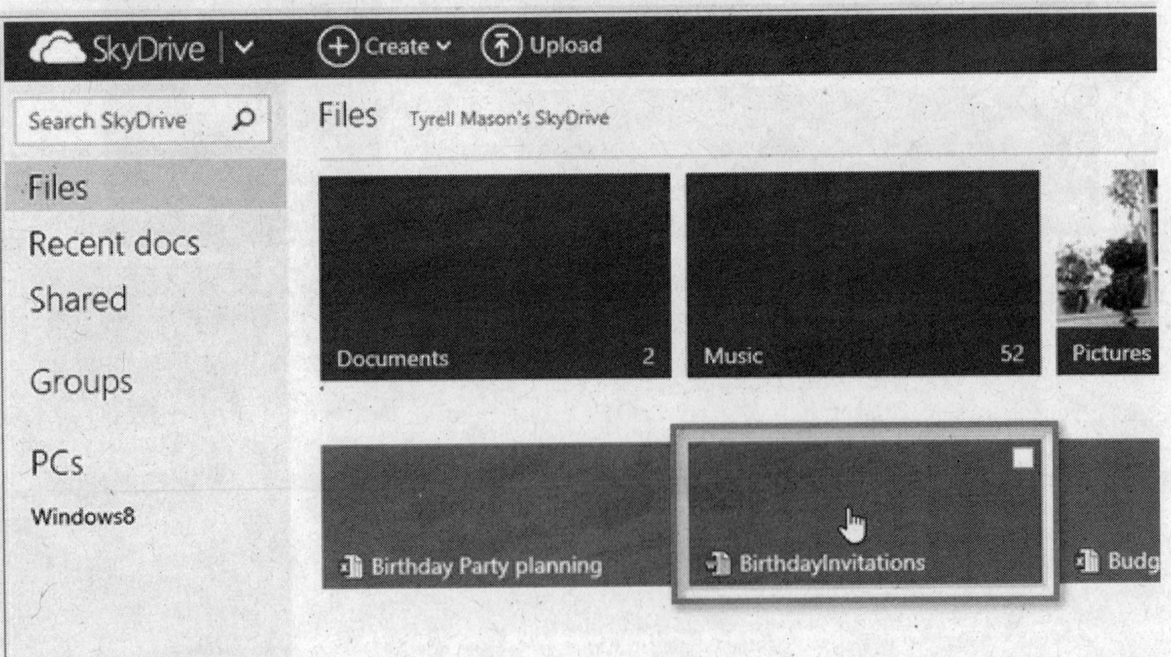

Opening a Word document

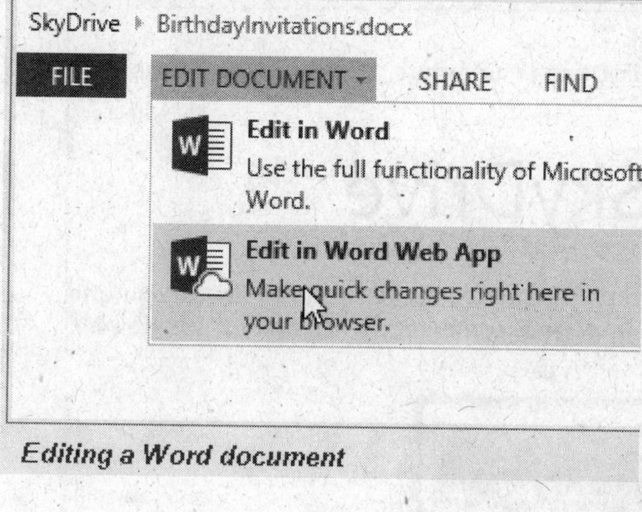

Editing a Word document

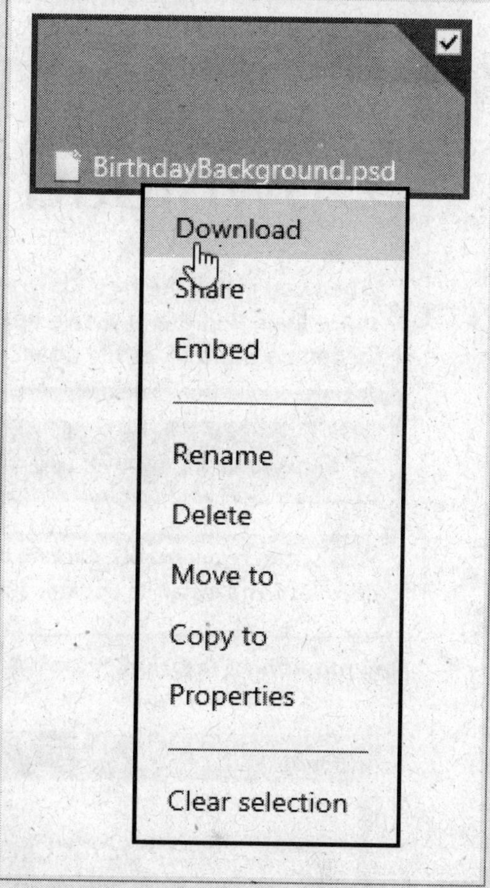

Downloading a file

The SkyDriveSetup.exe download has completed. Run Close

Opening the SkyDrive Installer

Meet SkyDrive Compare Download Mobile

Download SkyDrive

When you install the free SkyDrive app on your computer, you can access your ph
share them. Put the SkyDrive app on all your computers— Windows 7, Windows V
forgetting a photo or file again.

Download SkyDrive for Windows

View system requirements. Clicking the download button means you agree to the Microsoft s
download and install its updates automatically.

Downloading SkyDrive

Clicking Get Started

Clicking Next

Clicking Done

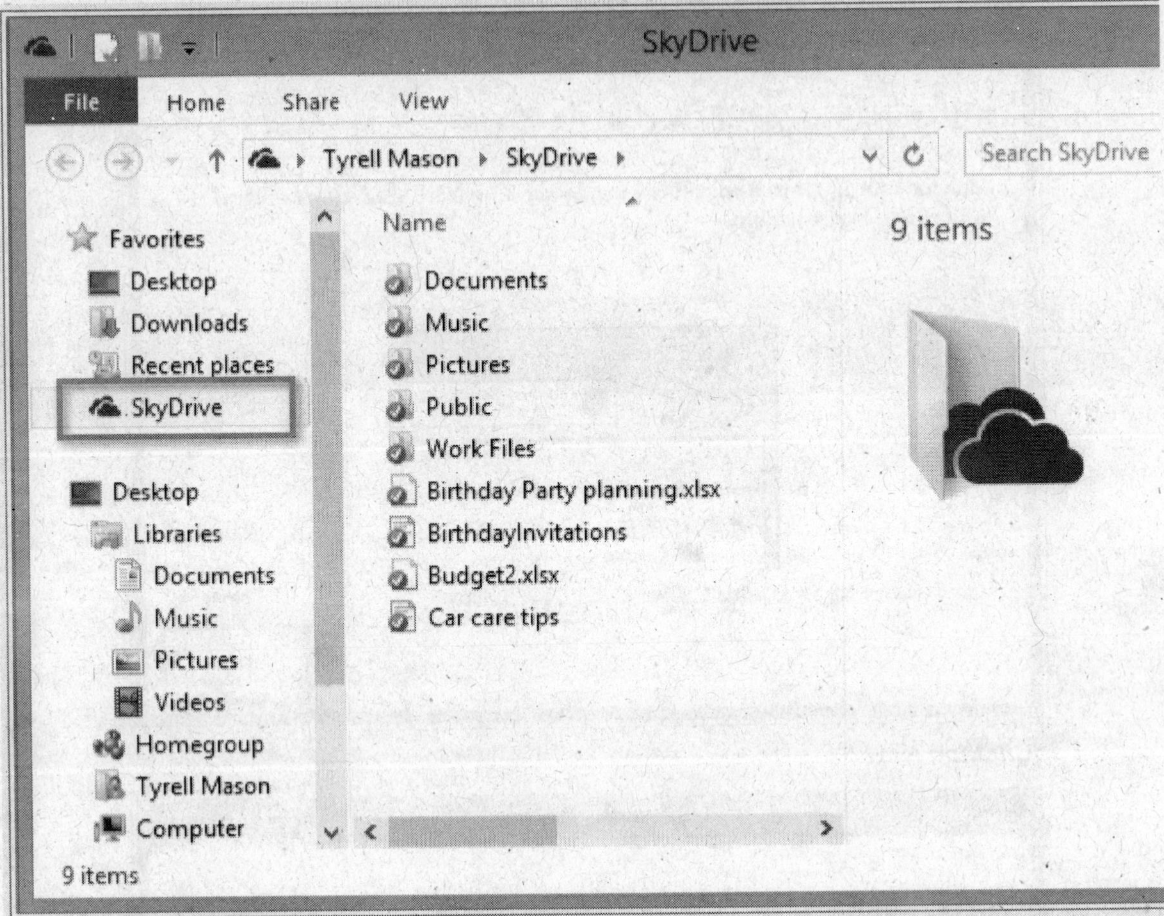

The SkyDrive Folder

CHAPTER 4

Using Search Engine

In this chapter you will read about:

- Using Search Engine
- Searching from Desktop.
- Searching from Tablet.

Introduction

Once you've used Windows 8 for a while, you'll start to have more and more files, such as music, photos, and documents. It may sometimes be difficult to find the exact file that you want. You may even have trouble finding a specific app, since Windows 8 has moved everything around. Luckily, there is a built-in search feature, which can help you find files, apps, or almost anything else on your computer.

To Search From the Start Screen:

- From the Start screen, type what you're looking for. Your search results will instantly appear on the left side of the screen, and search options will appear on the right.

Using Different Search Options

- By default, the search results will show apps. However, you can select different search options on the right side of the screen to find files, settings, and more:
- You can select Settings or Files to search for a setting or file.
- You can also use a specific app to search. For example, you can search the People app to find a friend's contact info.

Searching From the Desktop

- If you're on the Desktop, you will first need to press the Windows key to switch to the Start screen, and then type what you're looking for.

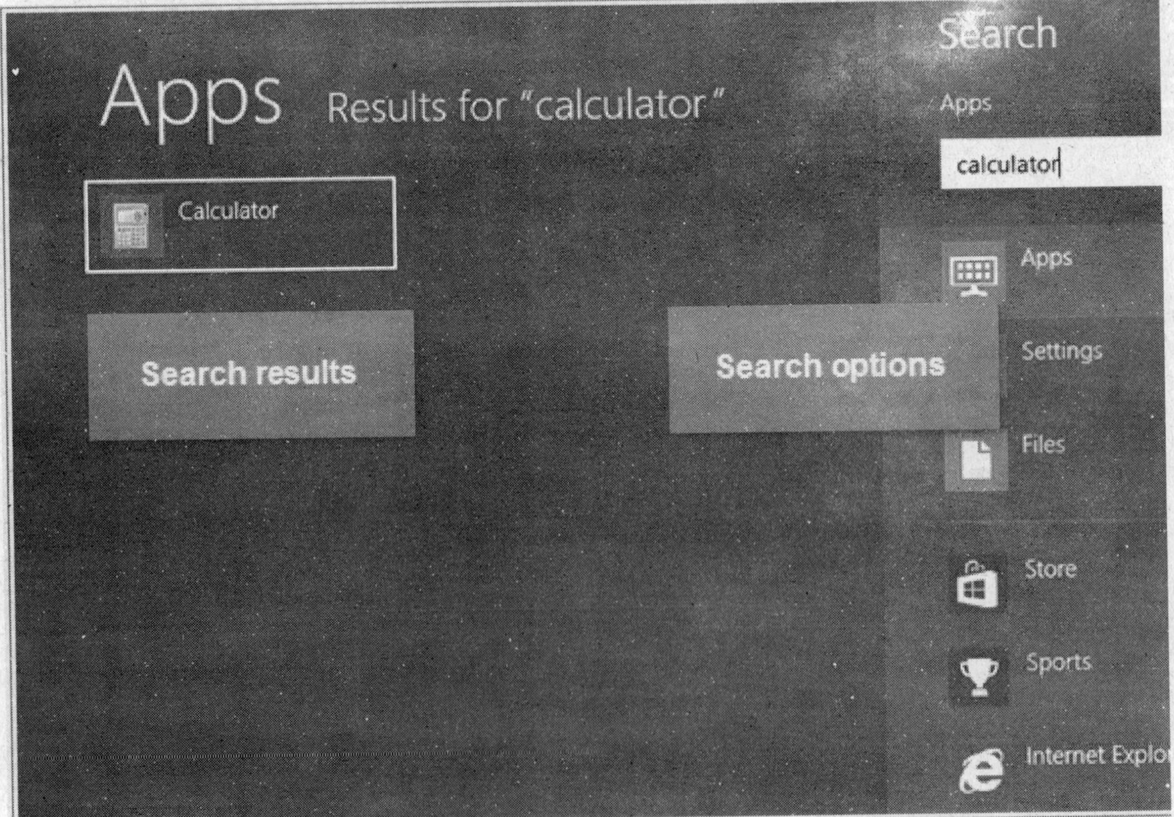

Searching for the Calculator app

Searching on a Tablet

- If you're using a tablet without an attached keyboard, you can search by swiping in from the right, and then selecting the Search charm. You can then type what you're looking for.

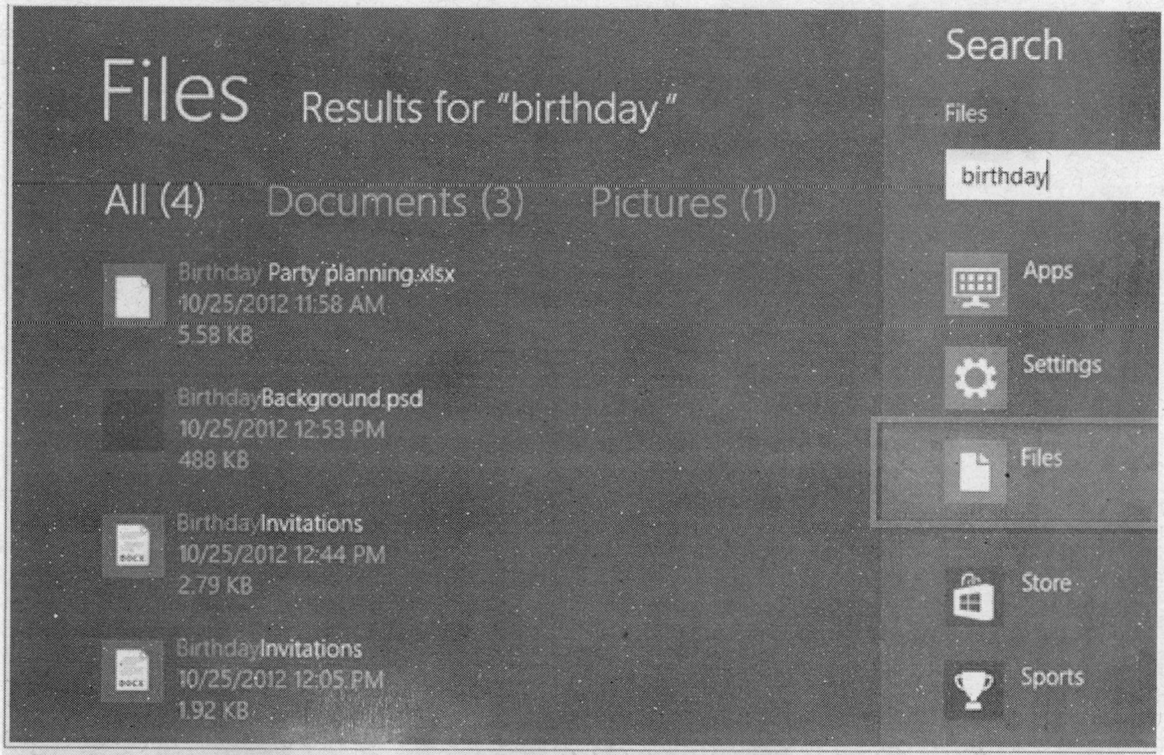

Searching for a file

Windows key

The Search charm

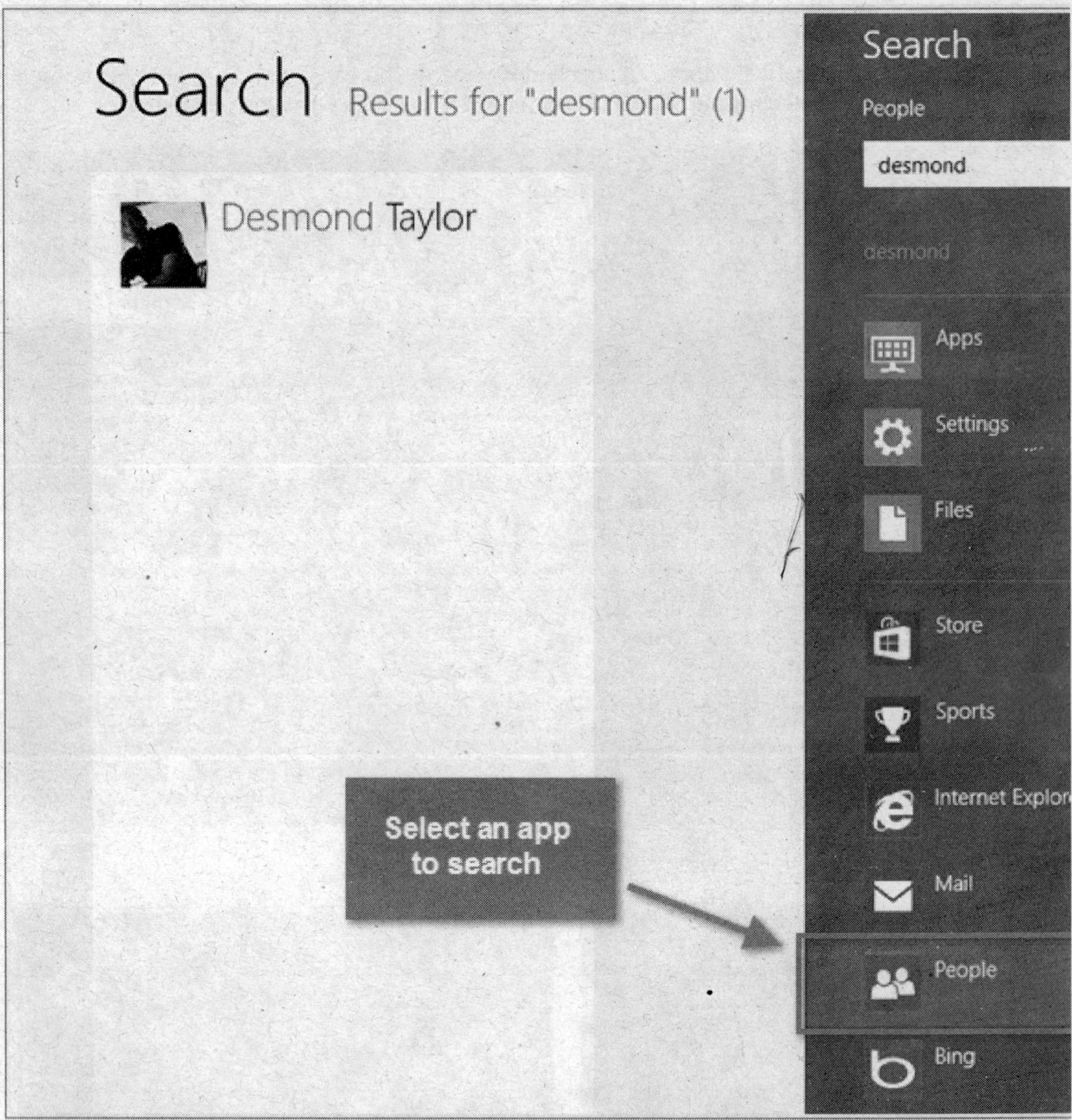

Searching the People app

CHAPTER 5

Personalizing Your Start Screen

In this chapter you will read about:

- Customizing Start Screen.
- Pinning Applications to the Start Screen.
- Creating Application Groups.

Introduction

You'll probably spend a lot of time on your Start screen, so you may want to personalize it so that it suits your taste. In this lesson, we'll show you several different ways to personalize it, including changing the background image and color, rearranging apps, pinning apps, and creating app groups.

To View Your Personalization Settings:

1. Hover the mouse in the lower-right corner to open the Charms bar, and then select the Settings charm.
2. Click Change PC settings.

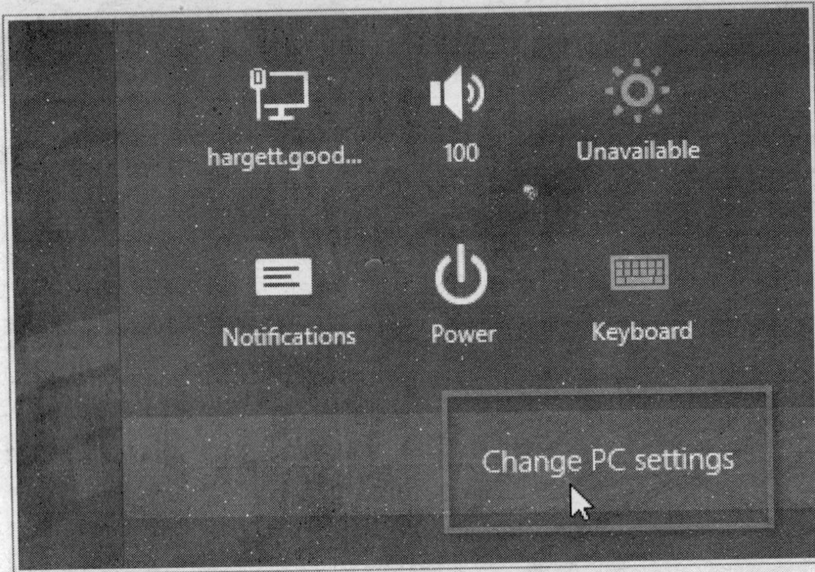

Clicking Change PC settings

Settings charm

3. Make sure Personalize is selected on the left side of the screen. Your settings will appear on the right side of the screen.

To Change Your Lock Screen Picture:

- From your personalization settings, select Lock screen at the top of the screen.
- Select the desired picture from the list of thumbnails. Alternatively, you can click Browse to select one of your own pictures.

The lock screen will appear whenever your computer is locked, which happens automatically after a few minutes of inactivity. You can also lock your computer by clicking your account name and selecting Lock.

To Change Your Start Screen Background:

- From your personalization settings, select Start screen at the top of the screen.
- Select the desired background image and color scheme.

Windows 8 does not allow you to use one of your own photos as your Start screen background.

Personalization settings

To Change Your Account Picture:

- From your personalization settings, select Account picture at the top of the screen.
- Click Browse.
- To use a photo in your SkyDrive, click on the desired SkyDrive folder. To select a folder on your computer, click the drop-down arrow at the top of the screen and select a different location.
- When you have selected a photo, click Choose image.

If your computer or tablet has a built-in camera, you can click Camera to take a picture of yourself.

Customizing Your Start Screen Apps

If you don't like the way your apps are arranged on the Start screen, you can rearrange them by

Locking the computer

Selecting a lock screen picture

moving them wherever you want. You may also find that the animated live tiles are too distracting, and you can easily turn them off so that they will display a plain background with no animations.

To Move an App:

1. Click, hold and drag the app to the desired location.
2. Release the mouse. The app will move to the new location.

To Turn a Live Tile Off:

1. Right-click the app you want to change.
2. A toolbar will appear at the bottom of the screen. Click Turn live tile off, and the tile will change to a plain background.

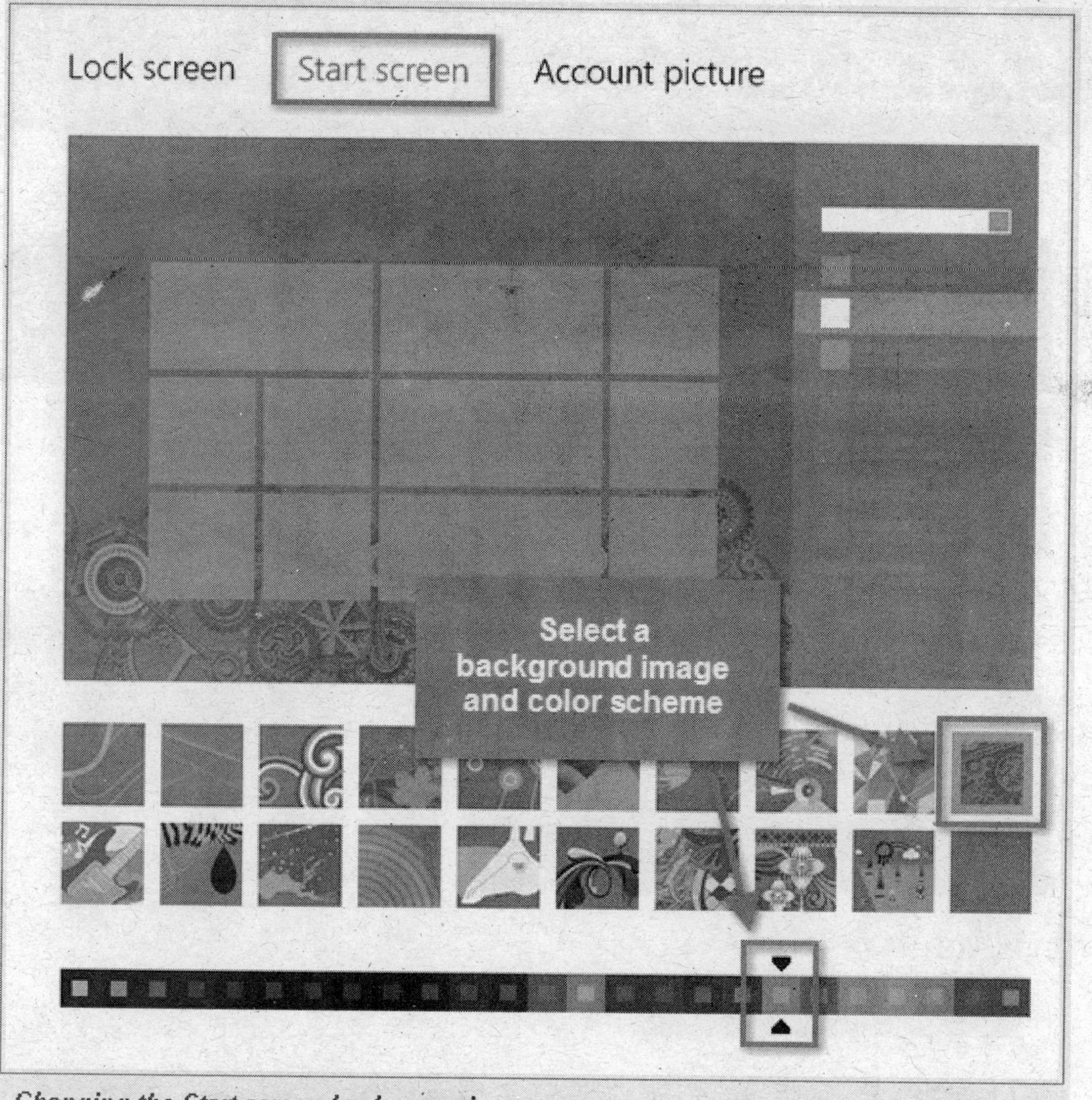

Changing the Start screen background

Pinning Apps to the Start Screen

By default, the Start screen doesn't show all of the apps on your computer. However, it's easy to pin your favorite apps to the Start screen so that you can open them quickly.

To Pin an App to the Start Screen:

1. Right-click anywhere on the Start screen background.
2. A menu will appear at the bottom of the screen. Click All apps to view all of the apps installed on your computer.
3. Locate and right-click the desired app.

Navigating to the desired folder

Changing the account picture

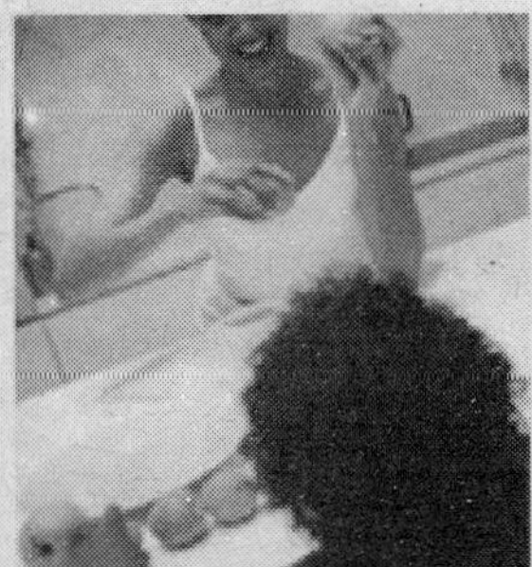

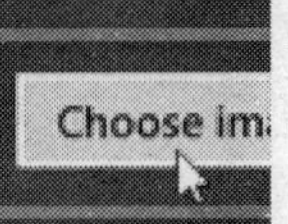

Selecting an image

Clicking the Camera button

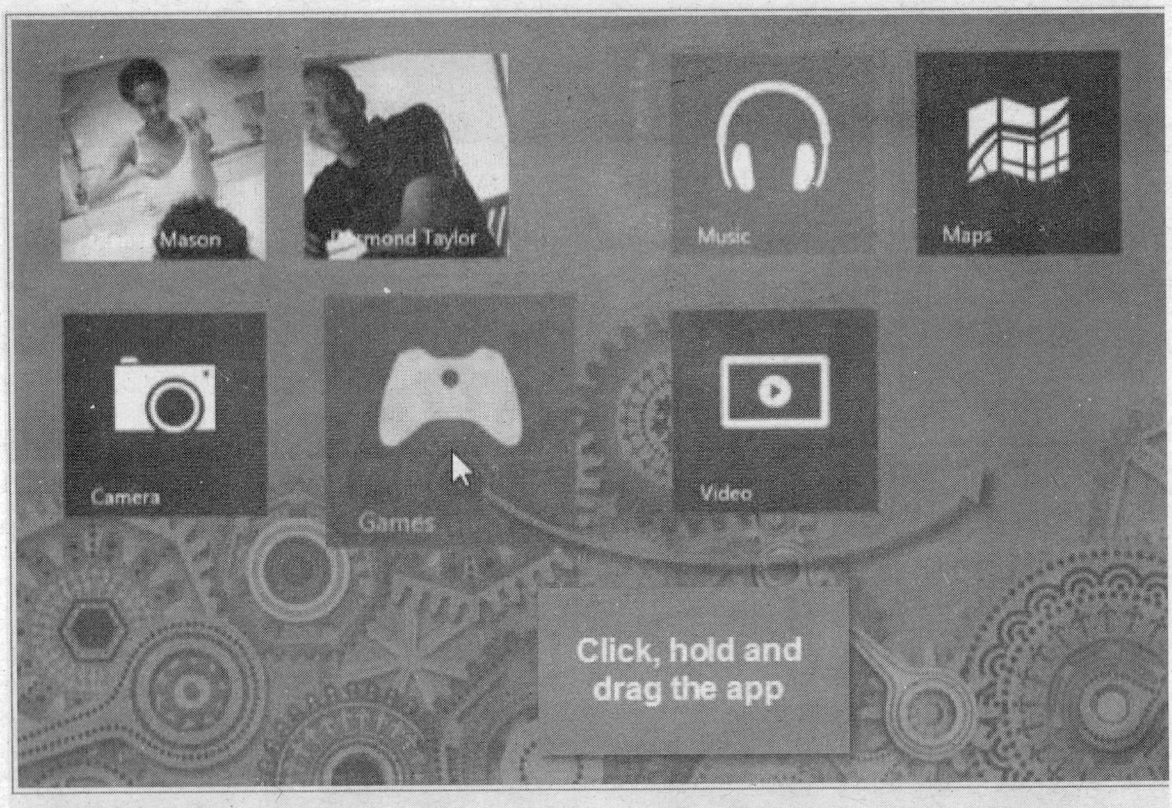

Moving an app

The app in its new location

Right-clicking a live tile

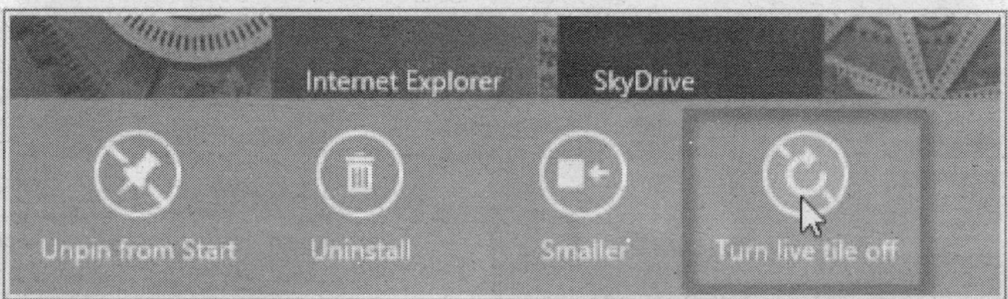

Turning a live tile off

Right-clicking the Start screen background

4. At the bottom of the screen, click Pin to Start.
5. Click the lower-left corner to return to the Start screen. Your app will now appear on the Start screen.

To Unpin an App from the Start Screen:

1. From the Start screen, right-click the desired app.
2. At the bottom of the screen, click Unpin from Start. The app will disappear from the Start screen.

Right-clicking an app

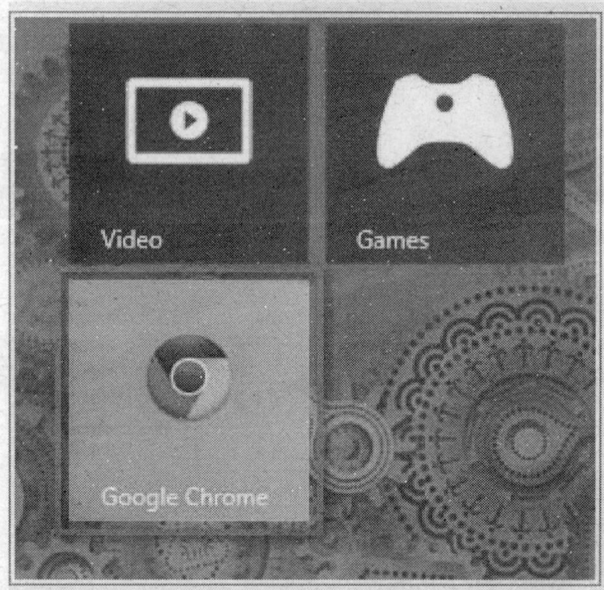

The pinned app

Clicking the All apps button

Pinning an app to the Start screen

Unpinning an app from the Start screen

Creating App Groups

To further organize your apps, you can put related apps into groups. You can also name your groups, and each group will display its name at the top.

Right-clicking an app

To Create a New App Group:

1. Click, hold and drag an app to the right, until it is on an empty area of the Start screen.
2. Release the mouse. The app will now be in its own app group, and you should see a space between the new group and the other groups. This space helps to visually separate the different groups.
3. You can now move more apps into the new app group.

To Name an App Group:

1. Click the lower-right corner of the screen to zoom out.
2. All of your Start screen apps will appear as small icons organized into groups. Right-click the desired group.
3. At the bottom of the screen, select Name group.
4. Type the desired name. Shorter names usually work best, so try to use a single word if possible. When you're done, click Name.
5. Click anywhere on the Start screen to return to the normal view. The new name will appear above the app group.

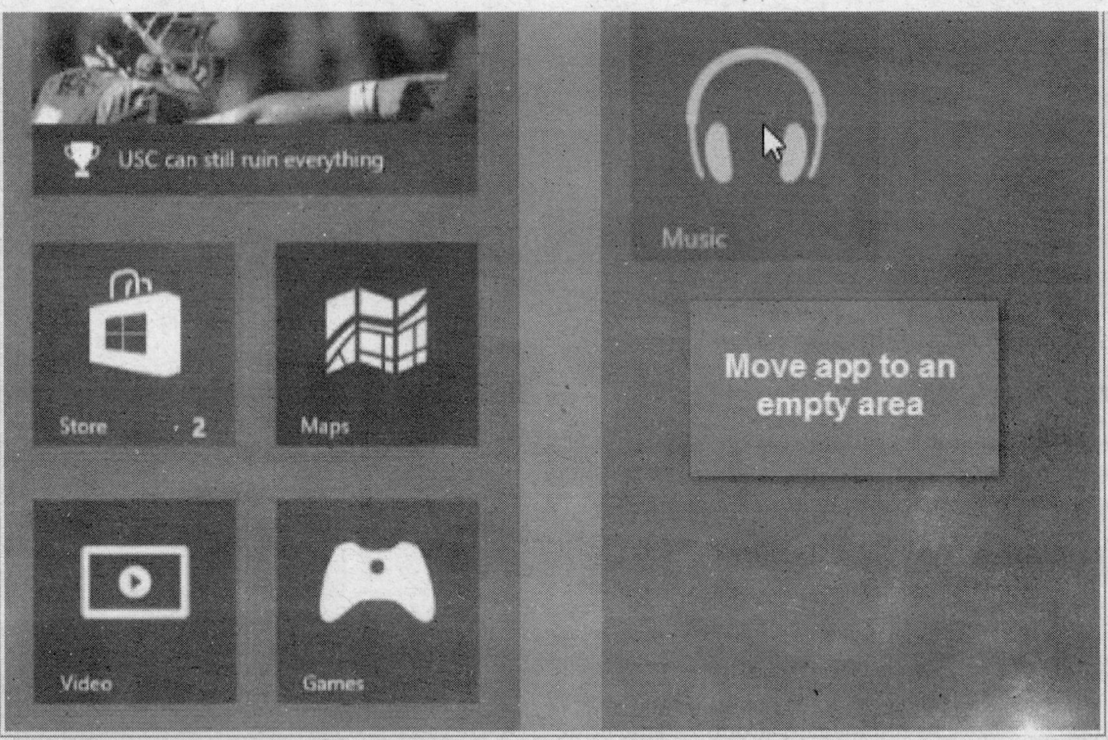

Moving an app

The new app group

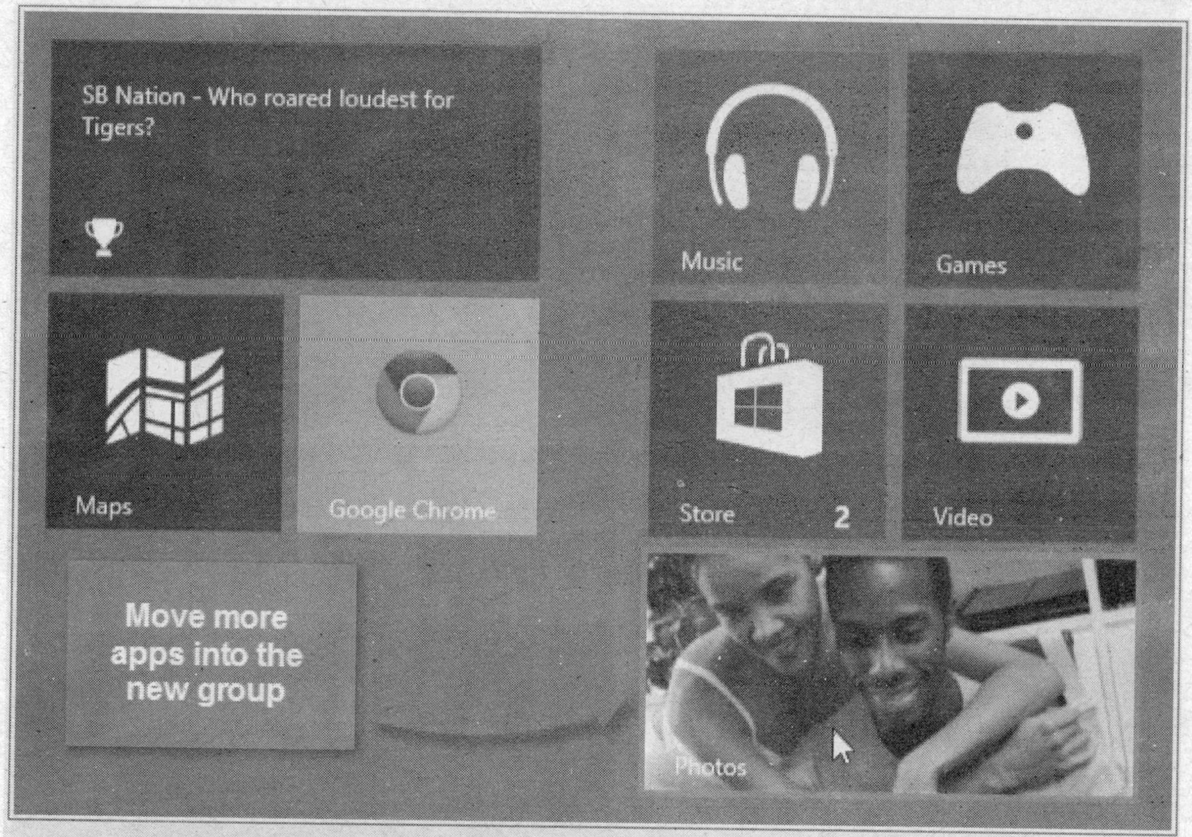

SB Nation - Who roared loudest for Tigers?
Music
Games
Maps
Google Chrome
Store
2
Video
Move more apps into the new group
Photos

Adding apps to the new group

Click the lower-right corner of the screen

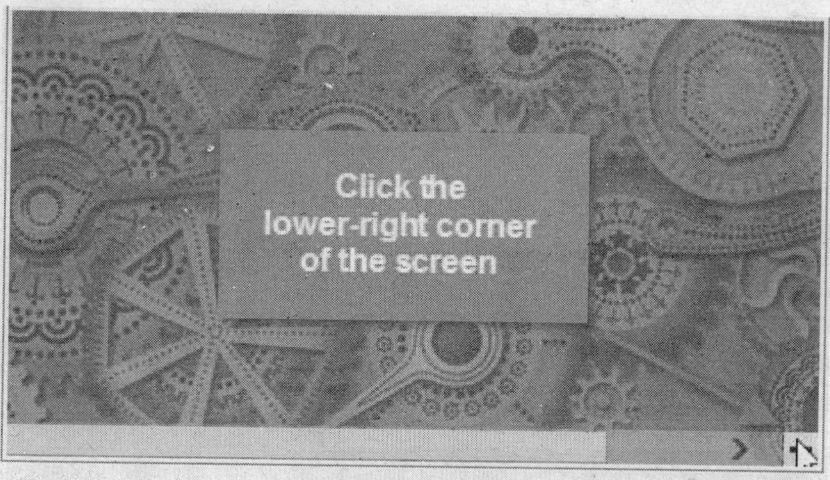

Zooming out

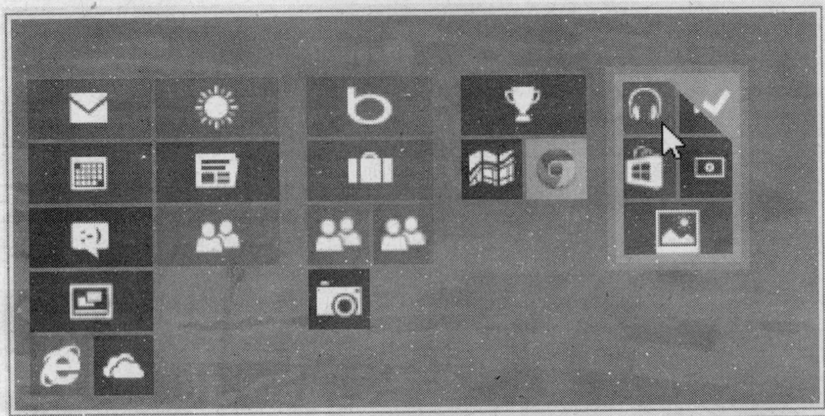

Right-clicking a group

Clicking the Name group button

The new group name

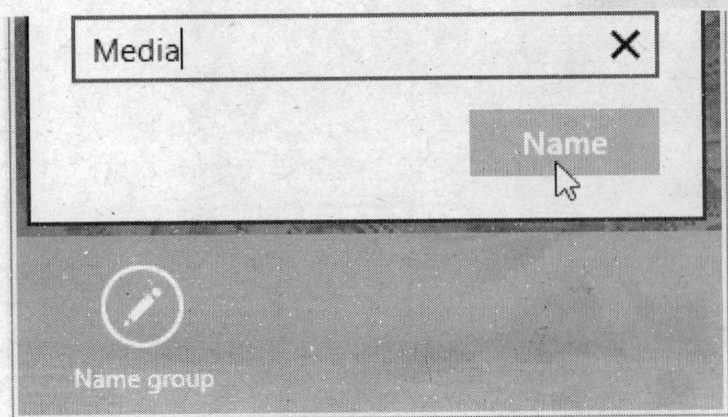

Typing a name for the group

CHAPTER 6

Desktop and Managing Files

In this chapter you will read about:

- Working with Files.
- Working with Desktop Applications.
- Taskbar Features.
- Searching the File Explorer.
- Working with Libraries.

Introduction

Although Windows 8 uses the Start screen for launching apps and other tasks, the Desktop view is still an important feature that you'll need to know how to use. In this lesson, we'll show you the basics of using the Desktop, including how to navigate with File Explorer, pin apps to the taskbar, and manage open windows with the built-in desktop effects.

To Switch to the Desktop:

1. Click the Desktop tile on the Start screen.

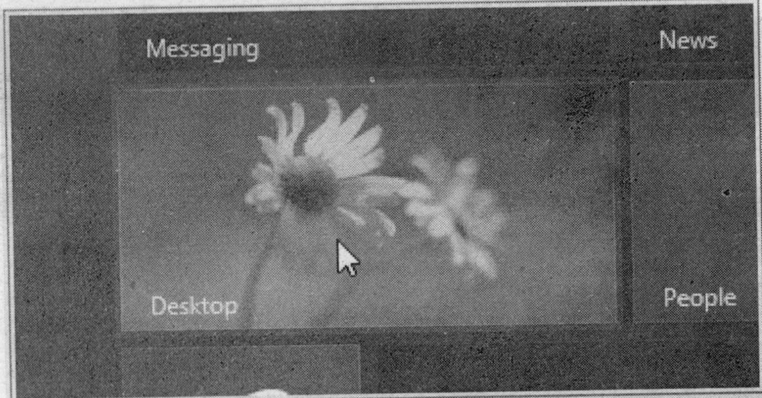

Switching to the Desktop

2. Click the buttons in the interactive below to learn more about the Desktop view in Windows 8.

Working with Files

To work with the files and folders on your computer, you'll use the File Explorer app. In File Explorer, you can navigate to different folders, open files, delete files, and more.

If you want to access your files from any computer, you may want to store your files online (in the cloud). To learn more, check out our lesson on Using SkyDrive with Windows 8.

To Open File Explorer:

1. Click the File Explorer icon on the taskbar, or double-click any folder on your desktop. A File Explorer window will open.

Basic Navigation:

1. If you see the file that you want, you can double-click it. Otherwise, you can use the Navigation pane on the left side of the window to select a different location.

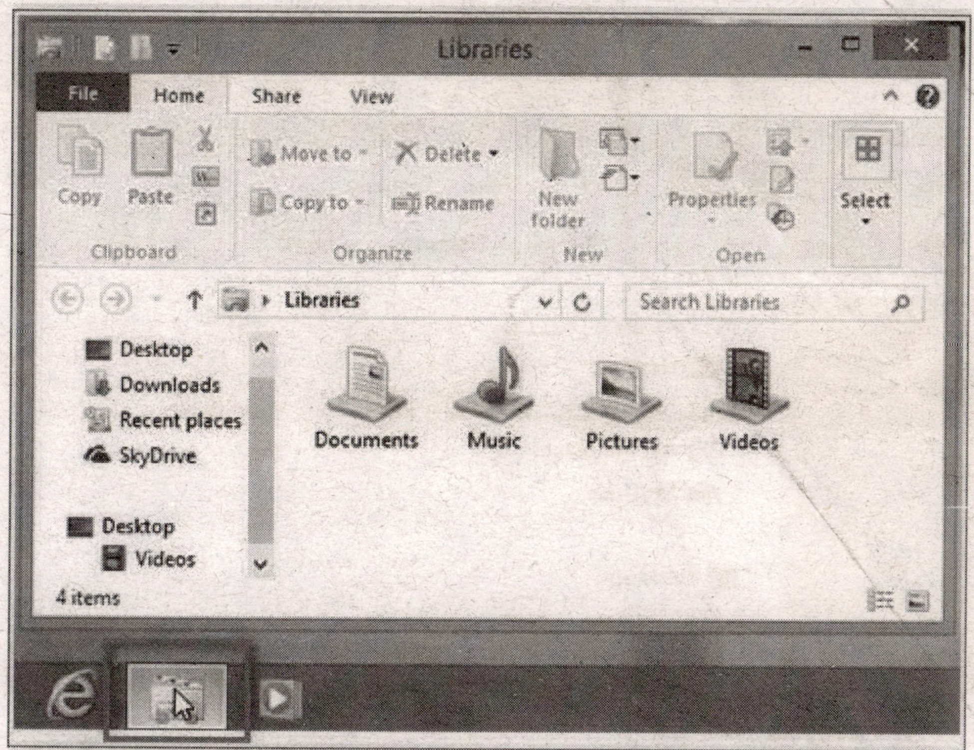

Opening File Explorer

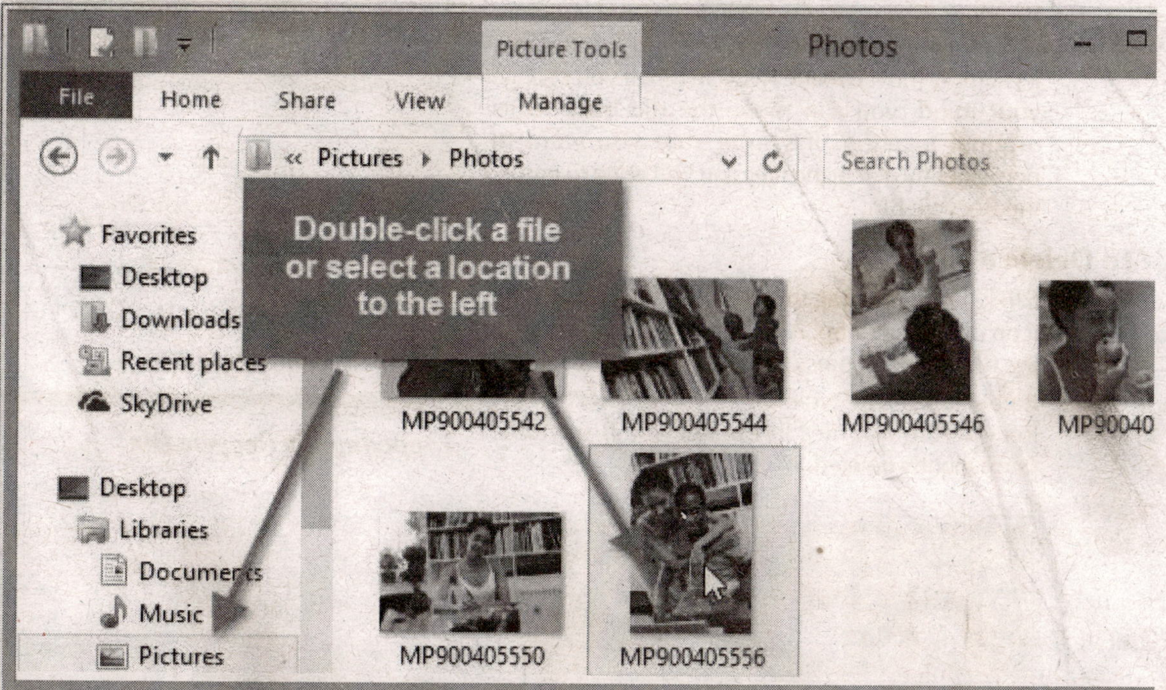

Navigating File Explorer

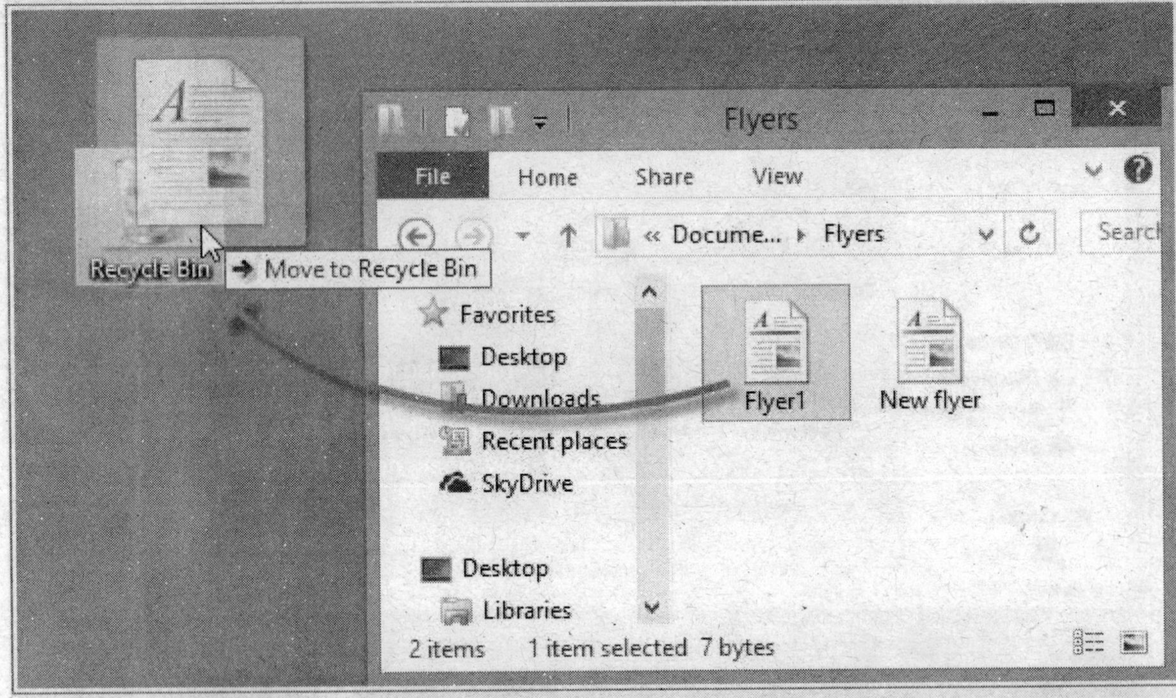

Dragging a file to the Recycle Bin

Deleting Files

1. Windows 8 uses a Recycle Bin to prevent you from accidentally deleting files. When you delete a file, it is simply moved to the Recycle Bin. If you change your mind, you can move the file back to its original location. If you're sure you want to permanently delete the file, you will need to empty the Recycle Bin.

Emptying the Recycle Bin

To Delete a File:

1. Click, hold and drag the file onto the Recycle Bin icon on the Desktop. Alternatively, you can select the file and then press the Delete key.
2. Right-click the Recycle Bin icon and select Empty Recycle Bin. All files in the Recycle Bin will be permanently deleted.

Working with Desktop Apps

Opening an app from a shortcut

Clicking All apps

While many applications run exclusively in the Start screen, you'll also need to know how to open apps from the Desktop view. If you've used previous versions of Windows before, this should feel more familiar.

To Open an App on the Desktop:

There are two ways to open an app in Desktop view:

1. Click the app icon on the taskbar.
2. Double-click the app shortcut on the Desktop.

To Pin Apps to the Taskbar:

By default, only a few apps will have icons on the taskbar. You can pin your favorite apps to the taskbar, which will create a convenient shortcut to the app from the Desktop view.

1. Right-click anywhere on the Start screen and a menu will appear at the bottom. Click the All apps button.
2. A list of apps will appear. Locate and right-click the desired app.
3. A menu will appear at the bottom of the screen. Click Pin to taskbar.

Pinning an app to the taskbar

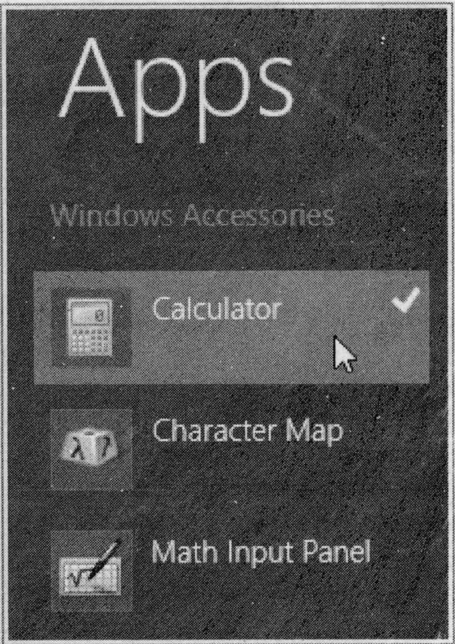

Right-clicking the desired app

4. The app icon will now appear on the taskbar.

The app pinned on the taskbar

Not all apps can be pinned to the taskbar. Apps that are designed to run from the Start screen, such as Messaging and Calendar, can only be pinned to the Start screen.

Using Desktop Effects

Windows 8 uses several desktop effects that make it easier to multitask and work with multiple windows. These were previously known as Aero effects in older versions of Windows. The desktop effects include Snap, Peek, Shake, and Flip.

Snap

Snap allows you to resize open windows quickly, which is especially convenient whenever you're working with multiple windows at the same time.

Overlapping windows

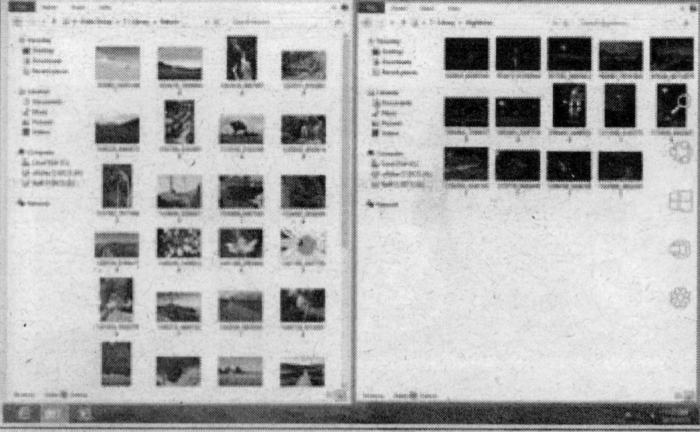

Side-by-side Snap view

1. Click, hold and drag the desired window to the left or right until the cursor reaches the edge of the screen.
2. Release the mouse. The window will snap into place.
3. To unsnap a window, click and drag the window down, then release the mouse.

Snapping a window to one side of the screen

MSN for Windows 8 - Windows...
National and Local Weather For...
CNN.com - Breaking News, U.S....
Amazon.
CNN
'Unthinkable devastation'

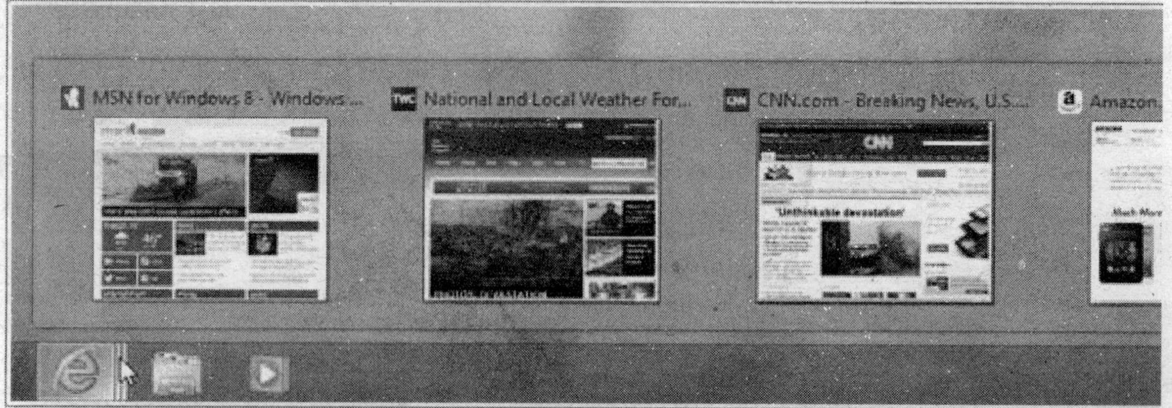

Viewing a thumbail preview with Peek

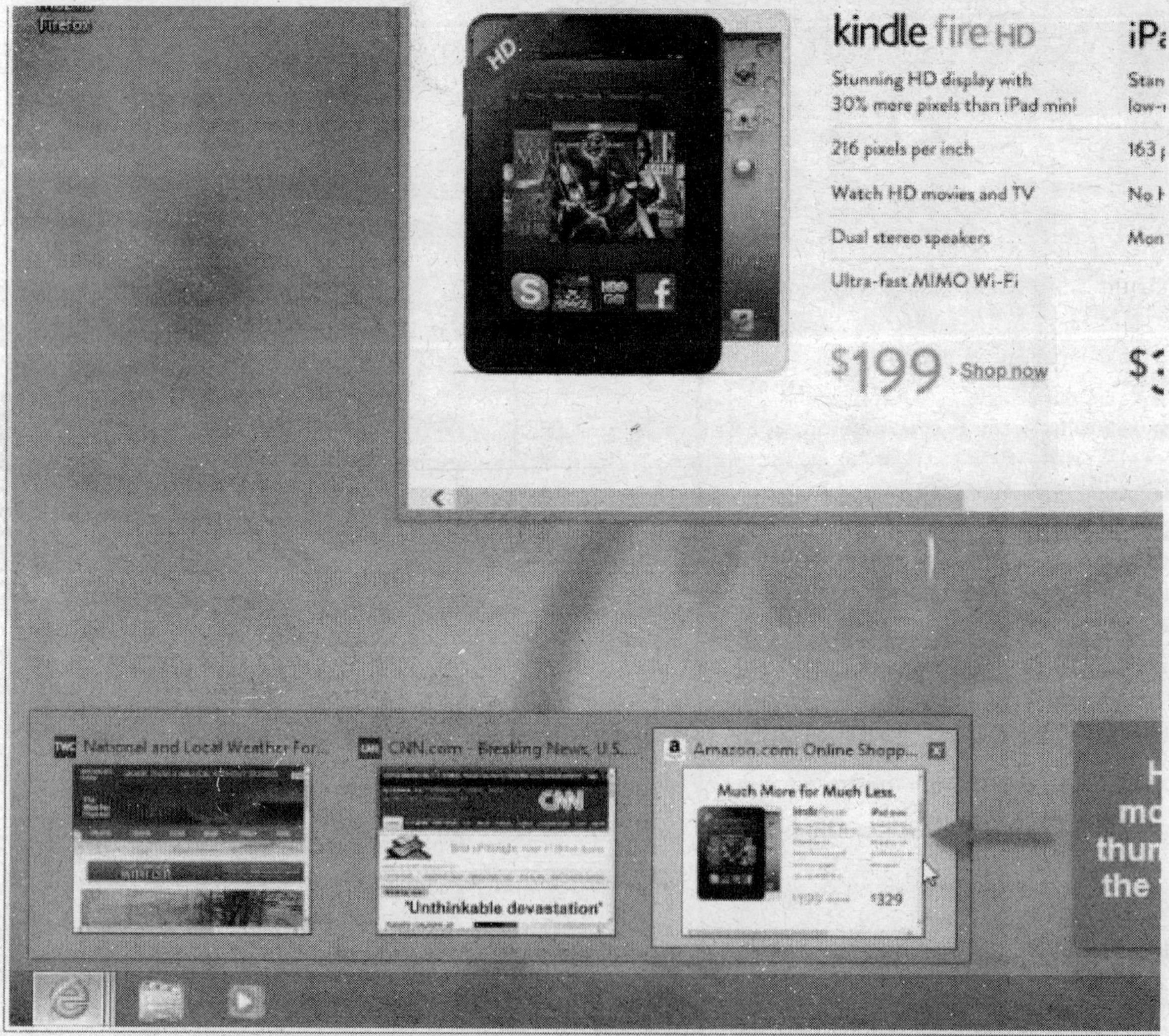

kindle fire HD
Stunning HD display with
30% more pixels than iPad mini
216 pixels per inch
Watch HD movies and TV
Dual stereo speakers
Ultra-fast MIMO Wi-Fi
$199 › Shop now
National and Local Weather For...
CNN.com - Breaking News, U.S....
Amazon.com: Online Shopp...
CNN
"Unthinkable devastation"
Much More for Much Less.
$329

Previewing a full-sized window from Peek view

You can also use Snap to maximize a window. Simply click and drag the window until the cursor reaches the top of the screen, then release the mouse.

Multiple windows cluttering the desktop

Peek

You can view your open windows on the taskbar by using Peek. Simply hover the mouse over an icon in the taskbar and a thumbnail preview of open windows will appear.

1. Hover the mouse over the window in the thumbnail preview. A full-sized version of the window will appear.
2. Select the thumbnail preview to open the window or click the X to close the window from Peek view.

Shaking to view a single window

Shake

When your desktop is cluttered with open windows, you can use Shake to select a single window and minimize the rest.

1. Locate and select the window you wish to focus on.
2. Gently shake the window back and forth. All other windows will be minimized.
3. Shake the window again and the minimized windows will reappear.

Flip

You can use Flip to scroll through a preview of your open windows. Any apps open on the Start screen will also appear in the Flip preview. While Snap, Peek, and Shake are designed to work exclusively in the Desktop view, Flip works the same way in both the Start screen and Desktop views.

1. Press and hold the Alt key and then press Tab. The Flip preview will appear.
2. While holding the Alt key, scroll through the open windows by pressing Tab.

3. Stop on the window or app you wish to select. The chosen window or app will appear.

Flipping through open apps

Taskbar Features

The taskbar includes several features that make it easier to view and manage desktop apps.

To Show the Desktop:

If you want to see the desktop, you can click the lower-right corner of the screen to minimize all open windows.

1. Move the mouse to the bottom-right corner of the screen and click.
2. All open windows will be minimized and the desktop will appear.
3. Click the bottom-right corner again to restore the minimized windows.

To Access a Jump List:

A Jump List is like a mini-menu that you can open from the taskbar. It allows quick access to recent files, frequently viewed items, performance tasks, and more. For example, you might open frequently used websites with just a few clicks from the Internet Explorer Jump List.

1. Right-click an app icon in the taskbar to open a Jump List.

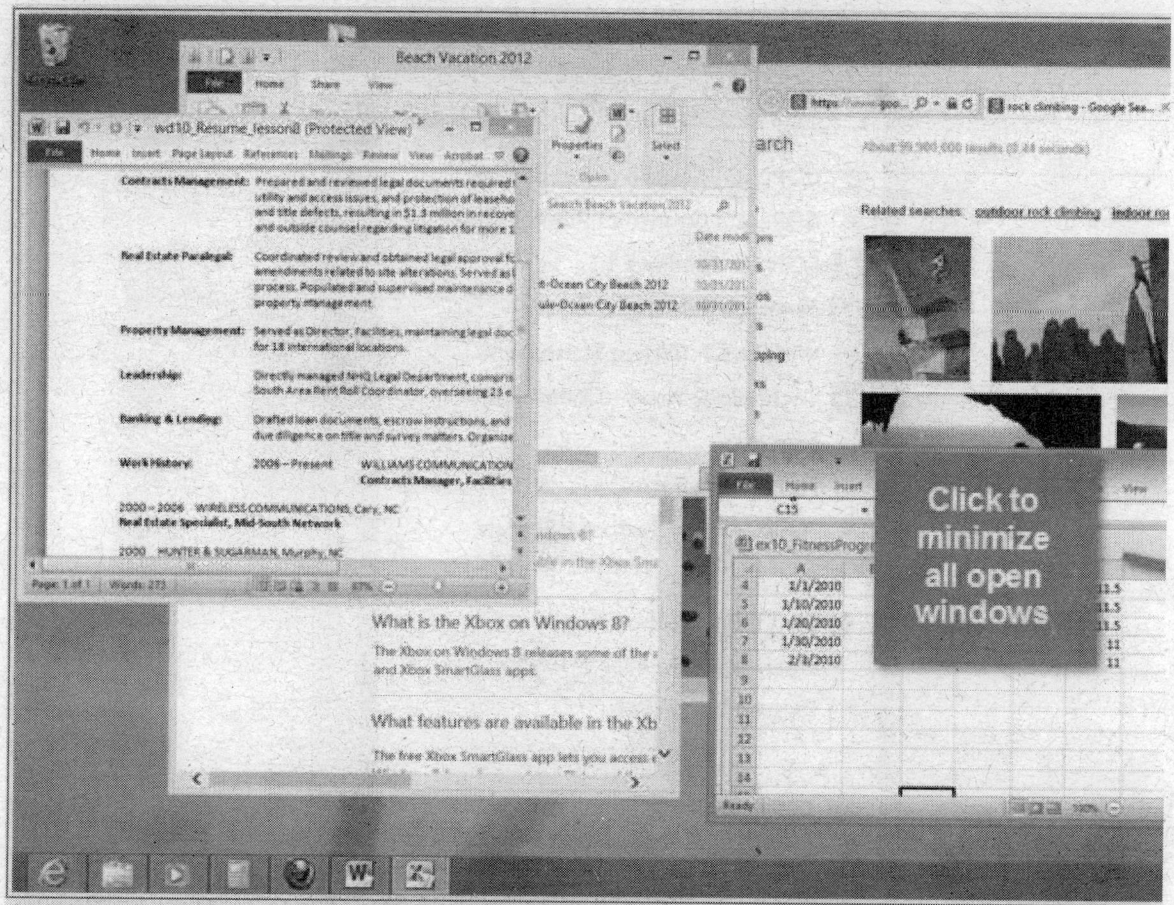

Click to minimize all open windows

Minimizing all open windows

The Desktop with all open windows minimized

The Jump List for Internet Explorer

Managing Your Files and Folders

You can easily manage your files and folders using File Explorer in the Desktop view. In this lesson, you'll learn how to view, organize, and search for files with File Explorer, and how to use libraries. We'll also talk about how libraries work with certain apps on the Start screen.

File Explorer

Opening File Explorer

File Explorer (previously known as Windows Explorer) allows you to open, access, and rearrange your files and folders in Desktop view. If you've used prior versions of Windows before, File Explorer should feel like a familiar way to manage and organize your files.

- Click the folder icon on the taskbar in Desktop view to open File Explorer.
- Click the buttons in the interactive below to become more familiar with the File Explorer interface.

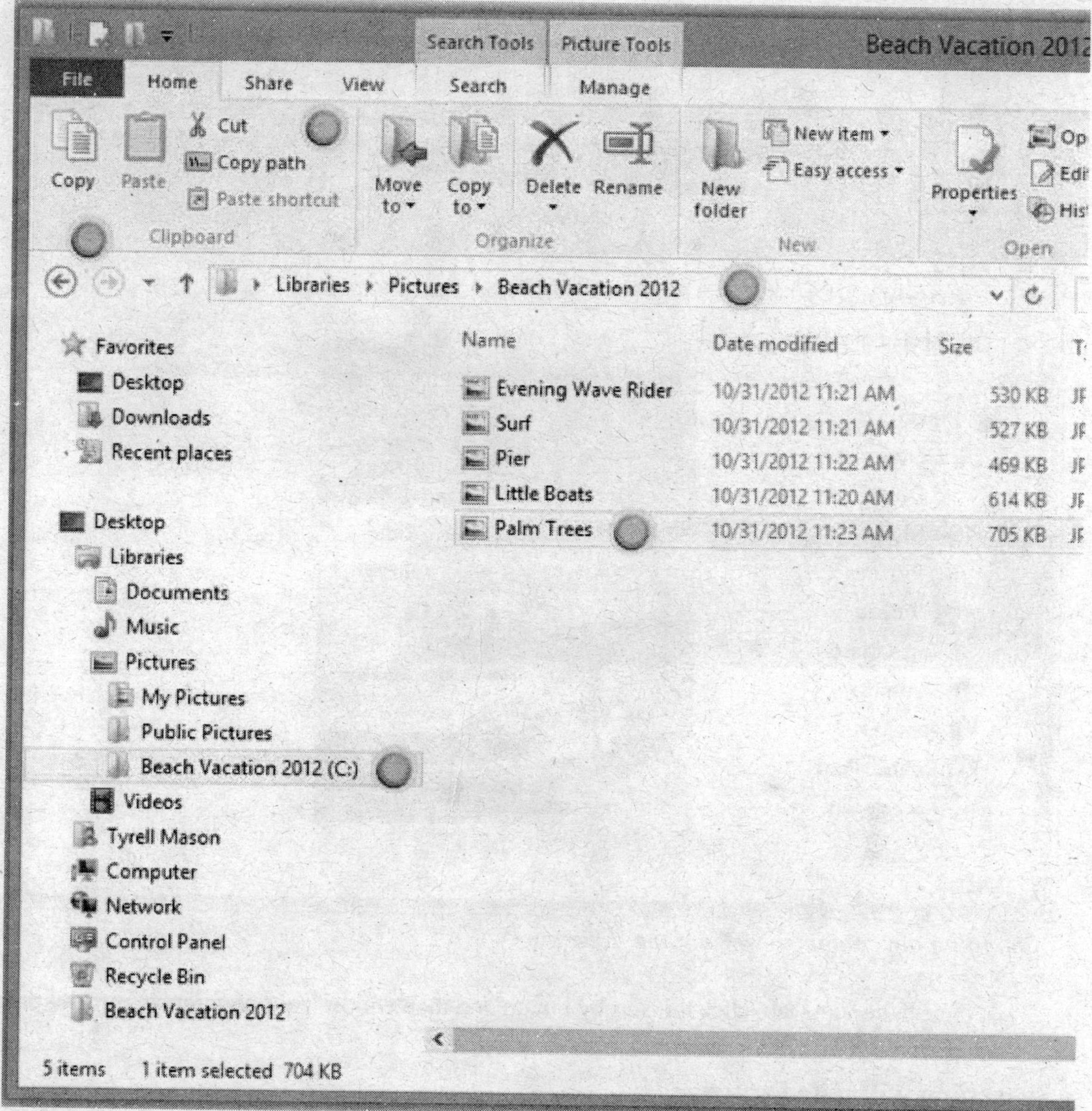

To Change the Content View:

The View tab makes it easy to change the way files are displayed within a folder. For example, you may prefer to see your files as a list when viewing documents and as large icons when viewing pictures.

1. Select the View tab and then choose your preference from the Layout group.

To Sort Files:

Depending on the folder, you may also want to sort your files. For example, you can sort files by size, name, date created, date modified, file type, and much more.

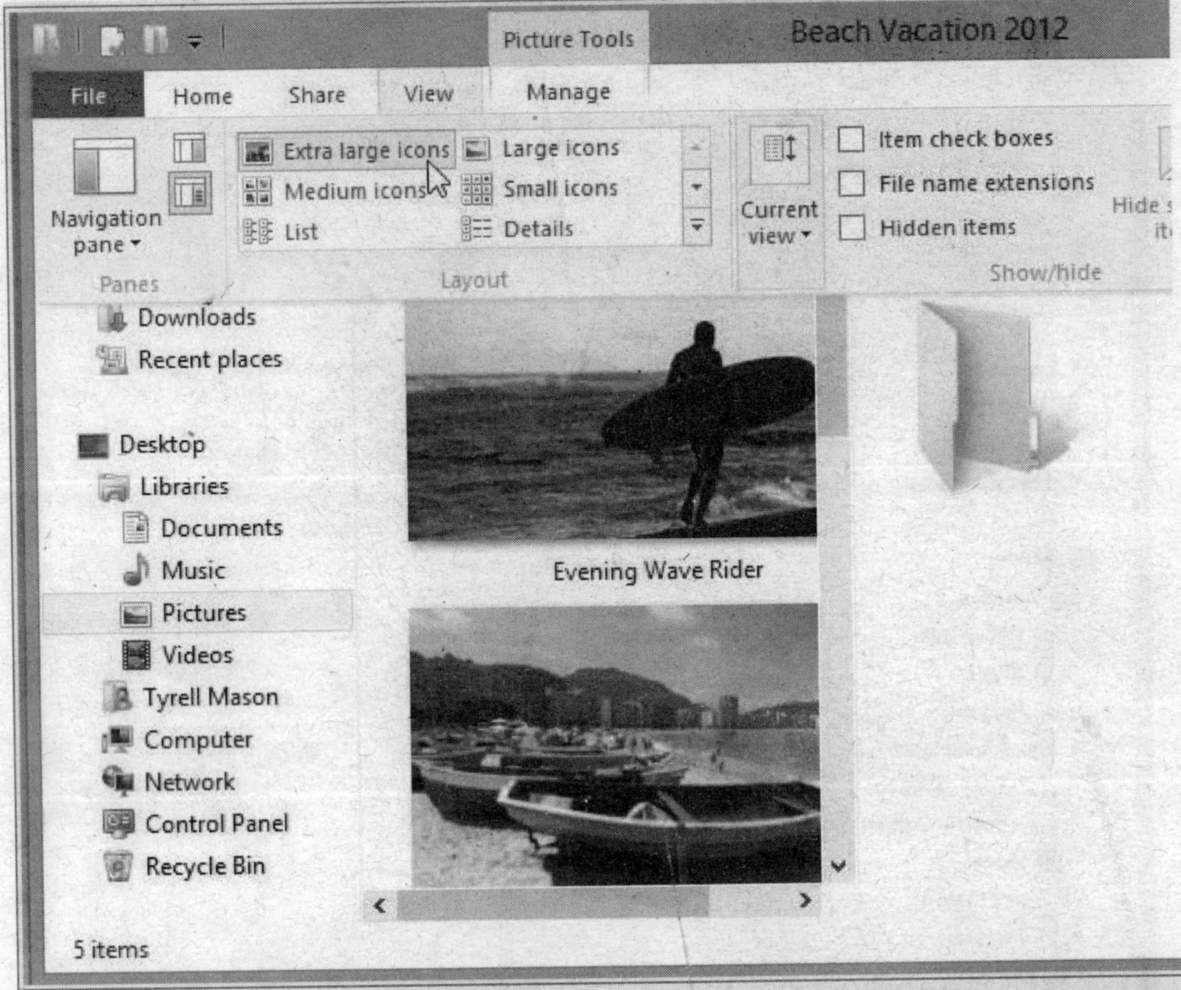

Changing the content view from the View tab

1. Select the View tab, click the Sort by button and then choose your preference from the drop-down menu.

Searching with File Explorer

In addition to the Search feature found on the Charms bar, you can also search for files directly from File Explorer using the Search bar. File Explorer also offers more advanced search options, which can be especially helpful if you're having trouble finding a specific file.

To Use the Search Bar:

1. Locate and select the Search bar in File Explorer.
2. Enter a file name or keyword. Your search results will appear as you type.

The Search Tools Tab

Whenever you enter a term into the search bar, the Search Tools tab will open automatically on the

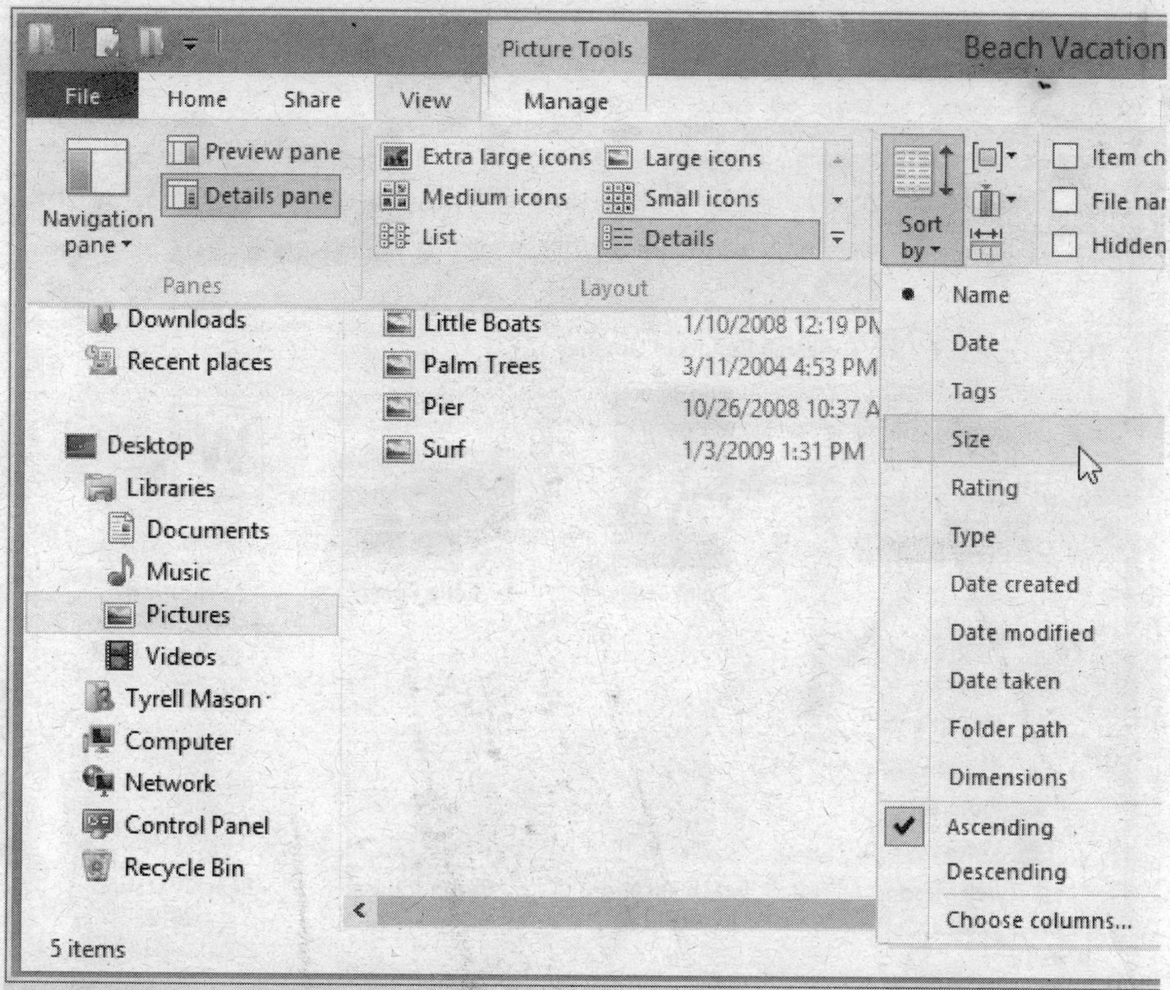

Sorting files by size

Ribbon. This tab gives you access to advanced search options, which allow you to limit your search by file type, size and date modified, view your recent searches, and more.

Working with Libraries

Libraries make it easier to find your files whenever you need them. Libraries are collections of content that can be easily accessed through File Explorer. There are four basic libraries in Windows 8: Documents, Pictures, Music, and Videos.

Libraries do not actually store your files and folders—they simply help keep them organized. You can include any of your folders within a library without changing where they're stored on your computer. For example, you might include a folder of important spreadsheets in the Documents library while still keeping the folder on the Desktop for quick access.

Libraries and the Start Screen

Libraries are especially important in Windows 8 because many of the apps on the Start screen—including

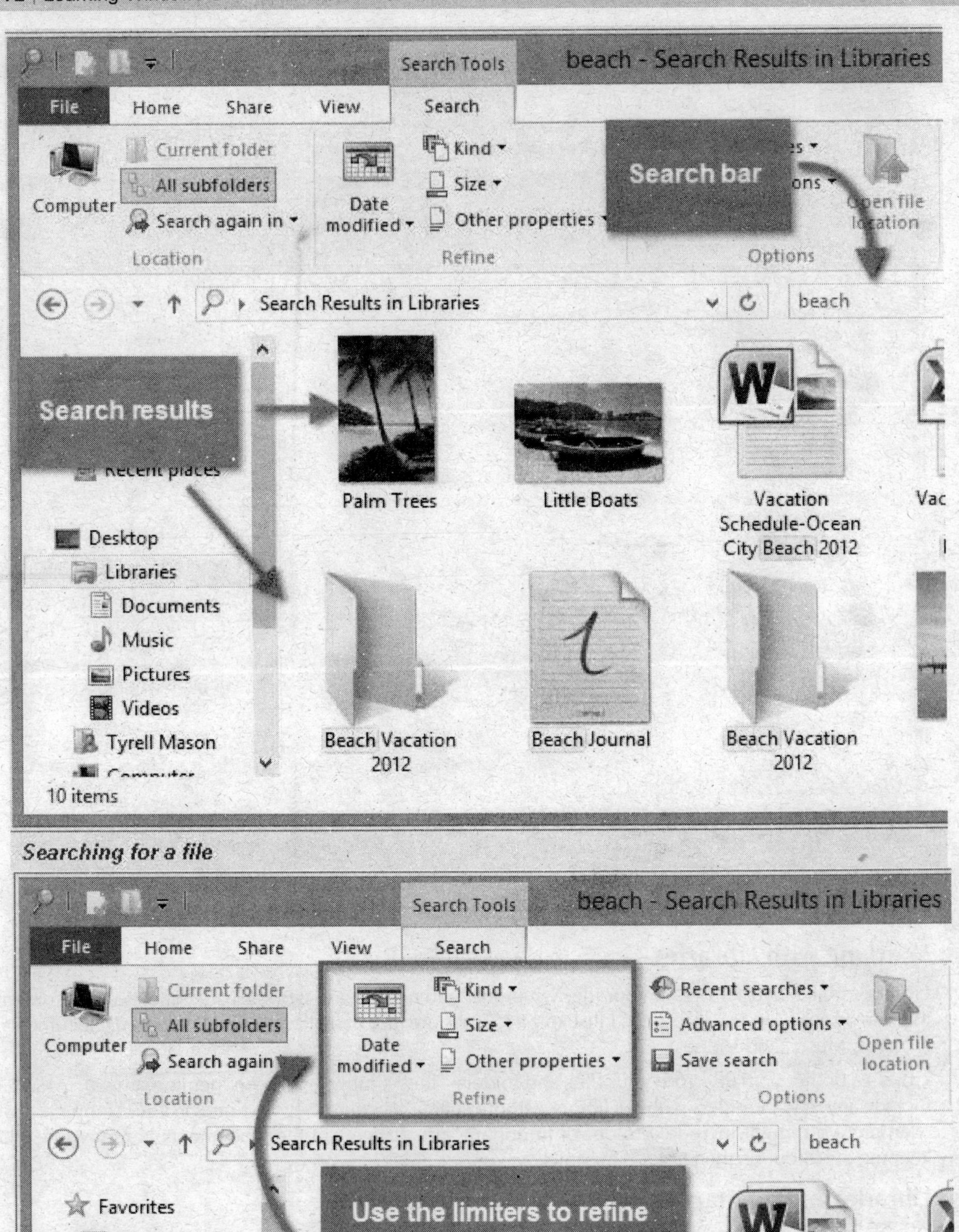

Searching for a file

The Search Tools tab

Music, Photos, and Videos—use your libraries to find and display content. For example, any songs or albums in the Music library will appear in the Music app.

The apps on your Start screen are optimized for media, making it easier than ever before to play music, watch videos, and view photos. File Explorer can help you organize your existing media files into libraries, so you'll be able to enjoy them from the Start screen.

To Add Folders to Libraries:

Some folders, such as My Documents and My Music, are included automatically in the appropriate library. If you want to include additional folders, you will need to add them to the library. In the example below, we'll include a folder on the Desktop in the Pictures library without changing the folder's location.

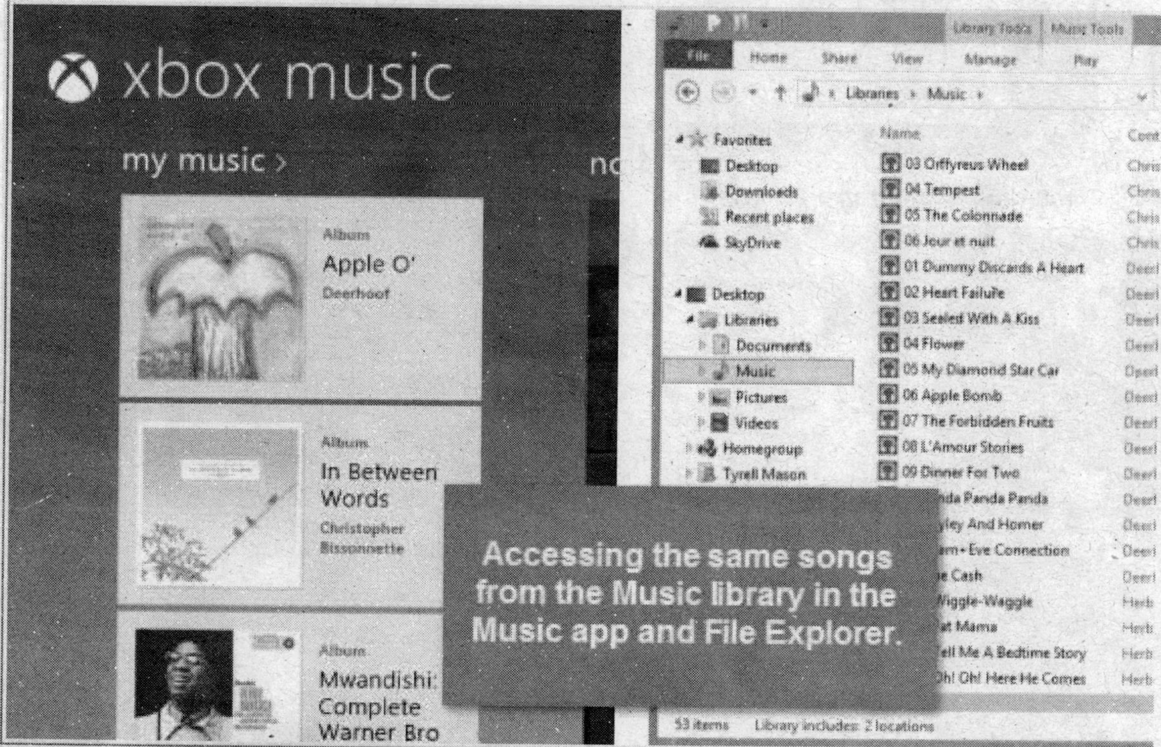

Files shared between the Music app and Music library

1. Locate and right-click the Folder.
2. Hover the mouse over Include in library in the drop-down menu and then select the desired library.
3. The folder will now be included in the chosen library.
4. The photos will also be viewable in the Photos app from the Start screen.

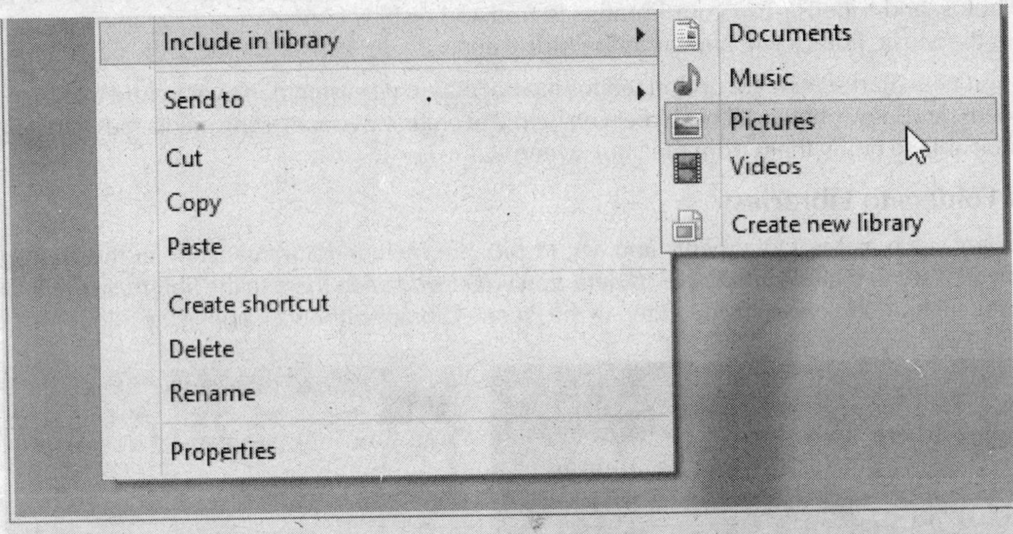

Including a folder in a library

The folder included in the chosen library

CHAPTER 7

Personalizing Your Windows

In this chapter you will read about:

- Font Size and Text Display Settings.
- Adding, Finding and Linking Contacts.
- Using Mail Applications.
- Using Email.
- Adding, Modifying Accounts.

Introduction

Windows 8 makes it easy to customize the look and feel of the Desktop view. In this lesson, you'll learn how to access the Personalization pane, which allows you to customize the theme, background image, and color of your Desktop. You'll also learn how to adjust your font size and text display.

Any changes you make to the appearance of the Desktop will not affect the Start screen. Check out our lesson on Personalizing Your Start Screen to learn more.

- To access the Personalization pane, right-click anywhere on the Desktop and then select Personalize from the drop-down menu. The Personalization pane will appear.

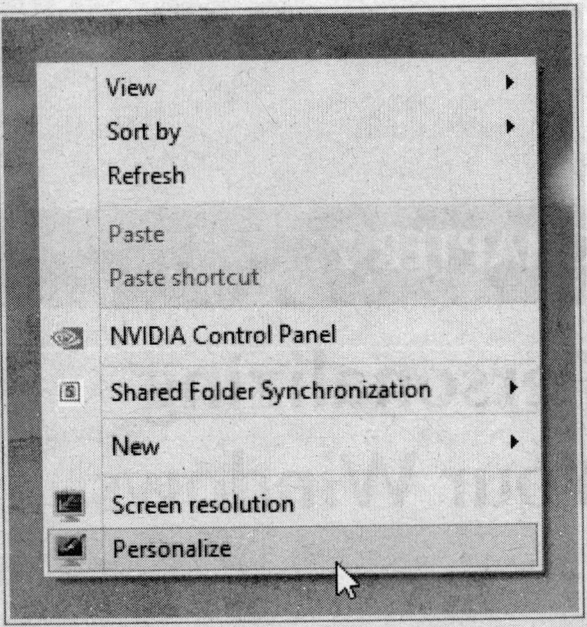

Accessing the Personalization pane

Click the buttons in the interactive below to learn more about using the Personalization pane to customize the appearance of the Desktop view.

Font Size and Text Display Settings

You can also use the Personalization pane to customize the font size and text display. Again, it's important to note that these settings will only affect the Desktop view, not the Start screen.

To Change the Font Size:

If you have difficulty seeing the text on your Desktop, you can increase the font size. Increasing the font size will also increase the size of icons and other items on your Desktop.

1. Locate and select Display in the lower-left corner of the Personalization pane.
2. The Display settings will appear. Choose the desired size. Note that a larger size may interfere with the way some items appear on the screen.
3. Click Apply to save your changes.
4. You may need to restart your computer for these changes to take effect.

To Adjust ClearType Settings:

ClearType helps improve the readability of text on LCD monitors and screens.

1. Locate and select Display in the lower-left corner of the Personalization pane. The Display settings will appear.
2. Select Adjust ClearType text from the left-navigation menu.
3. The ClearType Text Tuner dialog box will appear. Follow the instructions, choosing the text that appears best to you.
4. When you are done selecting text, click Finish. The ClearType settings will be applied.

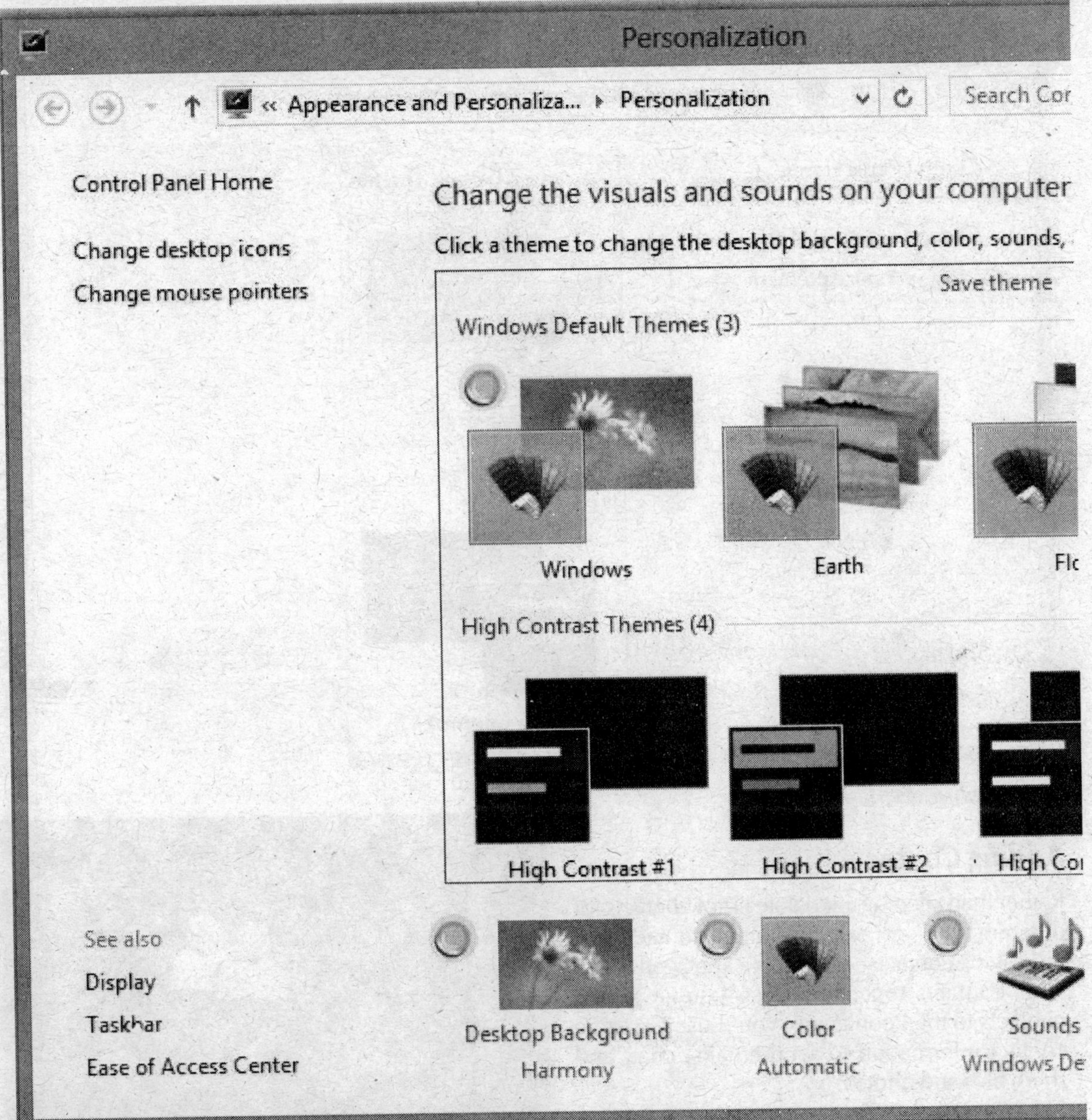

Using the People App

The People app is the central place for all your contacts, and it's one of the most important apps you'll use in Windows 8. The People app can also be integrated with your favorite social networks, such as Facebook and Twitter. In this lesson, you'll learn how to add, manage, and organize your contacts, and how to connect your social networks.

- To open the People app, locate and select People on the Start Screen. The People app will appear.
- Click the buttons in the interactive below to become more familiar with the People app interface.

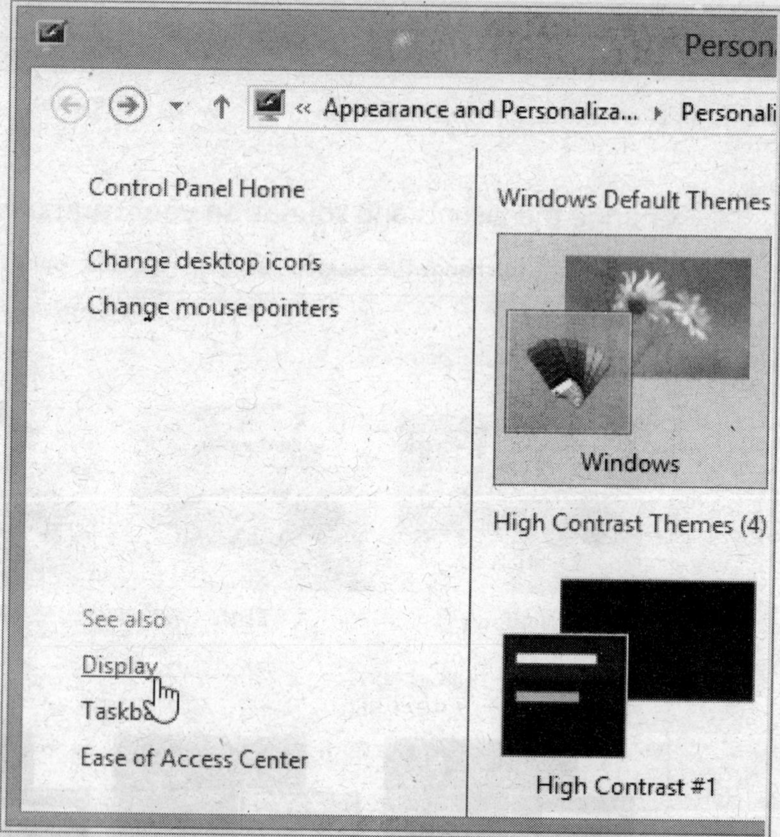

Accessing display settings

Adding Contacts

Rather than keeping a separate list of contacts for different apps—for example, email contacts and messaging contacts—the People app keeps all of your contacts together. Once you've added contacts to the People app, you'll use the same contact information to send emails, chat, and share files and photos.

Opening the People app

There are two ways to add contacts:

1. Manually entering information for each of your contacts.
2. Importing existing lists of contacts from other accounts, like Gmail, Facebook, Twitter, and LinkedIn. If you already have a lot of contacts saved with another account, this method can save you a lot of time and effort.

To Import Contacts from a Service:

Connecting to another account will import all of your existing contacts. If you choose to connect to a social network, your news feeds and updates will also be integrated into the People app.

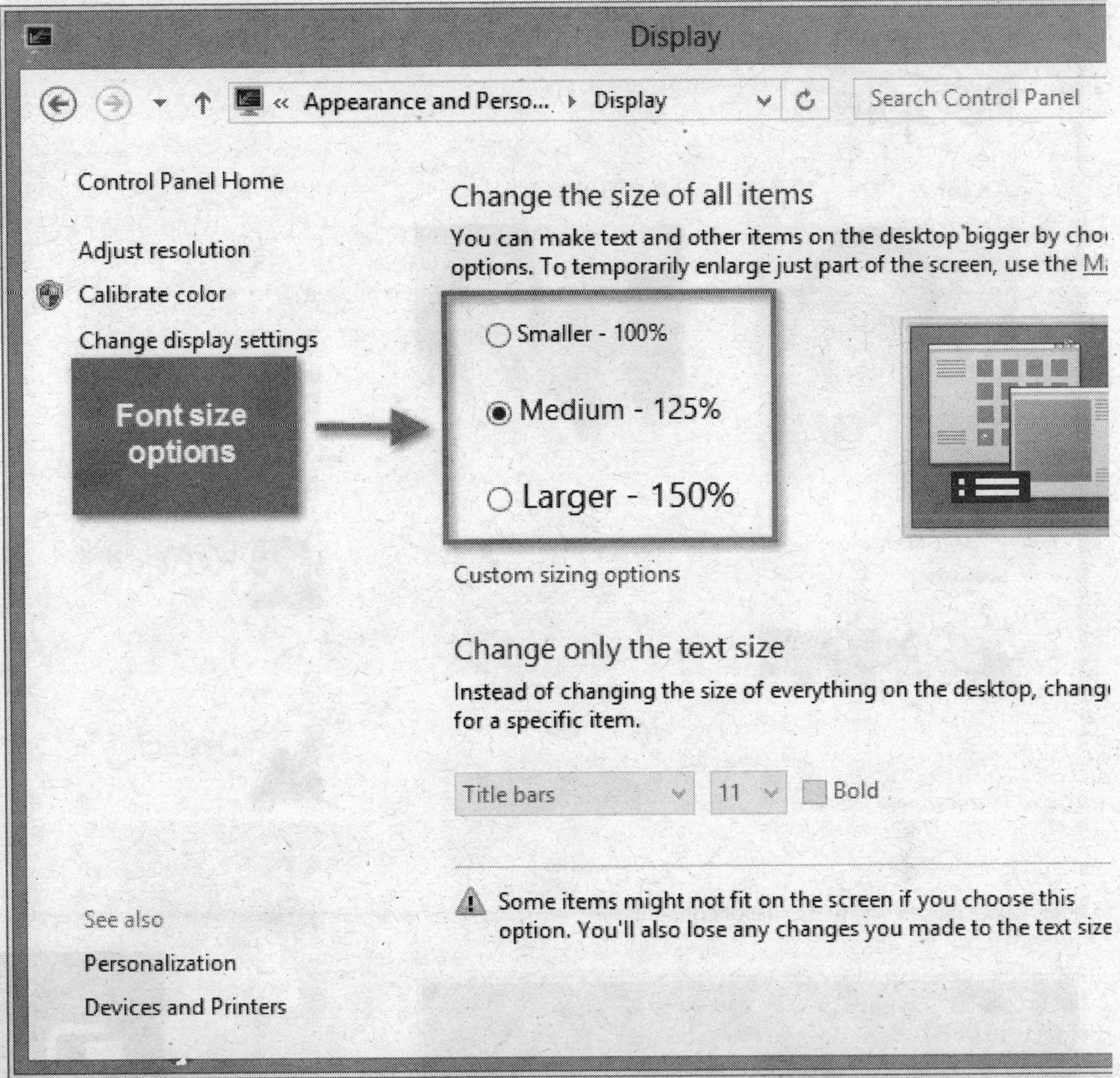

Changing the default font size

1. In the People app, hover the mouse in the lower-right corner to access the Charms bar, then select Settings.
2. The Settings pane will appear on the right. Select Accounts.
3. The Accounts pane will appear. Click Add an account.
4. Select the service you wish to use. In this example, we'll add a Facebook account.
5. The Connecting to a service page will appear. You will need to sign in to the chosen account.
6. The Request for Permission page will appear with options and permissions. This page will vary depending on which service you chose. Follow the instructions to give the People app permission to access your account.

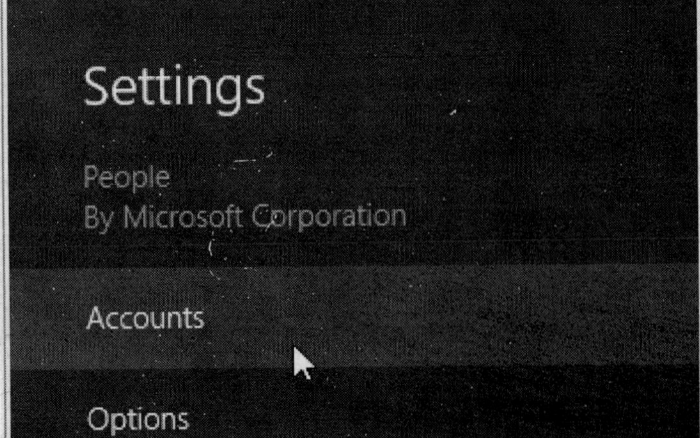

Clicking Accounts

Clicking settings

Clicking Add an account

7. Once you are connected, your contacts will be imported into the People app.

Unlike manually added contacts, any contacts imported from another service cannot be deleted. We've noticed that connecting to some services (especially Twitter) may import contacts that you don't actually need to communicate with. Be sure to consider how often you'll use all of your contacts before deciding to import from any given external service.

To Add a New Contact Manually:

If you don't have all of your contacts stored on your social networks, or if you just prefer to enter contact information on your own, it's easy to add contacts manually.

1. Right-click anywhere on the People app. A menu will appear at the bottom of the screen.
2. Locate and select New contact.

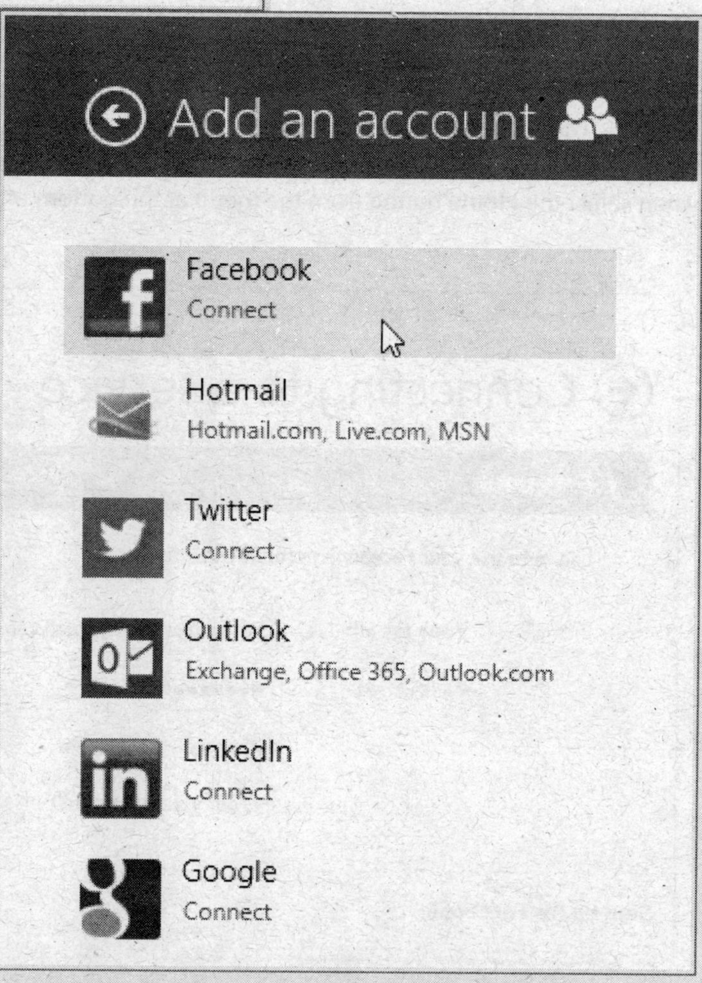

Adding a Facebook account

3. Enter the contact information. At the very least, you should enter a first and last name, as well as an email address. However, you can also enter other information, like phone numbers, alternate email addresses, and work info.
4. When you are finished filling out the contact information, click Save.
5. The contact will be added to the People app.

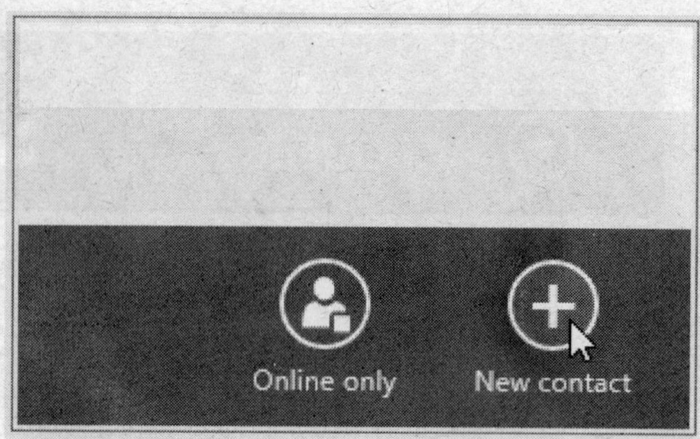

Clicking New contact

Viewing and Editing Contacts

Once you've added some contacts, you're ready to start using the People app. It's easy to connect with any of your contacts by navigating to their contact page. From there, you'll be able to see the contact's information, as well as updates and photos from any connected social networks. You can also edit a contact if you need to change or update their information.

To View a Contact Page:

1. Locate and select the desired contact.
2. The contact page will appear.

Sometimes the Back Arrow may not appear on a contact page. If this occurs, right-click the mouse and then select the Home button from the menu at the bottom of the screen.

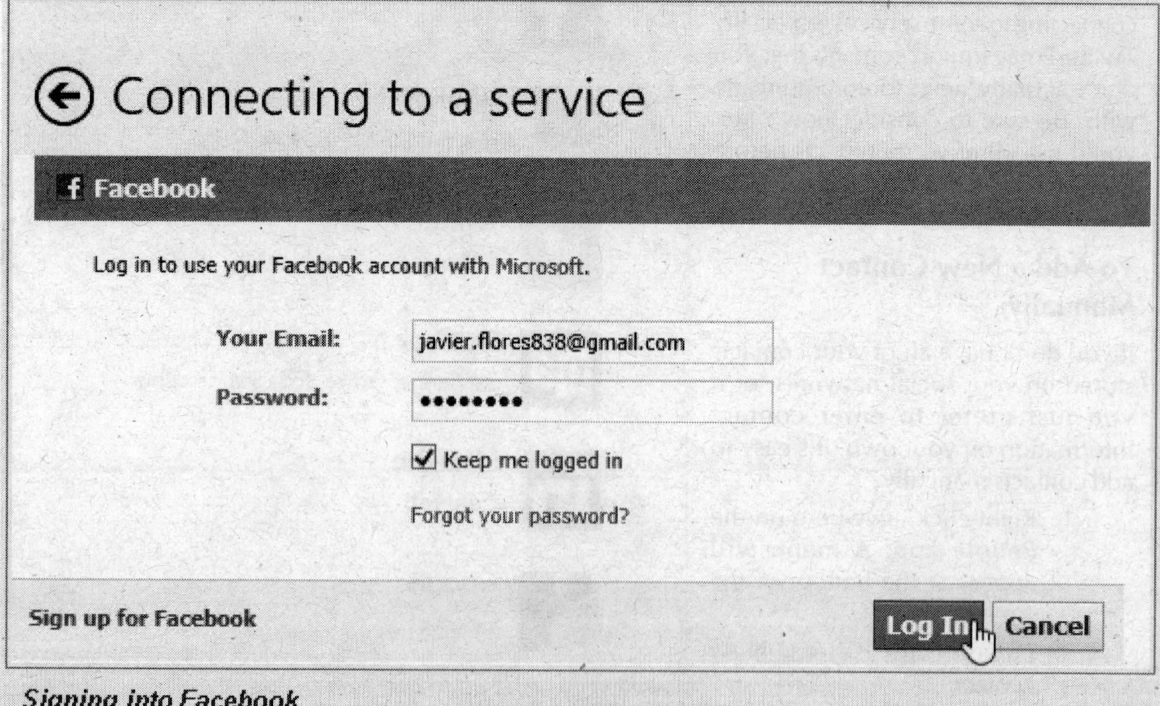

Signing into Facebook

All

A

Amelia Jones

G

Grace Ellington

B

Bryan Durand

H

Henri Rousseau

D

Desmond Taylor

J

Jessie Reese

Julia Fillory

Facebook friends imported into the People app

You can also use the contact page to connect with a contact. Click the buttons in the interactive below to learn about different ways to communicate from the contact page.

To Edit a Contact:

1. Locate and select the contact you wish to edit.
2. The contact page will appear. Right-click and a menu will appear at the bottom of the screen.
3. Locate and select Edit.
4. Modify the contact information as desired, then click Save. The contact information will be saved.

Selecting the desired contact

Connecting to a service

Request for Permission

Microsoft is requesting permission to do the following:

Access my basic information
Includes name, profile picture, gender, networks, user ID, list of friends, and any other information I've made public.

Access my profile information
Birthday, Current City, Website and Work History

Access my photos
Photos Uploaded by Me

Access my videos
Videos Uploaded by Me

Access information people share with me
Birthdays, Current Cities, Work History, Websites, Photos and Videos

Post on my behalf
This app may post on my behalf, including status updates, photos and more.

Access posts in my News Feed

Access my data any time
Microsoft may access my data when I'm not using the application.

Access Facebook Chat

Microsoft

Logged in as Javier Flores · Log Out

Connecting Facebook with your Microsoft

New contact

Account

Account

Gmail

Name

First name

Merced

Last name

Flores

Company

Email

Personal

flores.merced@yahoo.com

Email

Phone

Mobile

Phone

Address

Address

Save

Saving contact details

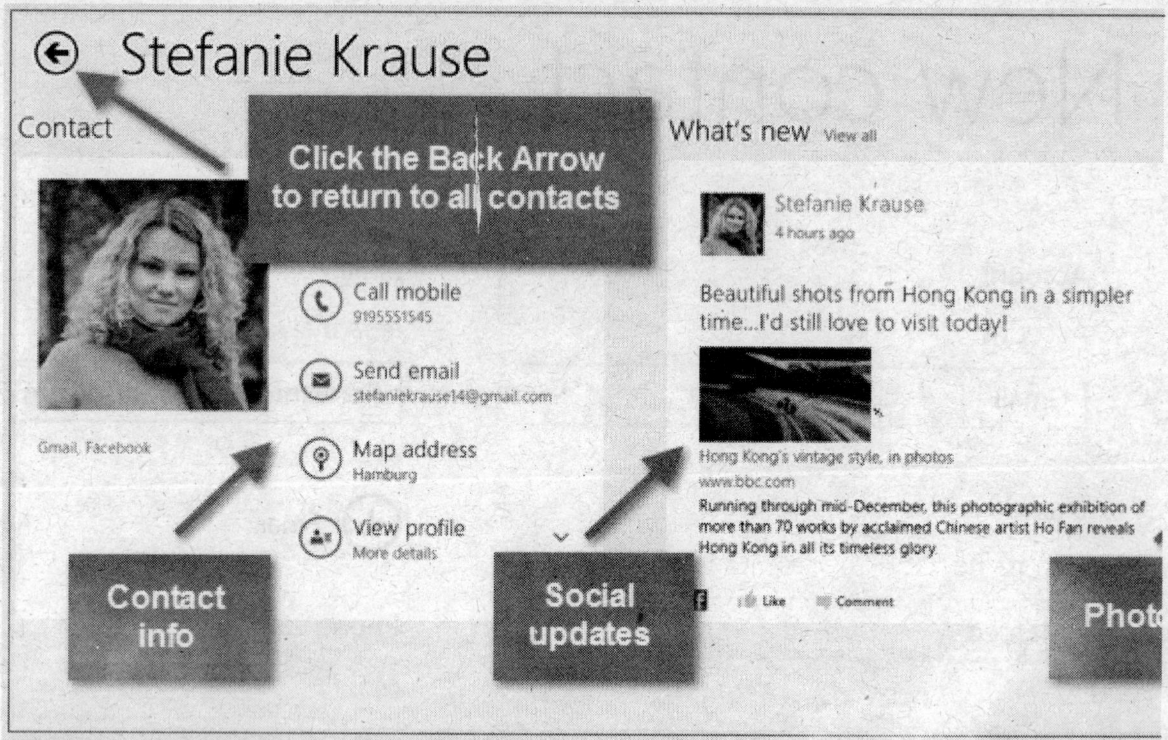

Viewing a contact page

The added contact

Finding Contacts

If you have a lot of different contacts, it can be difficult to locate the one you need. Fortunately, there are several ways to find your contacts quickly.

To Search for a Contact:

1. From the People app, type the contact you're looking for. Your search results will instantly appear on the left side of the screen. Simply click a contact to open the contact page.

Clicking the Home button

Editing a contact

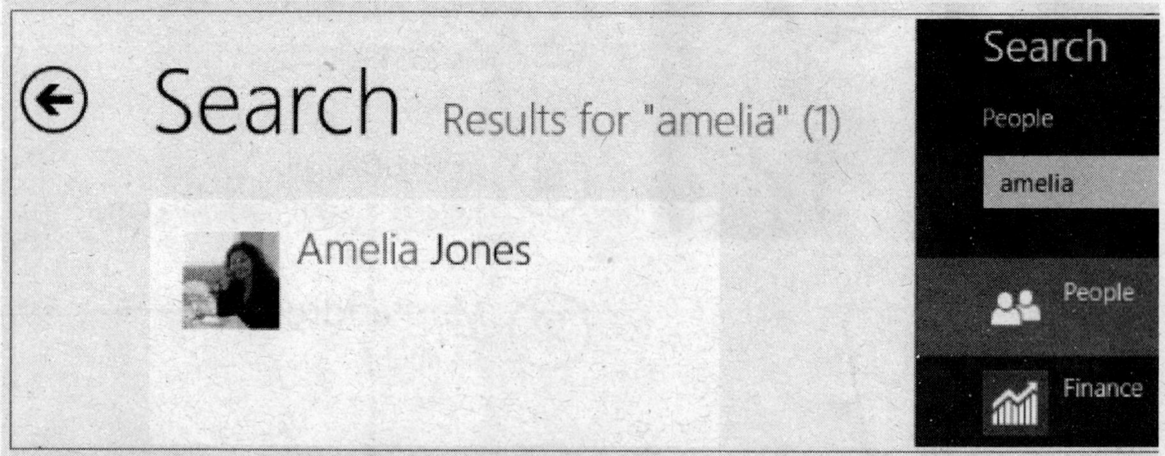

Searching for a contact in the People app

Edit contact info

Name

First name

Stefanie

Last name

Krause

Company

(+) Name

Email

Personal ⌄

stefaniekrause14@gmail.com

(+) Email

Phone

Mobile ⌄

(+) Phone

Address

(+) Address

Other info

Website

stefanifekrause.com

(+) Other info

Save

Saving the edited contact information

To Zoom Out:

If you want to jump directly to a specific place in your contacts list—for example, contacts whose names begin with the letter G—you can zoom out to see a simplified view of your contacts.

1. From the People app, locate and select the zoom button near the lower-right corner of the screen.
2. Your contacts list will zoom out. Simply click a letter to navigate to a specific set of contacts.

The zoom button

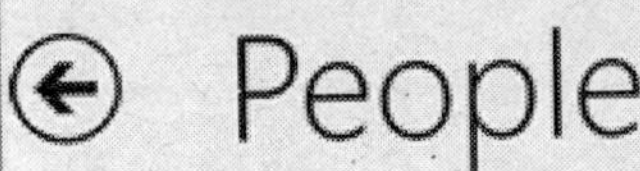

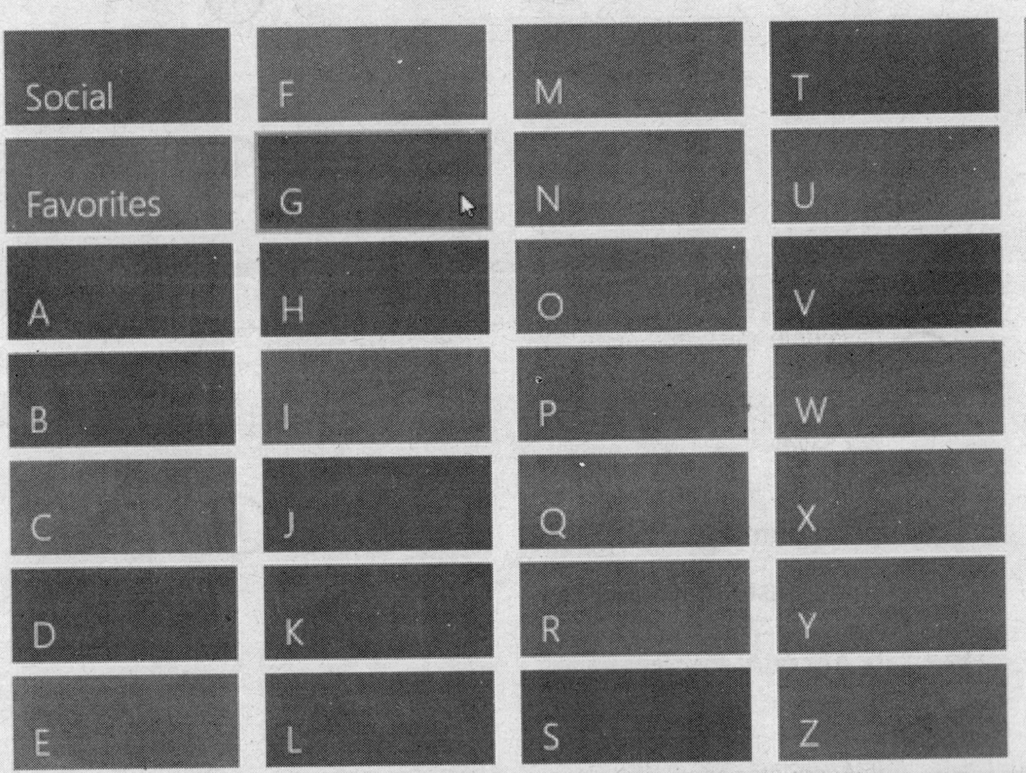

Zooming out to view all contacts

Linking Contacts

If you import contacts from multiple services, you may find that you have duplicate contacts. For example, you might have imported the same contact from both Gmail and Facebook. You can link these together to create a single contact.

To Link a Contact:

1. Locate and select the contact you wish to link.

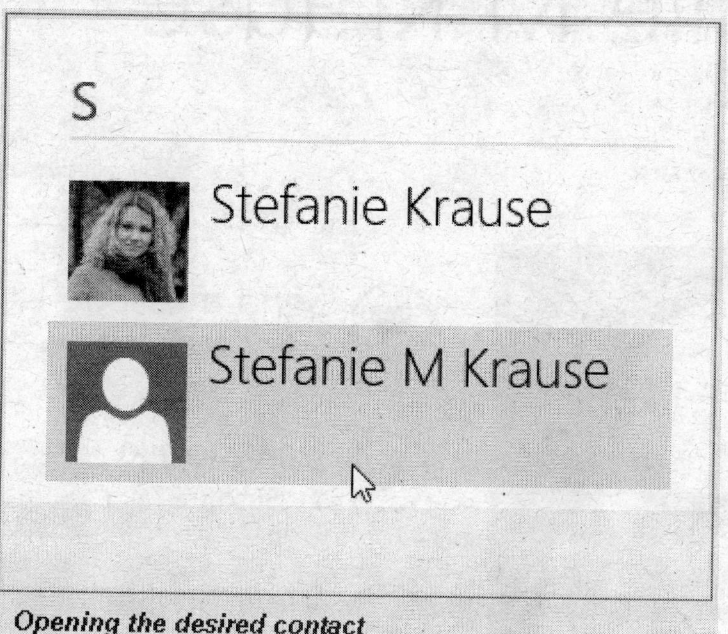

Opening the desired contact

2. The contact page will appear. Right-click and a menu will appear at the bottom of the screen.
3. Locate and select Link.
4. The People app will suggest contacts to link if they share common information, like a name or email address.
5. Click the suggested contact, or click Choose a contact to select a contact manually.
6. Click Save.
7. The information will be linked together into a single contact.

Changing Account Permissions

Once you have added an account, like Facebook or Twitter, you may want to modify how much information the People app can access. You can also choose to remove a linked account completely.

To Modify Account Permissions:

1. In the People app, hover the mouse in the lower-right corner to access the Charms bar, then select Settings. The Settings pane will appear on the right. Select Accounts.
2. The Accounts pane will appear. Select the account you wish to modify.
3. The account details will appear. Click Manage this account online to modify the account permissions.
4. Internet Explorer will open and the account permissions page will appear. This page will vary depending on which account you select. You can either:
   - Click the boxes to set specific account permissions (if applicable).

Stefanie M Krause

Contact

Gmail

Clicking Link

Linked profiles

Stefanie M Krause
Gmail

Suggestions

Stefanie K
Gmail, Facebook

Choose a contact

Choosing a suggested contact

Links for Stefanie M Krau

Linked profiles

Stefanie M Krause
Gmail

Stefanie Krause
Gmail, Facebook

Suggestions

Choose a contac

Clicking Save

S

Stefanie M Krause

The linked contact

- Locate and select Remove this connection completely to remove the connection from your Microsoft account.

5. Once you are satisfied with the changes, click Save. Your account permissions will be saved.

Removing a linked account will also remove all contacts imported from that service.

Clicking Accounts

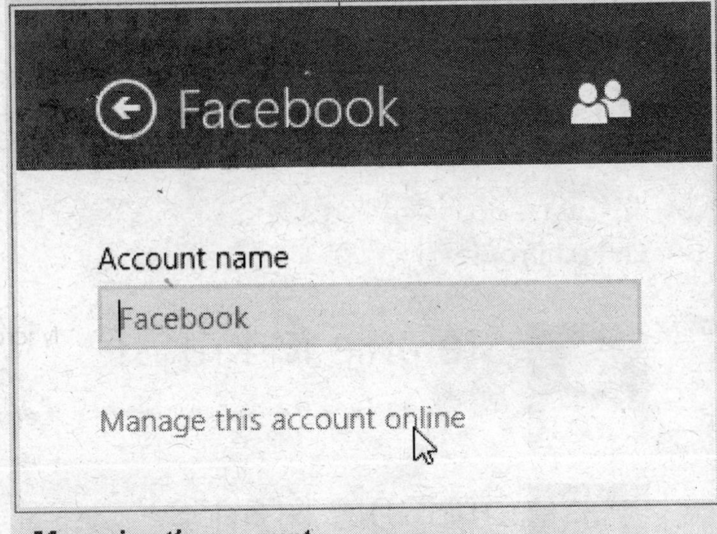

Managing the account

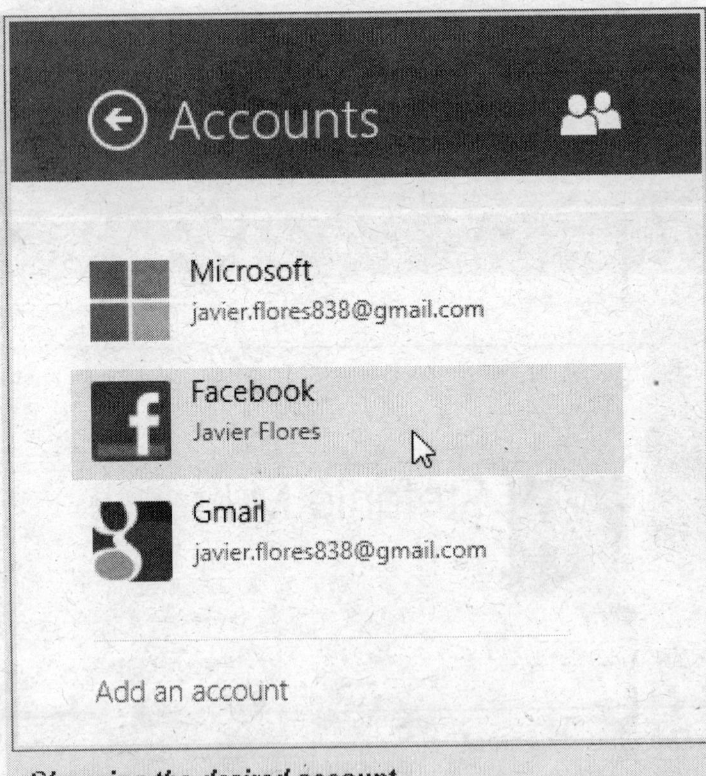

Choosing the desired account

Favoriting and Pinning Contacts

If you have certain contacts that you use very frequently, you may wish to favorite or pin those contacts for quick access.

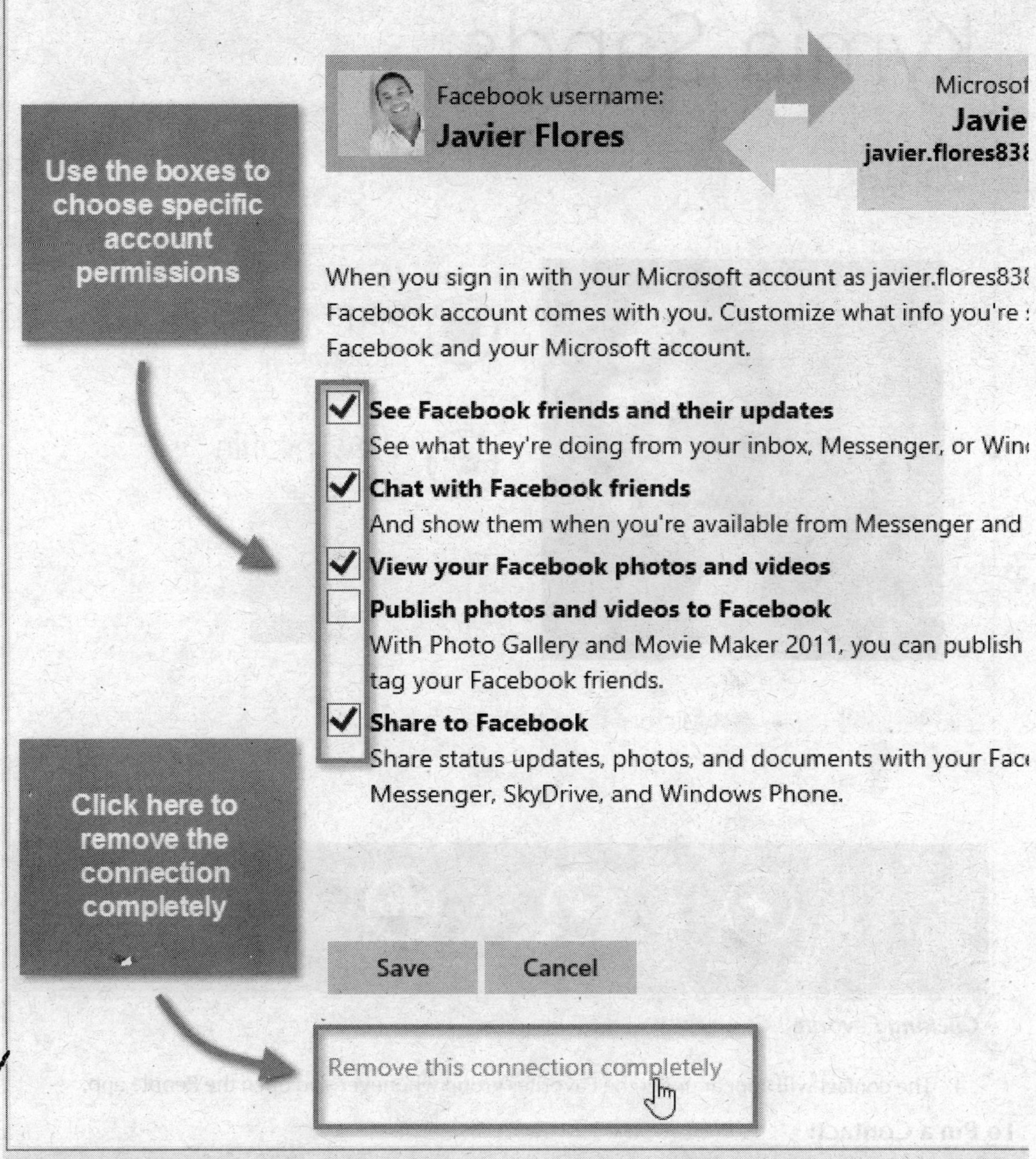

Managing linked account settings

To Favorite a Contact:

1. Locate and select the contact you wish to Favorite.
2. The contact page will appear. Right-click and a menu will appear at the bottom of the screen.
3. Select Favorite.

Kymia Sands

Contact

Facebook

Clicking Favorite

4. The contact will appear under the Favorites group whenever you open the People app.

To Pin a Contact:

Just like apps, you can also pin a contact to the Start screen.

1. Locate and select the contact you wish to pin.
2. The contact page will appear. Right-click and a menu will appear at the bottom of the screen.
3. Select Pin to Start.
4. A dialog box will appear. Click Pin to Start to continue.

The contact added to Favorites

5. The contact will be pinned to the Start screen. Simply click a contact on the Start screen to view their contact page.

To unpin a contact from the Start screen, right-click on the contact page and then select Unpin from Start from the menu.

Viewing Your Social Feeds

The social page makes it easy to see a quick summary of the latest information from your connected social networks. From here, you can edit your profile picture, post status updates, view your notifications, like and comment on posts, and more.

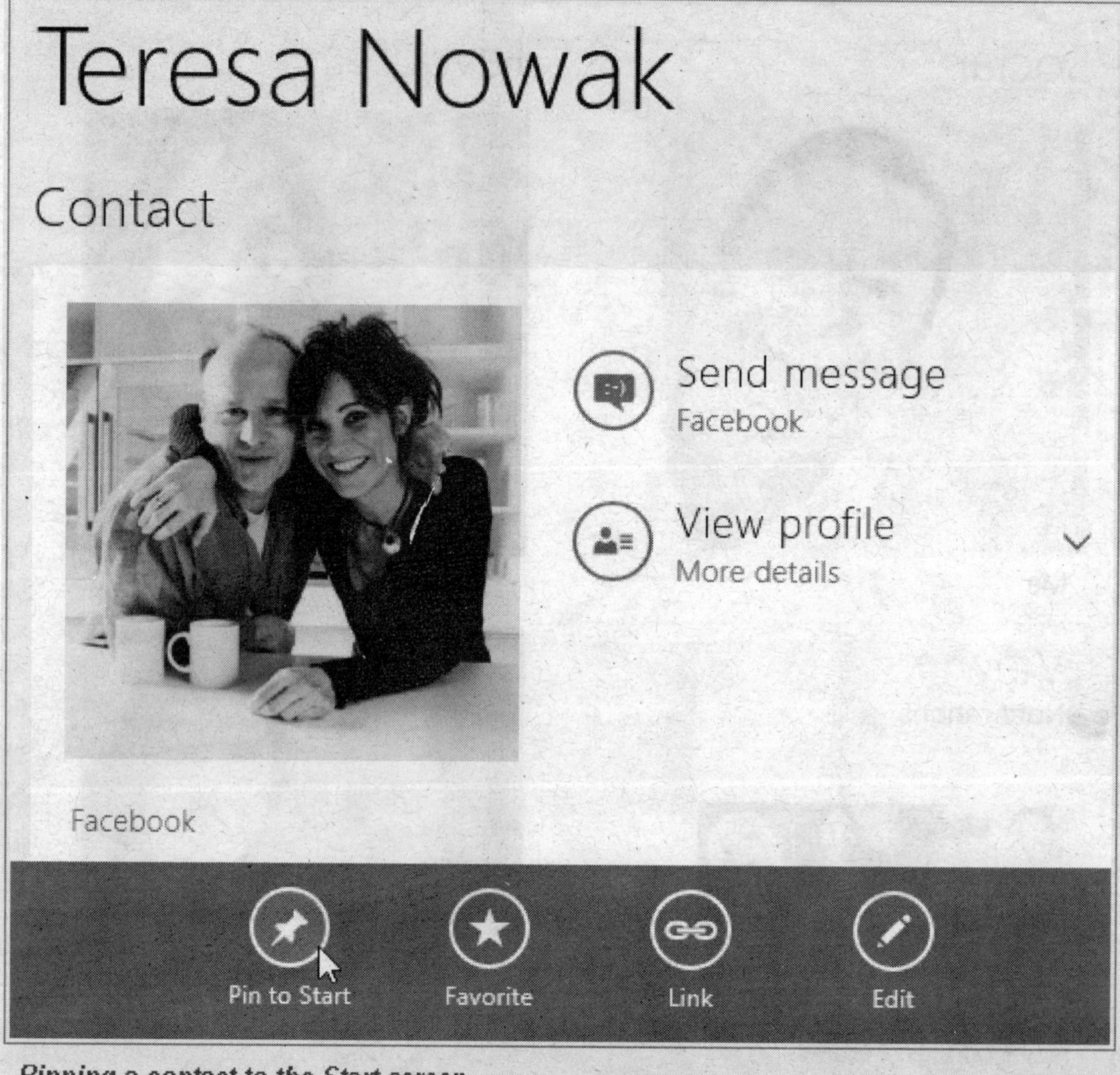

Pinning a contact to the Start screen

To Access the Social Page:

1. From the People app, click your profile picture.
2. The social page will appear.

To Change your Profile Picture:

It's easy to change your profile picture from the social page, but it's important to note that this will only change your Microsoft account profile picture, not connected accounts like Gmail or LinkedIn.

1. From the social page, select your profile picture.
2. The Change your account picture page will appear.
3. Click Browse to choose a new photo. If your computer or tablet has a built-in camera, you can click Take a Photo to take a picture of yourself.

Clicking Pin to Start

The contact pinned to the Start screen

Unpinning a contact from the Start screen

4. When you are satisfied, click Save. Your profile picture will be updated.

Using the Mail App

The Mail app offers a new way to view and manage your email messages. In many ways, the Mail app is very similar to other email applications, such as Outlook or Gmail, but its redesigned interface may feel a little confusing at first. In this lesson, you'll learn how to send, receive, and reply to email messages using the Mail app. You'll also learn how to organize your inbox, add multiple email accounts, and modify your account settings.

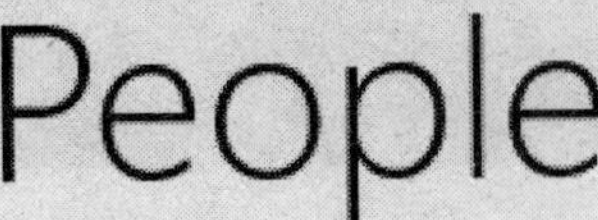

Accessing the social page

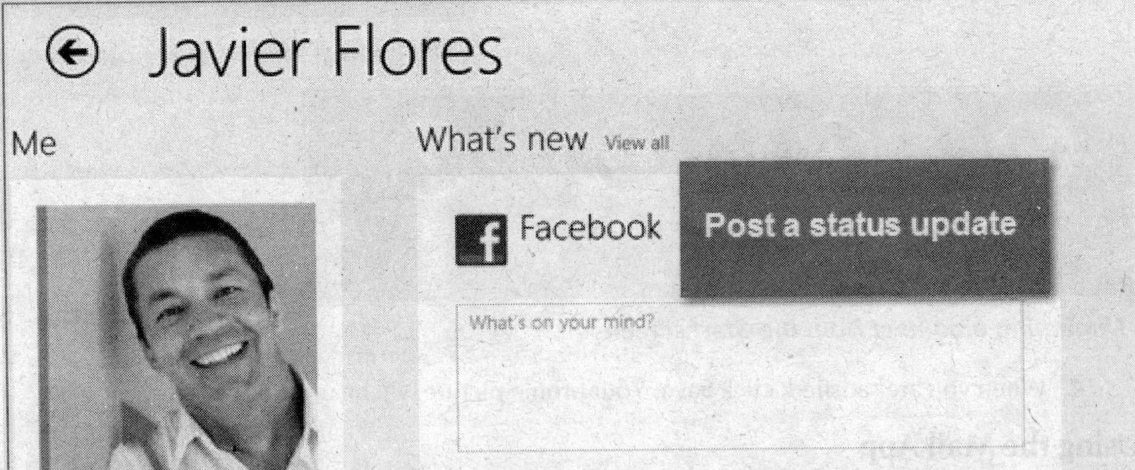

The social page

Clicking the profile picture

Opening the Mail app

Getting Started with Mail:

1. To open the Mail app, locate and select Mail on the Start screen. The Mail app will appear.
2. The first time you open the Mail app, you will need to connect an email account to start sending and receiving email. If you are signed into Windows 8 with a Microsoft account, the Mail app will request to connect with that email address. Enter your account information and then click Connect. Your inbox will appear.

Change your account pic

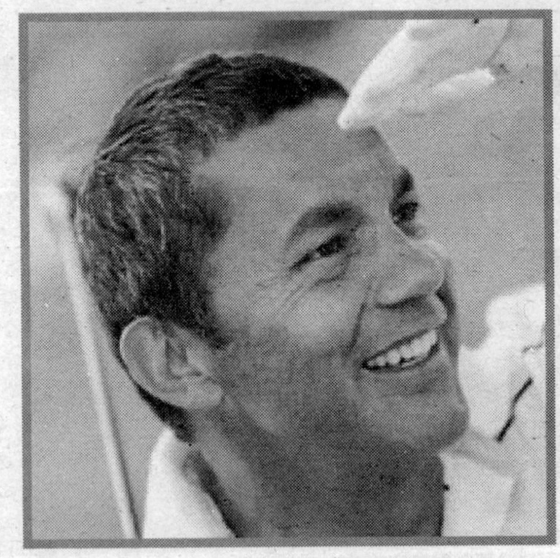

Changing the profile picture

3. If you have already connected an email service with the People app, such as Hotmail or Gmail, you will not need to connect to the account again.
4. Click the buttons in the interactive below to become more familiar with the Mail app interface.

Sending Email:

You'll use the Compose pane to write and send messages from the Mail app. From here, you'll add the email address of the recipient(s), the subject, and the body of the email, which is the message itself.

To Compose a New Message:

1. Locate and select the New Message button.
2. The Compose pane will appear.

Add your Google account

Enter the information below to connect to your Google account.

Email address

javier.flores838@gmail.com

Password

•••••••••

Include your Google contacts and calendars

Connect Cancel

Connecting an email account to the Mail app

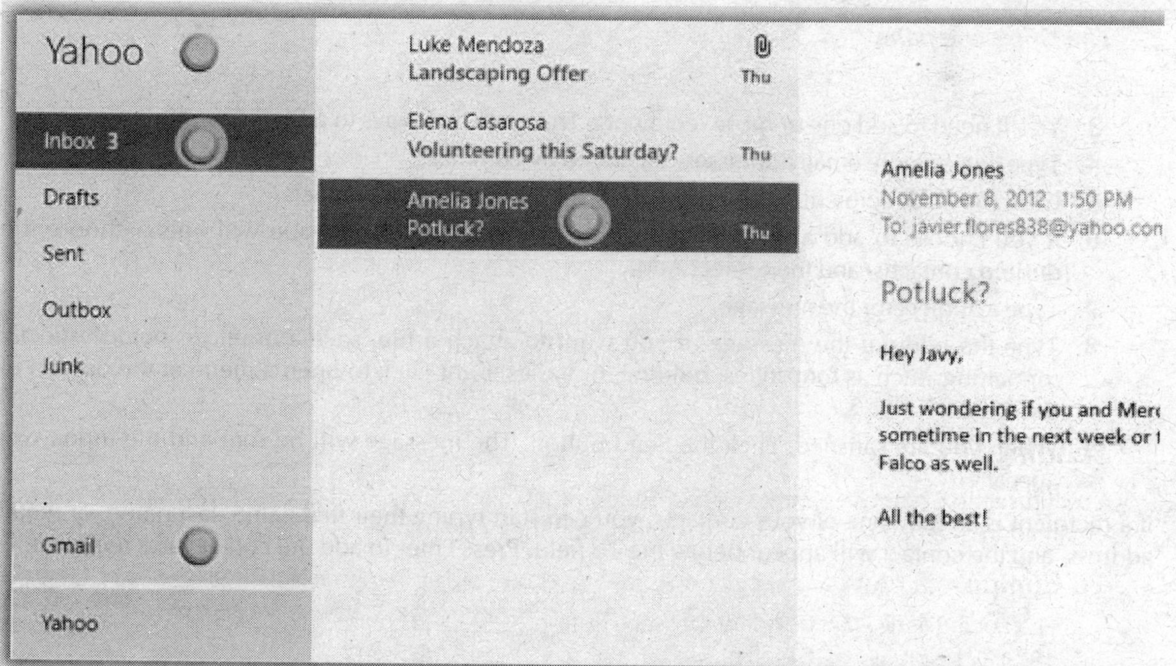

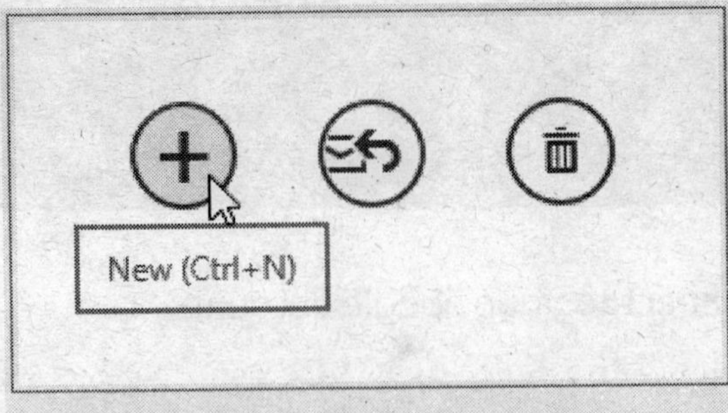

Clicking the New Message button

Add a subject

Add a message

Sent from Windows Mail

The Compose pane

3. You'll need to add one or more recipients. There are two ways to add recipients:
4. Type one or more email addresses, separated by commas.
5. Click the Add recipient button to select recipients from your contacts.
6. If you choose to add a recipient from your contacts, the People app will open. Choose the desired contact(s) and then select Add.
7. Type a Subject for the message.
8. Type the body of the message. If you want to attach a file, save a draft, or include special formatting, such as font styles, bolding, or italics, right-click to open a menu at the bottom of the screen.
9. When you are satisfied, click the Send button. The message will be sent and the inbox will appear.

If a recipient is already one of your contacts, you can start typing their first name, last name, or email address, and the contact will appear below the To field. Press Enter to add the contact as a recipient.

Yahoo
javier.flores838@yahoo.com
To
amelia.jones88@gmail.com henri.rousseau30@gmai
Cc
Show more

Adding recipients

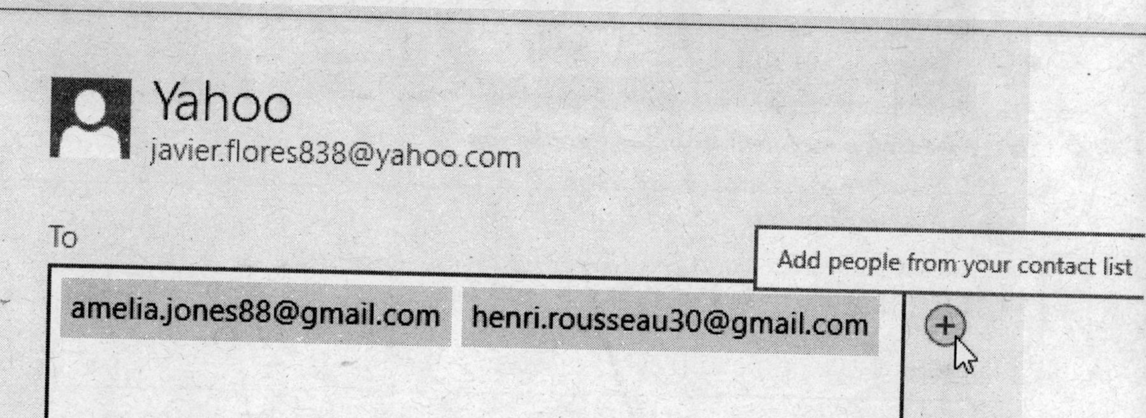

Adding a recipient from your contacts

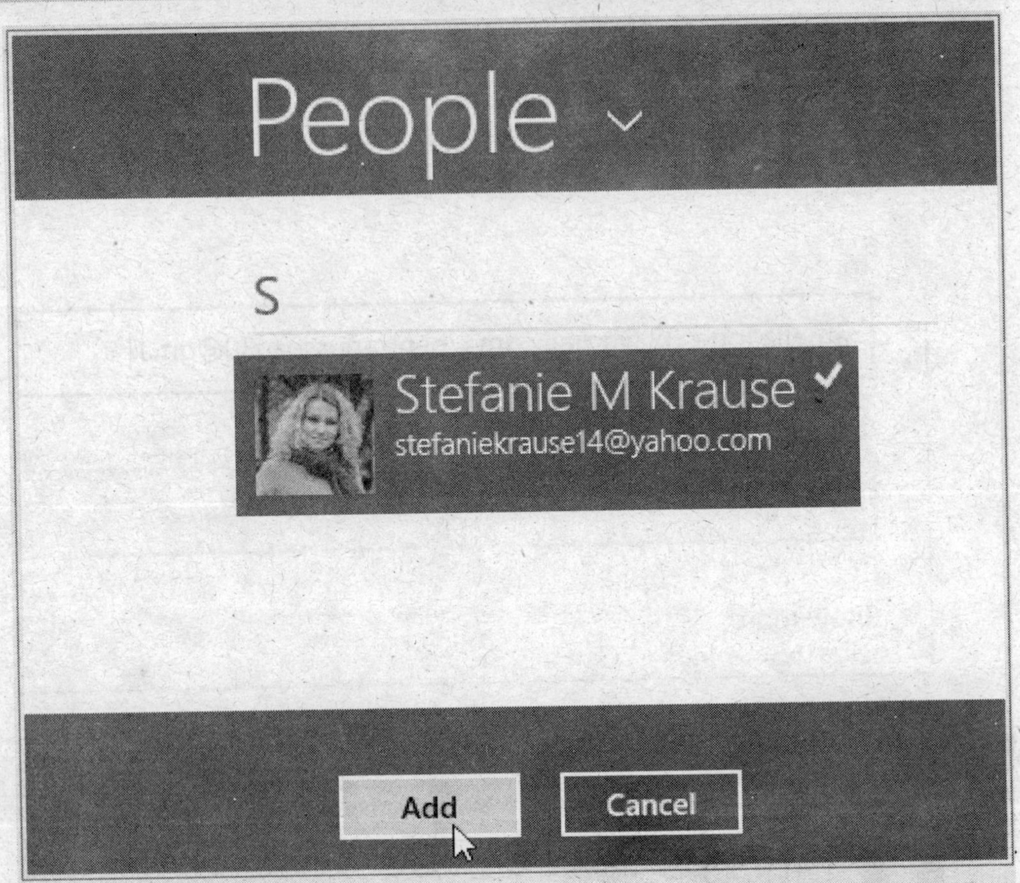

People

S

Stefanie M Krause
stefaniekrause14@yahoo.com

Add Cancel

Adding a recipient from the People app

Upcoming Charity Eve

Add a message

Sent from Windows Mail

Adding a Subject to the message

Upcoming Charity Event

Hey Everyone!

I just wanted to send out a reminder about the upcoming charity ball sponsorec

nt s ... Saturday at th ... loyd Stre

Save Draft

Include attachment

Formatting options

Compose options with the right-click menu

Upcoming Charity Event

Hey Everyone!

I just wanted to send out a reminder about the upcoming charity ball sponsored by the The event starts at 7:00pm on Saturday at the Old Smith Ballroom on Lloyd Street. The will be benefitting our local Parks and Recreation department, which is hoping to build playground in our neighborhood.

Hope to see you all there!

Javier Flores

Clicking the Send button

Adding an existing contact as a recipient

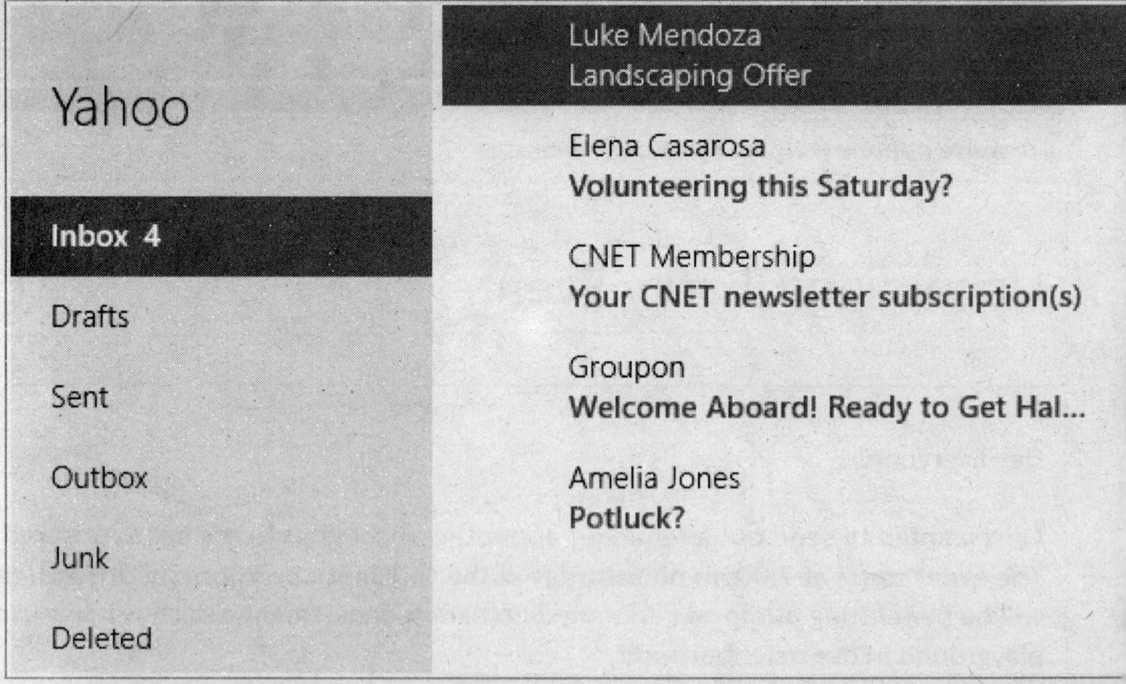

Unread emails in the inbox

Reading and Replying to Messages

By default, any email you receive will go to your inbox. Unread emails are always bold.

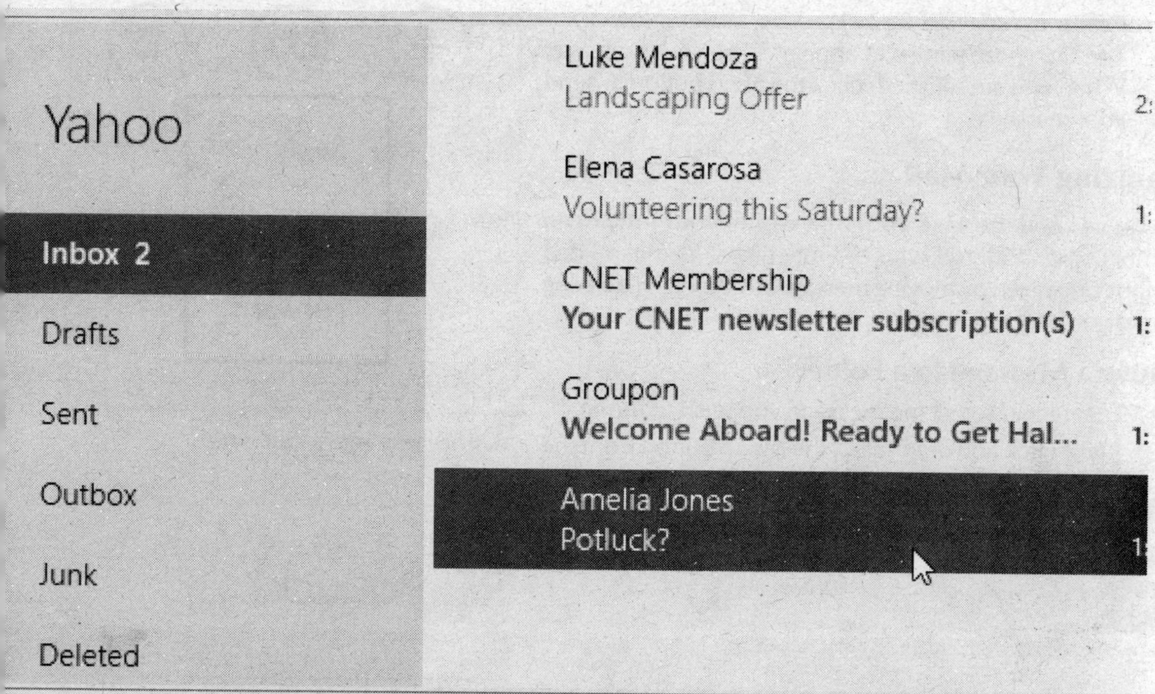

Yahoo

Inbox 2

Drafts

Sent

Outbox

Junk

Deleted

Luke Mendoza
Landscaping Offer 2:

Elena Casarosa
Volunteering this Saturday? 1:

CNET Membership
Your CNET newsletter subscription(s) 1:

Groupon
Welcome Aboard! Ready to Get Hal... 1:

Amelia Jones
Potluck? 1:

Selecting a message

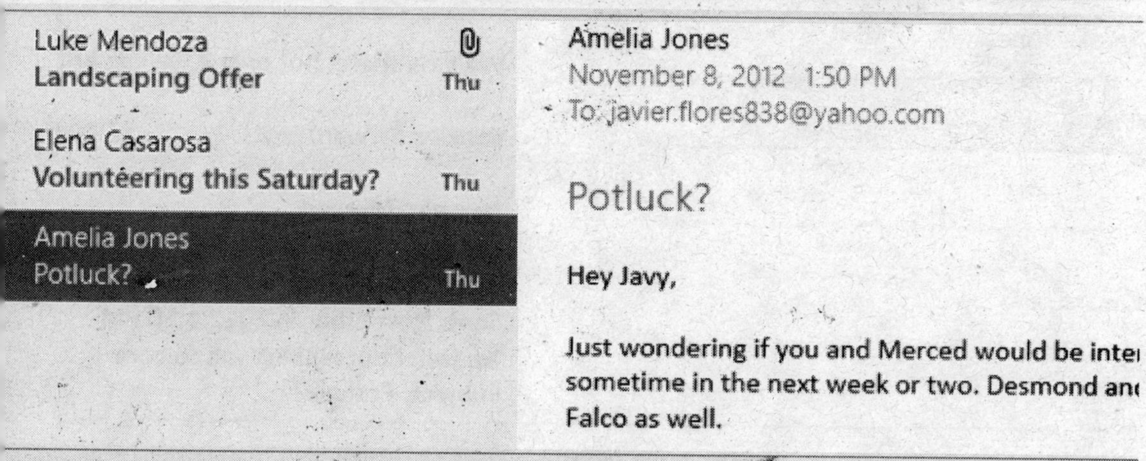

Luke Mendoza
Landscaping Offer Thu

Elena Casarosa
Volunteering this Saturday? Thu

Amelia Jones
Potluck? Thu

Amelia Jones
November 8, 2012 1:50 PM
To: javier.flores838@yahoo.com

Potluck?

Hey Javy,

Just wondering if you and Merced would be inte sometime in the next week or two. Desmond an Falco as well.

Viewing the selected message in the Message pane

o Read and Reply to a Message:

1. From the Mail app, locate and select the message you want to read.
2. The message will appear on the right-side of the screen in the Message pane.

3. To reply to the message, click the Reply button and then select your reply option from the drop-down menu.
4. The Compose pane will appear. Type your message. When you are satisfied, click the Send button to send your message.

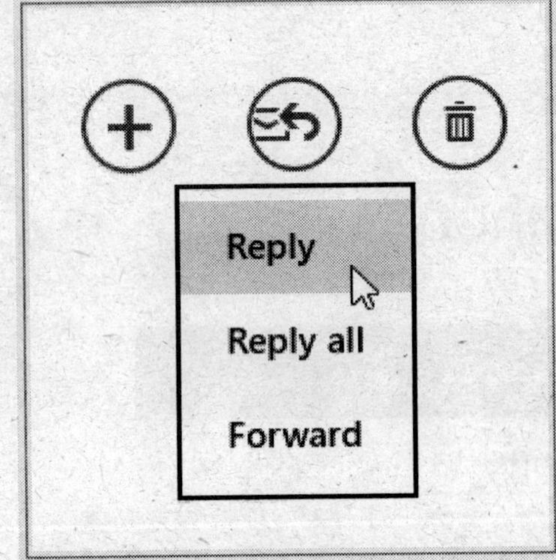

Choosing reply options

Organizing Your Mail

After you've used the Mail app for a while, your inbox can start to become cluttered with old messages. You can keep your inbox organized by moving messages to folders or deleting messages you no longer need.

To Move a Message to a Folder:

1. Locate and select the message you wish to move.
2. Right-click and then select the Move button from the menu at the bottom of the screen.

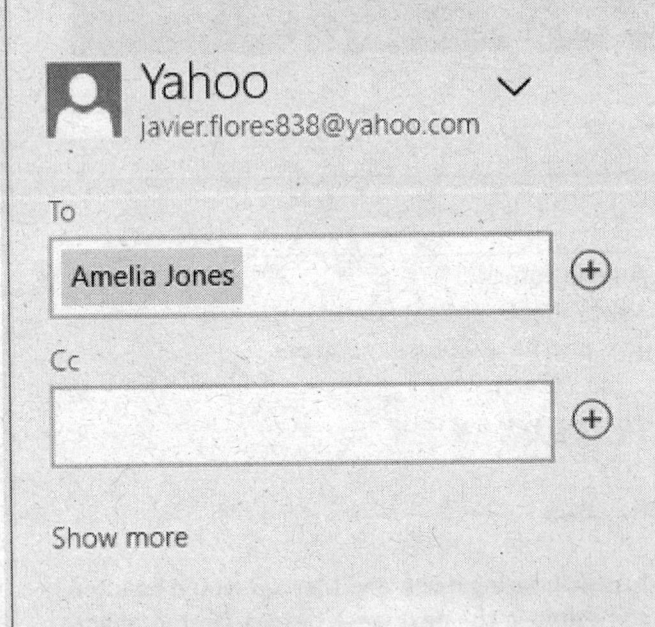

Replying to a message

Clicking the Move button

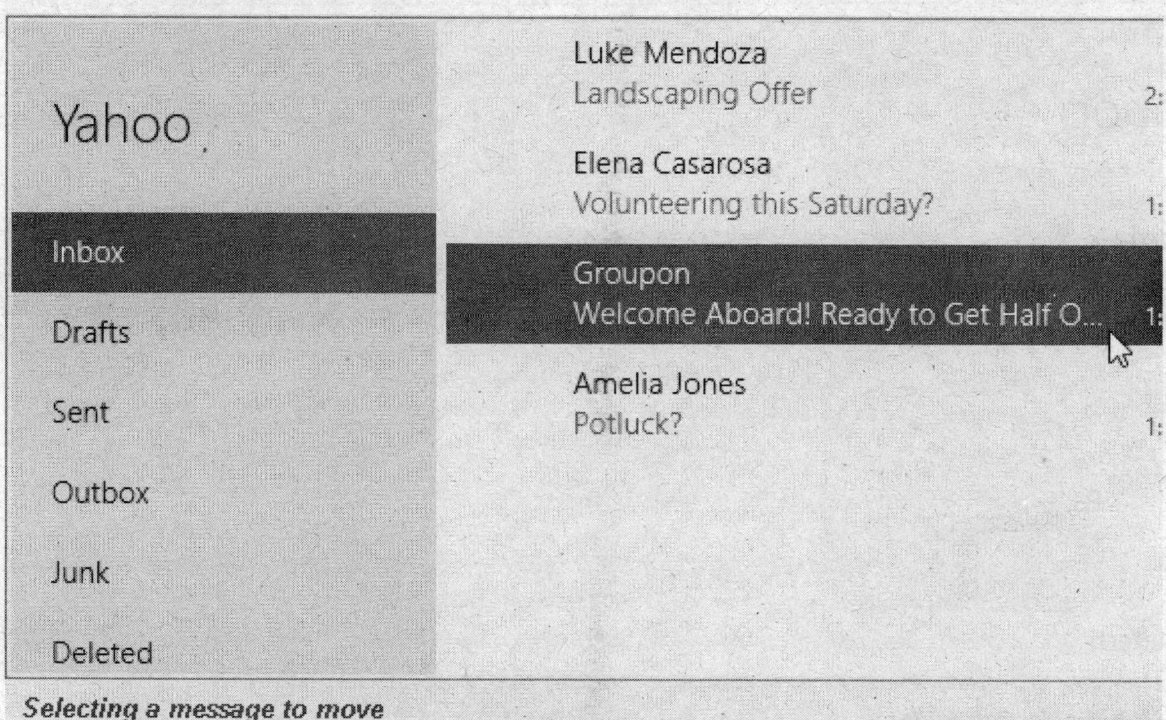

Selecting a message to move

3. Select the desired folder for the message.
4. The message will be moved to the selected folder.

To Delete a Message:

1. There are two ways to delete a message. You can either:
2. Click the Delete button when viewing any email.

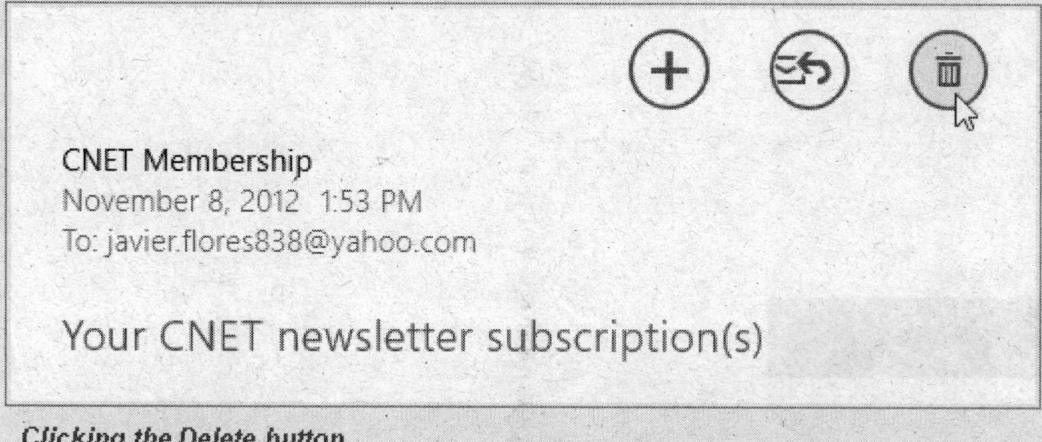

Clicking the Delete button

3. Select the desired message(s) and then press the Delete key on your keyboard.
4. To delete messages permanently, you'll need to access the Deleted folder and then delete the messages again.

Yahoo

Inbox

Drafts

Sent

Outbox

Junk

Deleted

Luke Mendoza
Landscaping Offer

Elena Casarosa
Volunteering this Saturday?

Groupon
Welcome Aboard! Ready to Get Half O...

Amelia Jones
Potluck?

Choosing the desired folder

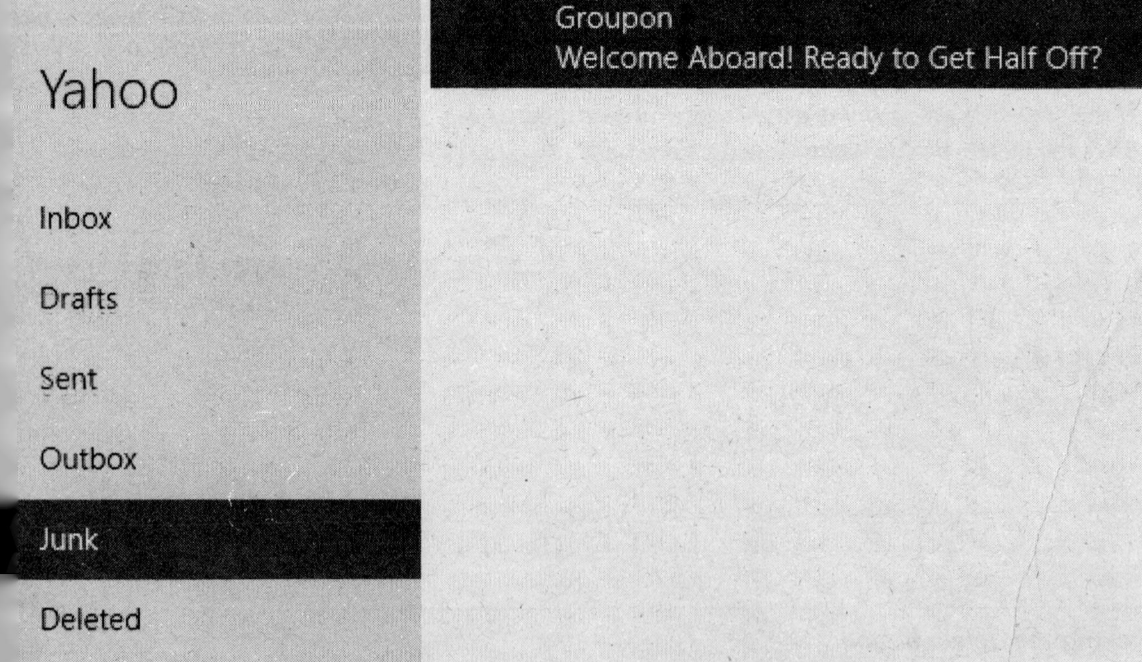

The message moved to the selected folder

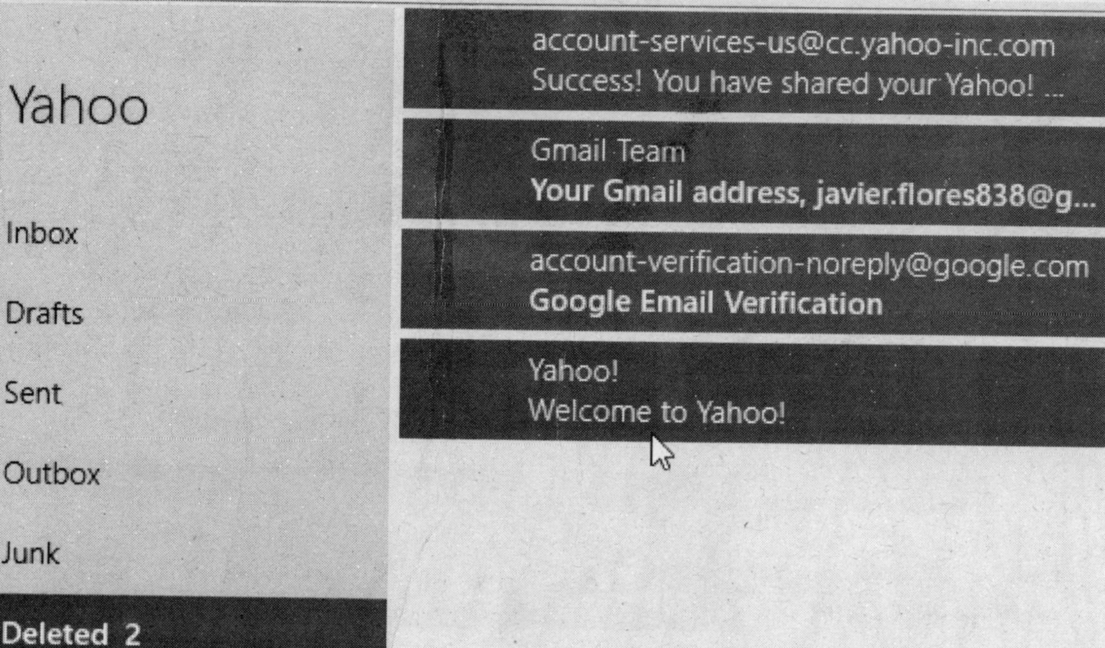

eleting messages permanently

dding Multiple Accounts

ou use more than one email account—for example, one for personal email and one for work email—ı can add multiple accounts to the Mail app, allowing you to read all of your messages from the same ce.

Add an Account:

1. In the Mail app, hover the mouse in the lower-right corner to access the Charms bar, then select Settings.
2. The Settings pane will appear on the right. Select Accounts.

Clicking settings

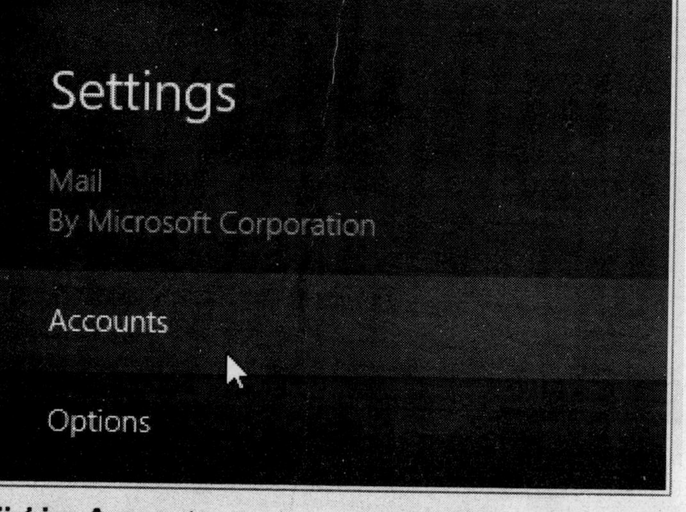

icking Accounts

3. The Accounts pane will appear. Click Add an account.

Adding an account

4. Select the service you wish to use. In our example, we'll add a Yahoo! account.
5. Enter your username and password, then click Connect.
6. Your account will be connected and email will appear automatically in your inbox. Any contacts from the account will also be imported into the People app.

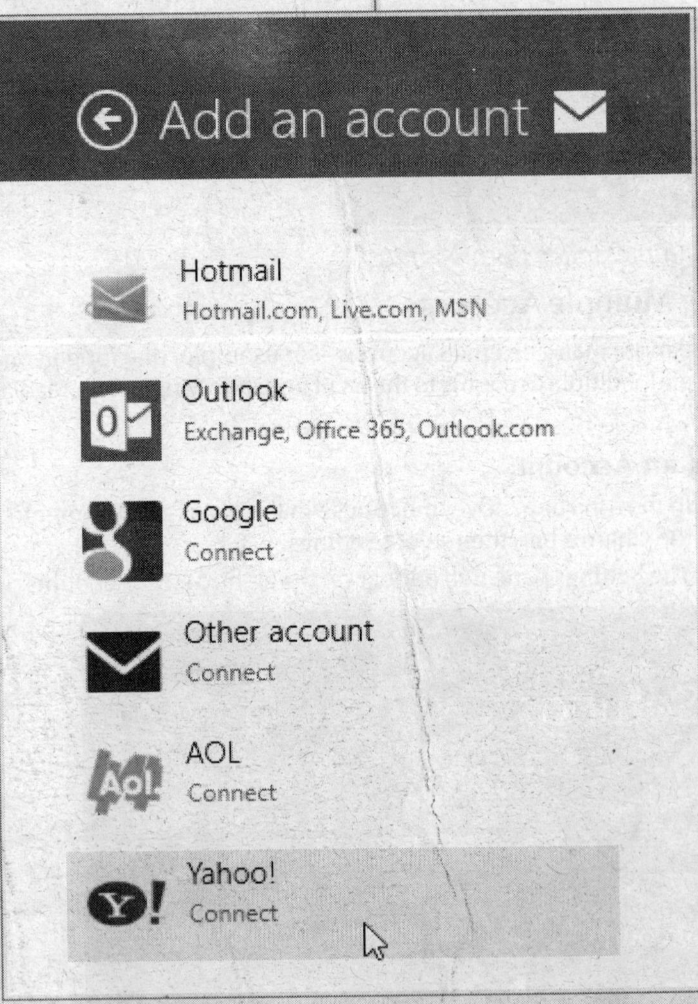

Selecting an account

To Switch Between Inboxes:

If you have multiple email accounts connected to the Mail App, you will need to switch between inboxes to view all your messages.

1. Locate and select the desired account in the lower-left corner of the Mail app.
2. The selected inbox will appear.

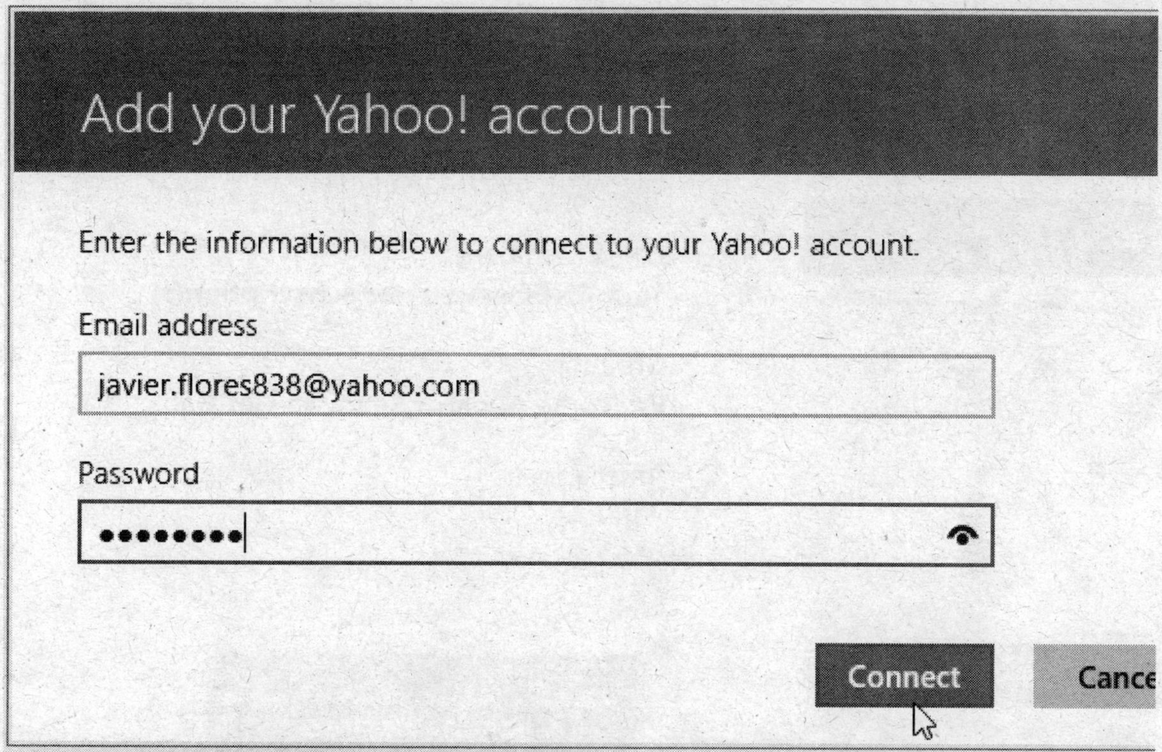

Add your Yahoo! account

Enter the information below to connect to your Yahoo! account.

Email address

javier.flores838@yahoo.com

Password

••••••••

Connect Cance

Clicking Connect

Yahoo

Inbox 3

Drafts

Sent

Outbox

Junk

Deleted

Luke Mendoza
Landscaping Offer 2:

Elena Casarosa
Volunteering this Saturday? 1:

CNET Membership
Your CNET newsletter subscription(s) 1:

Groupon
Welcome Aboard! Ready to Get Hal... 1:

Amelia Jones
Potluck? 1:

To get messages older than two weeks, go tc
Settings

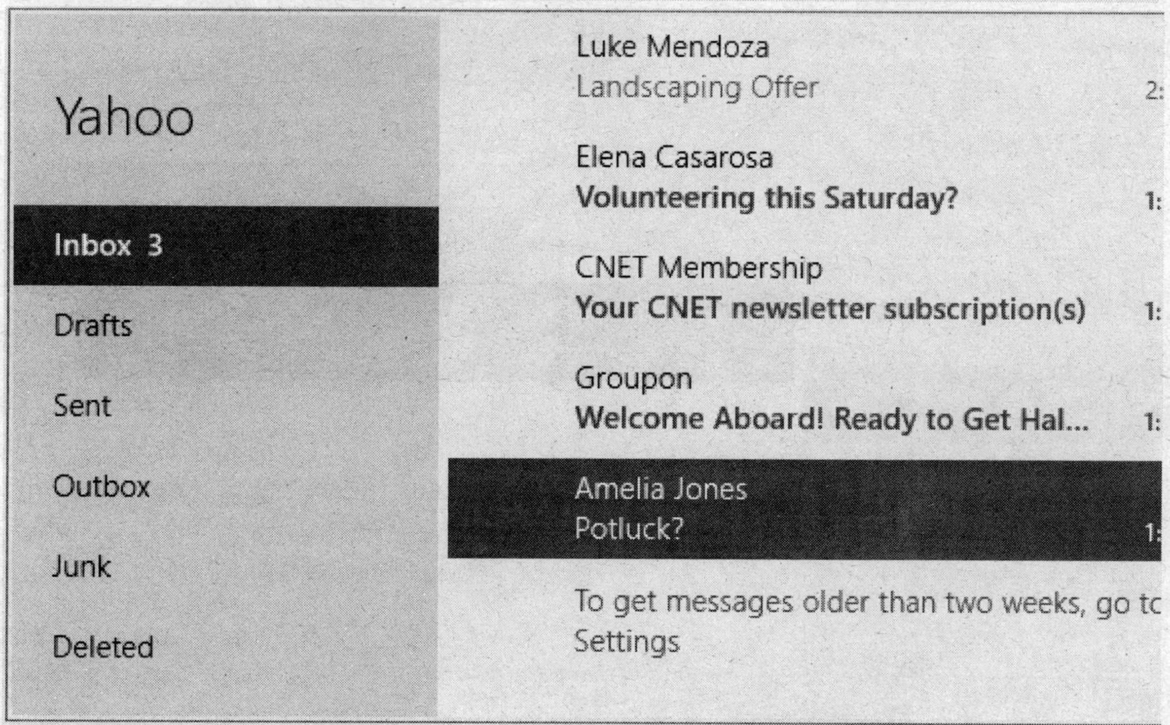

The synced inbox

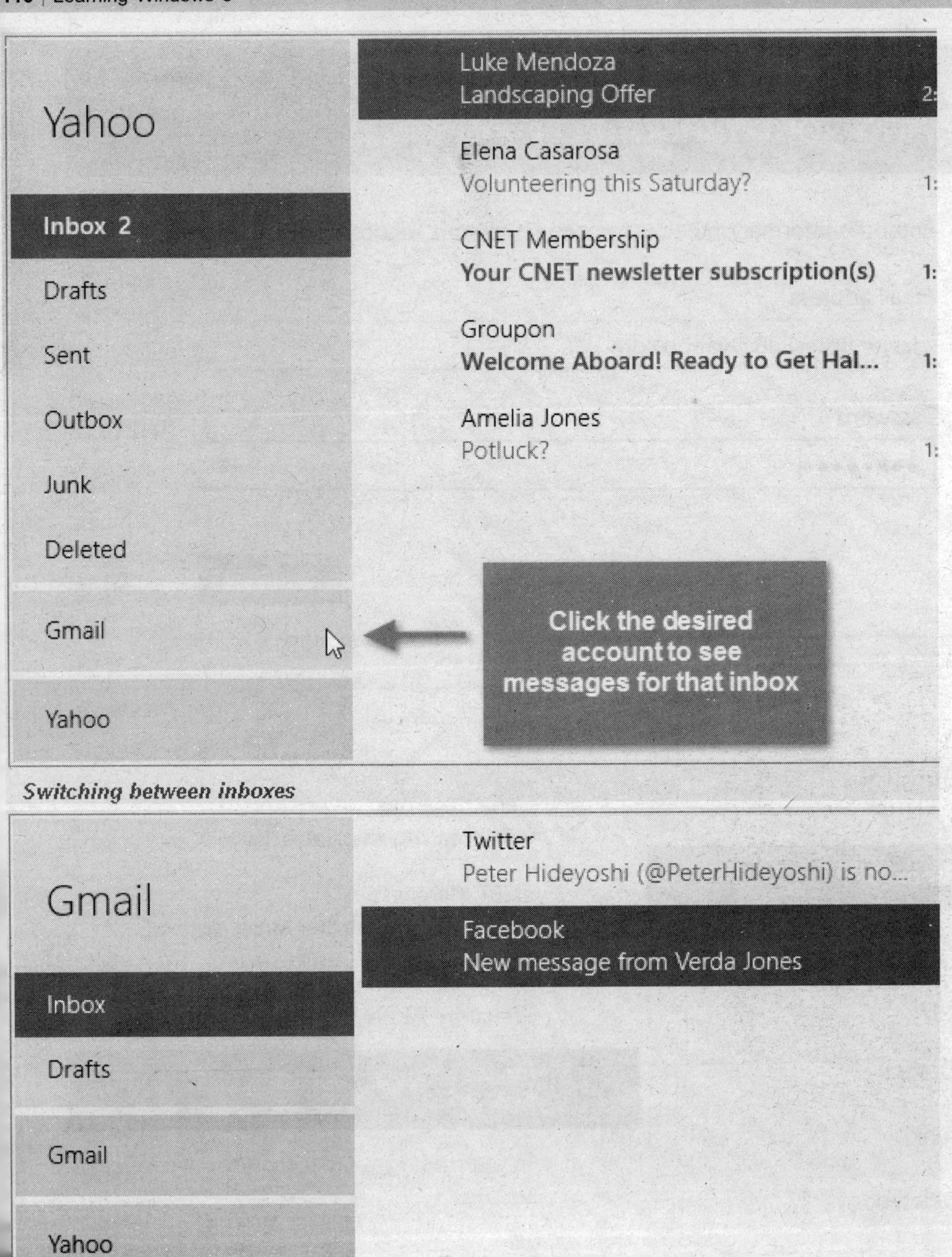

Switching between inboxes

The selected inbox

Modifying Account Settings

If you want to control how often email will be downloaded to the Mail app, change your email signature, or choose additional options for your connected email accounts, you'll need to modify your account settings.

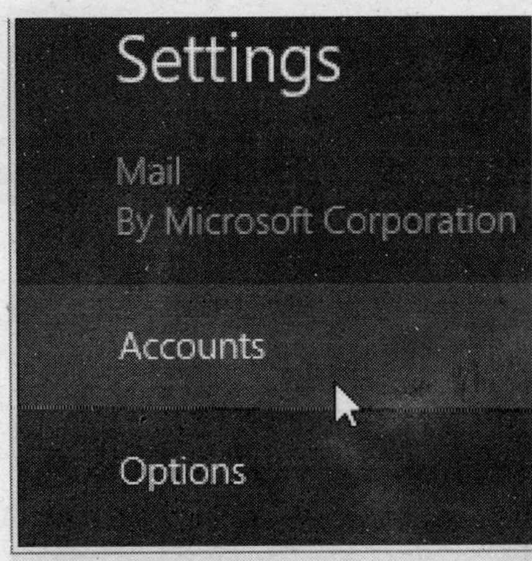

Clicking Accounts

To Modify Account Settings:

1. In the Mail app, hover the mouse in the lower-right corner to access the Charms bar, then select Settings. The Settings pane will appear. Select Accounts.
2. The Accounts pane will appear. Select the account you wish to modify. In our example, we'll choose Gmail.
3. The account settings will appear. You may have to scroll down to see all of the settings. Change the settings as desired.

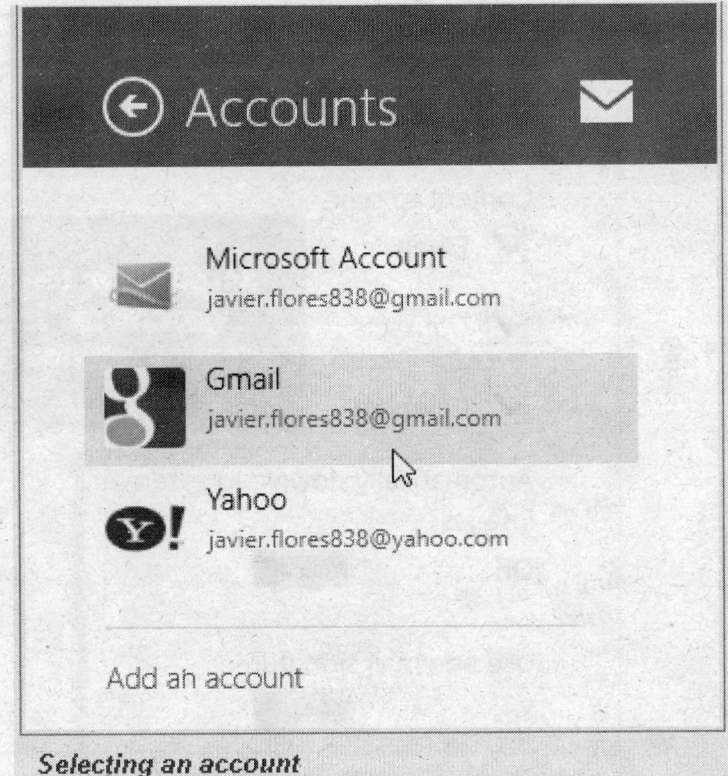

Selecting an account

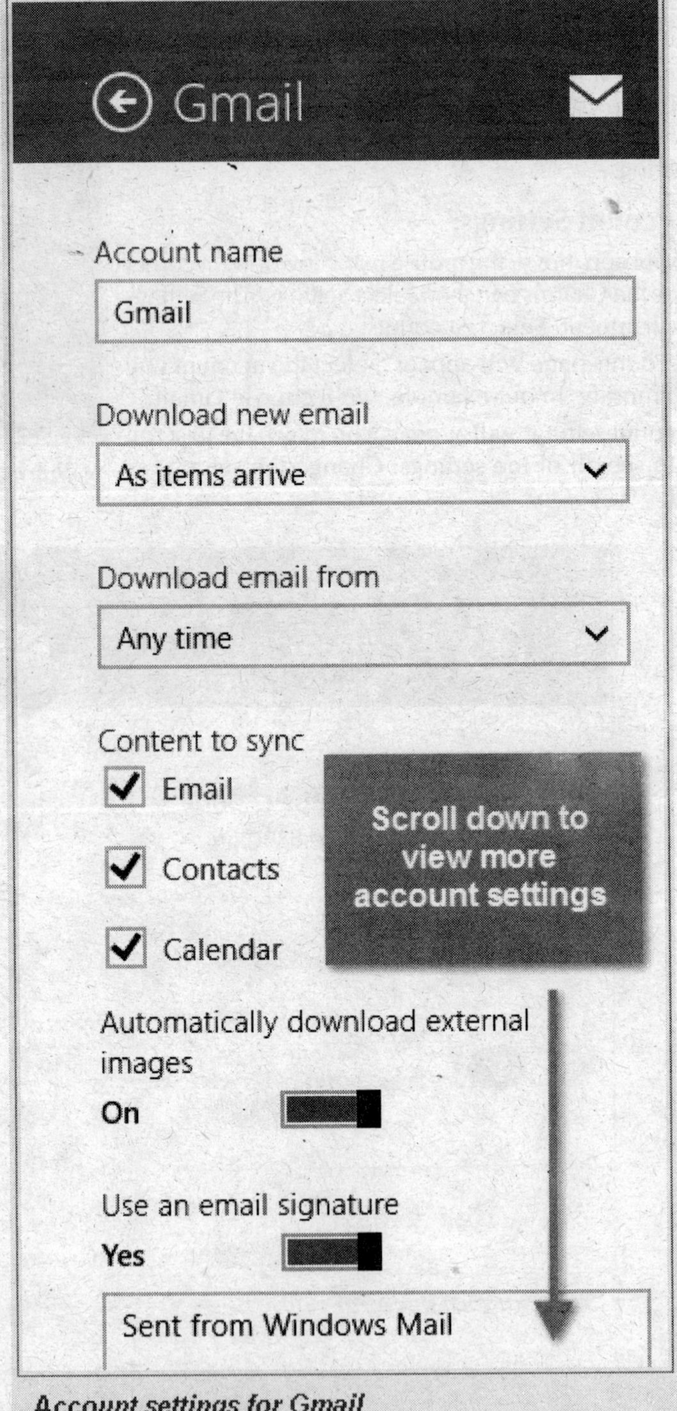

Account settings for Gmail

CHAPTER 8

Using Internet Explorer

In this chapter you will read about:

- Using Internet Explorer.
- Using the Address Bar.
- Using Tabs.
- Setting Favorite Websites.
- Privacy and Security.

Using Internet Explorer

Internet Explorer—also known as IE—is the default web browser in Windows 8. While IE offers many the same features you would expect to find in any browser, the simplified interface may be a litt confusing at first. In this lesson, you'll learn how to use the address bar, open and move between tab and save your favorite websites for quick access. We'll also talk about how to clear your browsing histor

Windows 8 comes with two versions of IE, with an app for both the Start screen and the Desktop. Th lesson will focus on the Start screen app. The Desktop version of IE offers a more traditional web browsi experience, as well as advanced options for bookmarking and privacy. Check out our lesson on Getti Started with the Desktop to learn more about using Desktop apps.

Getting Started with IE:

- To open IE, locate and select Internet Explorer on the Start screen. IE will appear.
- Click the buttons in the interactive below to become more familiar with the IE interface.

Opening IE

The Address Bar

Most browsers use an address bar for navigating to webpages and a search bar for conducting we searches. IE combines both of these elements into the address bar. By integrating Bing search technolog the address bar will offer suggestions for webpages as you type, which makes navigating the web fast and easier.

To Use the Address Bar:

- From IE, right-click and then select the address bar at the bottom of the screen.
- Enter a web address or search term. Suggestions will appear above the address bar as you typ Click a suggestion to navigate to a suggested site.
- Suggested pages from your browsing history will appear with their own icon.
- Suggested pages from Bing search results will appear with the Internet Explorer icon.

You can also press Enter to conduct a web search or type a complete web address and then press Enter navigate to a webpage.

Tabs

You can open multiple websites at the same time using tabs. Right-click anywhere in IE to view yo current tabs at the top of the screen.

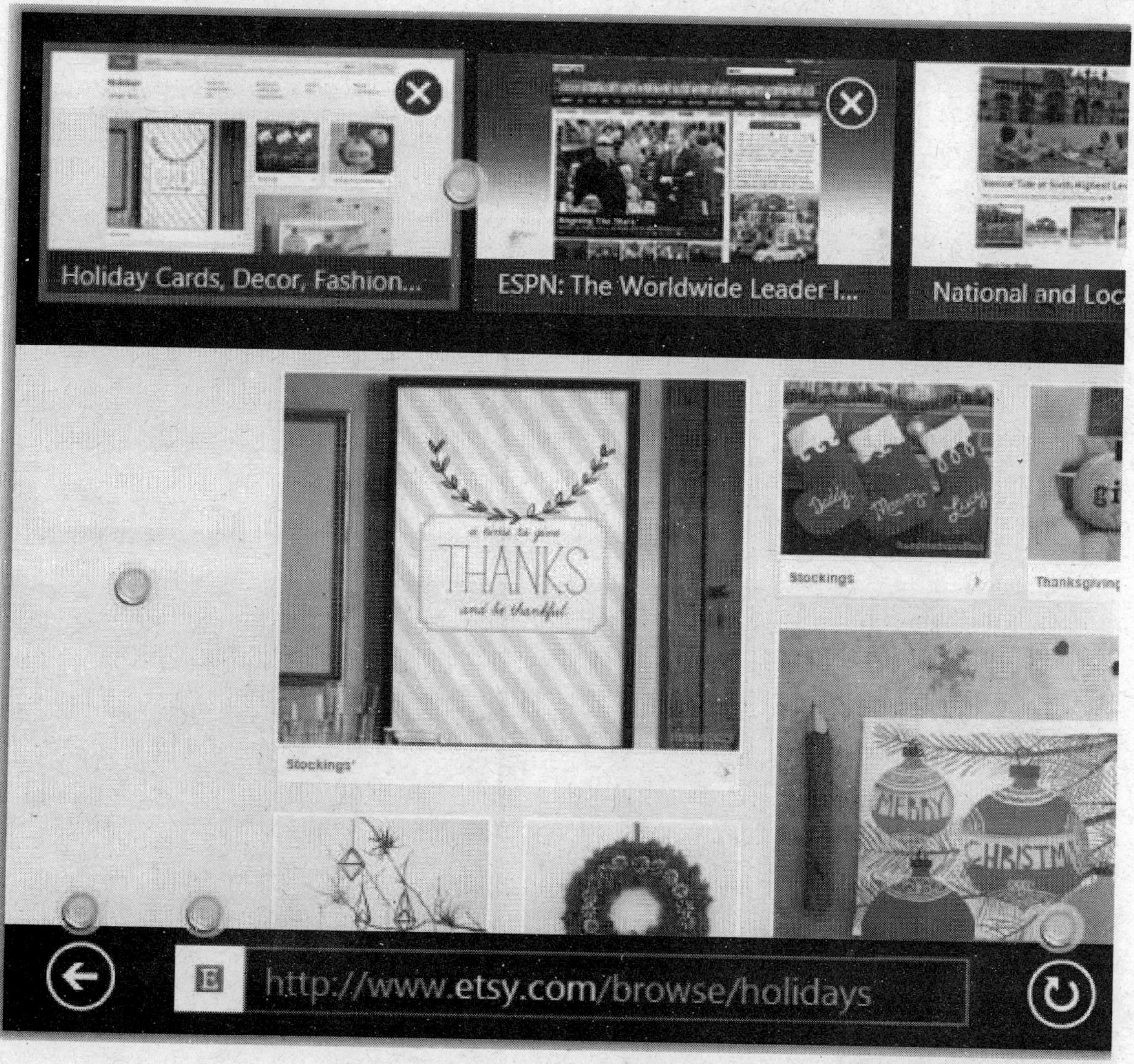

Holiday Cards, Decor, Fashion...

ESPN: The Worldwide Leader I...

National and Loc

Stockings

Thanksgiving

Stockings'

http://www.etsy.com/browse/holidays

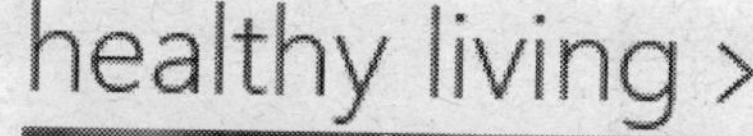

Clicking the address bar

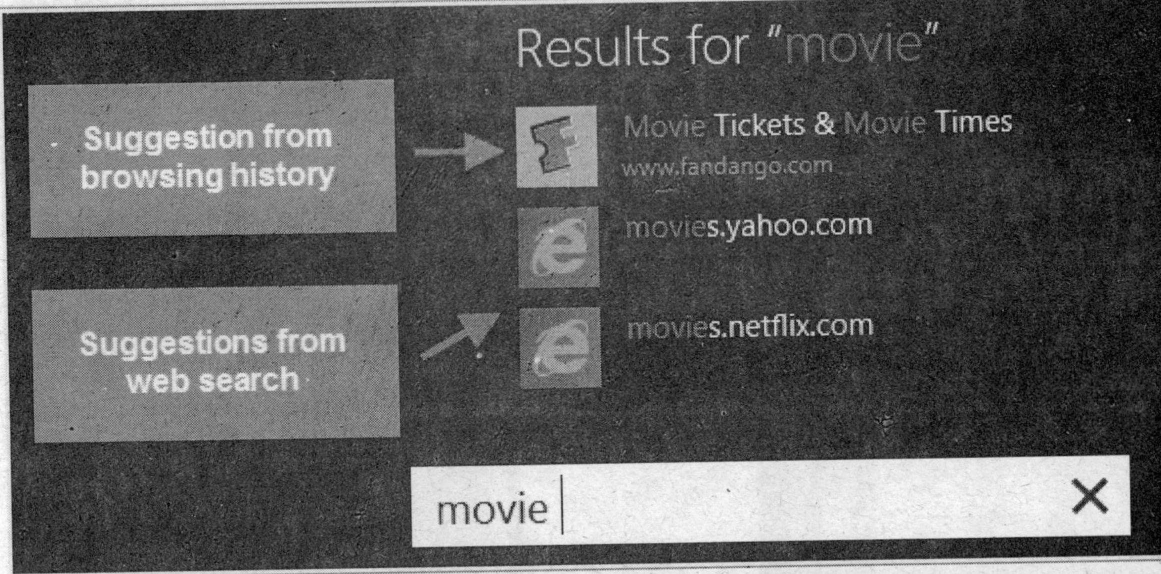

Entering a complete web address

To Open a New Tab:

1. Right-click and then select the New Tab button at the top of the screen.
2. The address bar will appear at the bottom of the screen. Type an address and press Enter or select a Frequently visited site to navigate to a new page. In our example, we'll navigate to Facebook.
3. The page will appear below the open tabs.

Multiple tabs open in IE

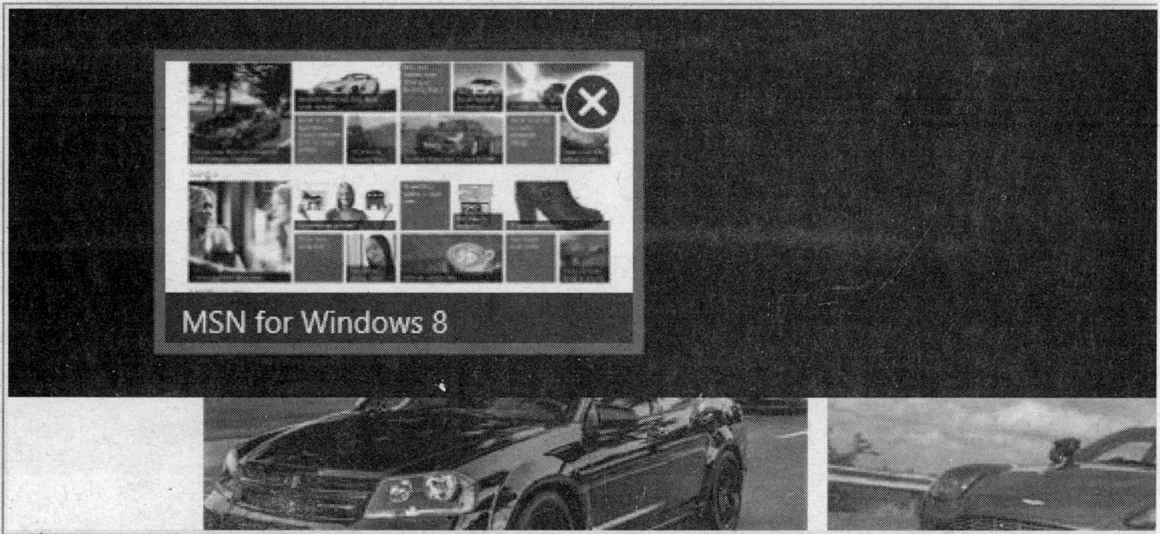

Clicking the New Tab button

Navigating to a frequently visited site

To Switch Between Tabs:

1. Right-click and then select the desired tab.
2. The tab will be selected and the page will appear below the open tabs.

The new tab

Switching between open tabs

The switched tab

To Close a Tab:

- Right-click and then select the close tab button in the top-right corner of the desired tab.

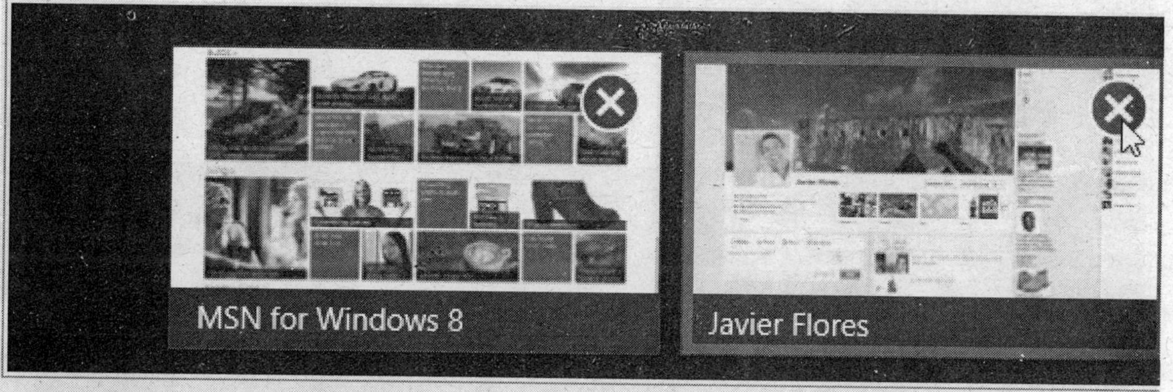

Closing a tab

Favoriting Websites

If you find a website you'd like to visit later, you can add it to your bookmarks, which are known as favorites in IE. Instead of having to remember an exact web address, you can just scroll through your favorites until you see the site you want. You can favorite a website to create a shortcut in the address bar or pin a site directly to the Start screen.

To Favorite a Website:

1. Navigate to the website you wish to favorite.
2. Right-click and then select the Pin button from the menu at the bottom of the screen.
3. A dialog box will appear. Select Add to Favorites.
4. The website will be added to your favorites list. Whenever you begin navigating to a new page, your favorites will appear above the address bar.

Clicking the Pin button

To Pin a Website:

1. Navigate to the website you wish to pin.
2. Right-click and then select the Pin button from the menu at the bottom of the screen.
3. A dialog box will appear. Select Pin to Start.
4. A dialog box will appear. Type a name for the pin and then click Pin to Start to continue.
5. The website will be pinned to the Start screen. Simply click to open that site in IE.

Privacy and Security

Like all browsers, IE keeps browsing history for the websites you visit. You may want to clear your browsing history periodically for the sake of privacy.

To Delete Browsing History:

1. In IE, hover the mouse in the lower-right corner to access the Charms bar, then select Settings.
2. The Settings pane will appear on the right. Select Internet Options.
3. The Internet Explorer settings will appear. Locate and select Delete to clear your browsing history.

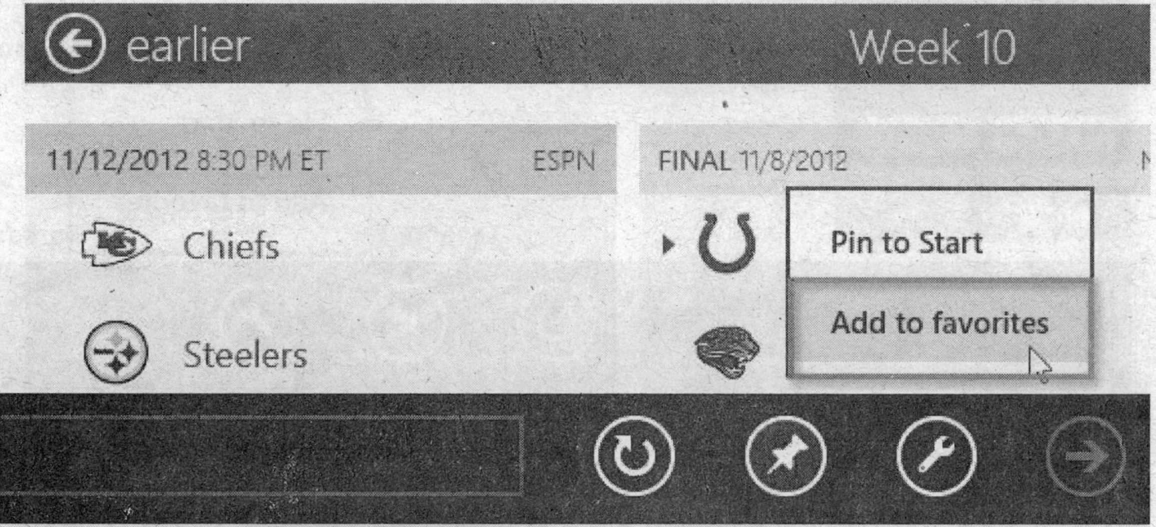

Favoriting the site

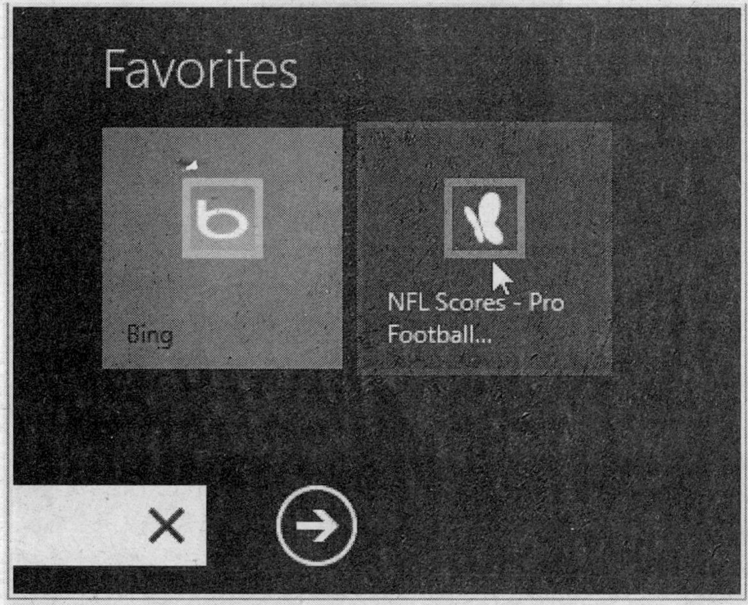

Viewing Favorited sites

If you want to remove specific sites from your browsing history, or if you need to set advanced privacy and security options, you'll need to access Internet Options in the Desktop version of IE.

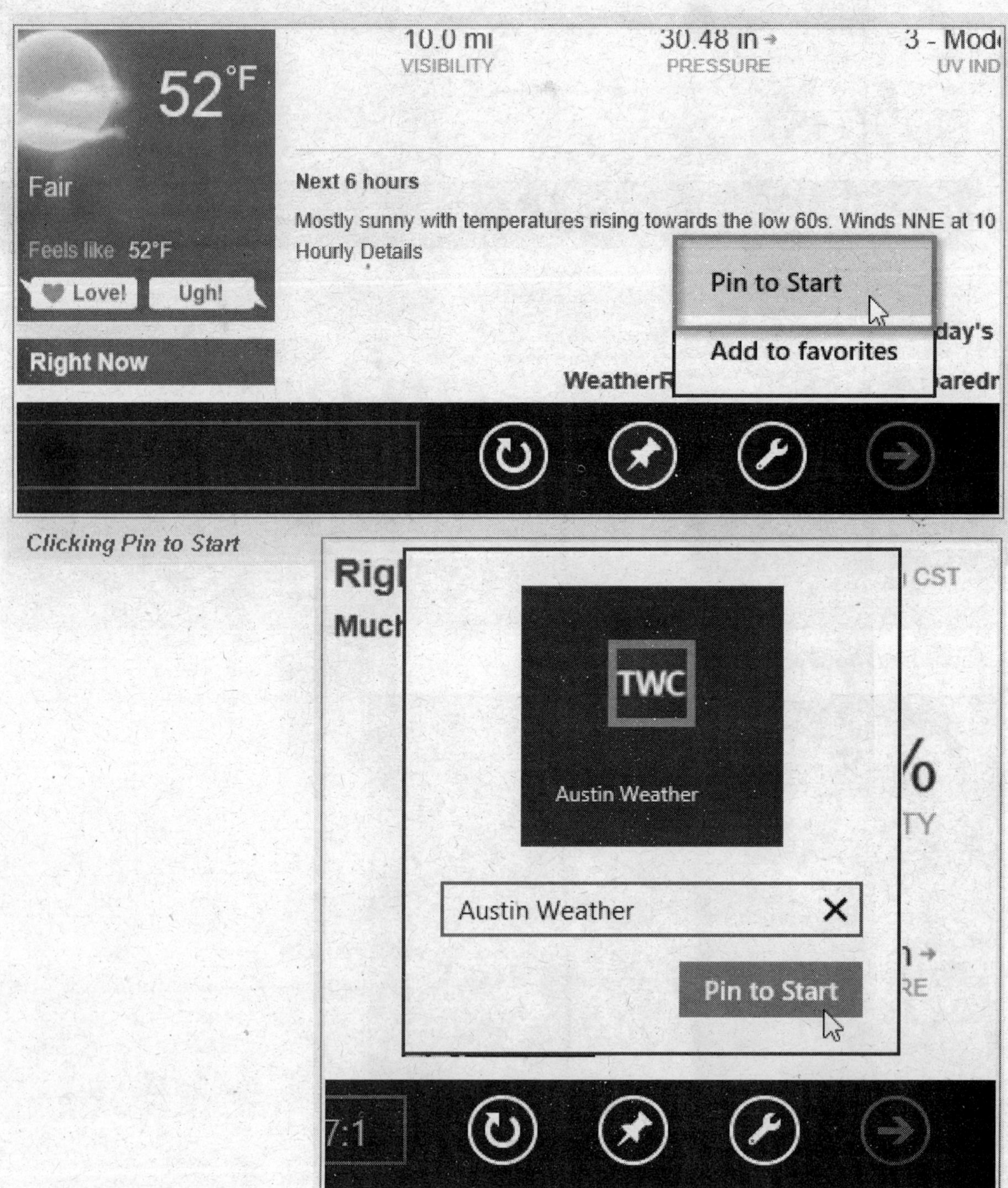

Clicking Pin to Start

Pinning the site to the Start screen

Clicking settings

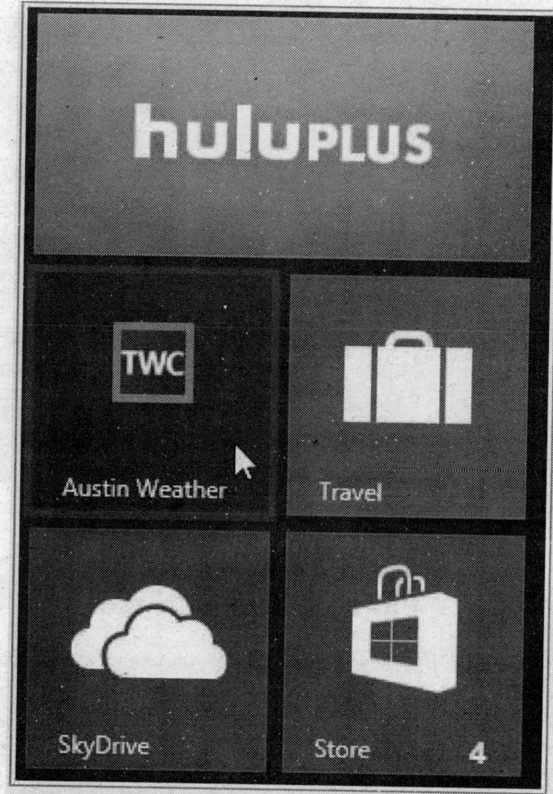

Opening the site from the Start screen

Internet Explorer Settings

Delete Browsing History

Delete

Permissions

Sites can ask for your physical location.

Ask for location

On

Clicking Delete

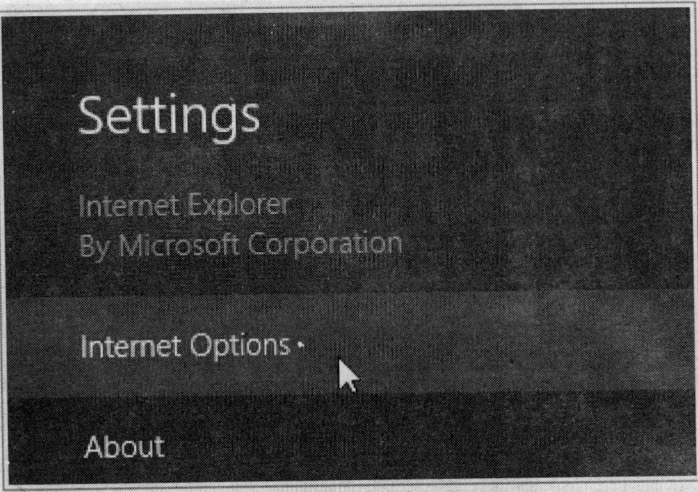

Clicking Internet Options

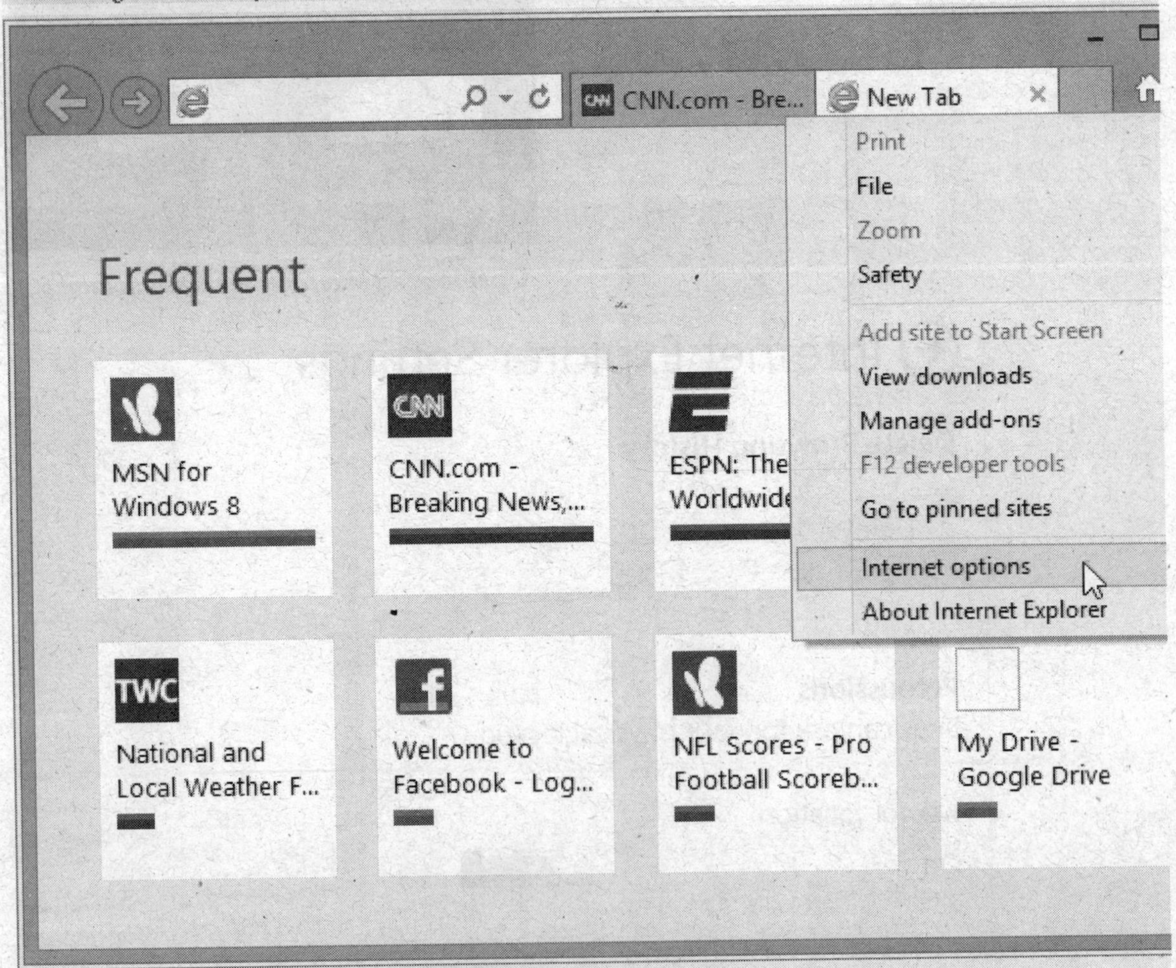

Accessing Internet Options in the Desktop version of IE

CHAPTER 9

The Music and Video Applications

In this chapter you will read about:

- Using the Music Applications.
- Buying Music.
- Using the Video Applications.

Introduction

To play and buy media in Windows 8, you'll use the built-in Music and Video apps. If you already have purchased music, TV shows, and movies, you can easily access them from these apps. You can also buy music and videos, and even listen to music for free (with ads). In this lesson, we'll show you how to access your media and use the Music and Video apps to find and buy music, TV shows, and movies.

Accessing Your Music and Video Libraries

Windows 8 lets you organize your media files by placing them into libraries. To do this, you'll need to go to the Desktop view and add files to your Music and Videos libraries. Any files that are in these libraries can be played or viewed with the Music and Video apps. If you've already purchased music, movies, or TV shows, make sure to add those files to your libraries.

Creating an Xbox Profile

In order to use many of the features in these apps, you'll need to have an Xbox profile. The sign-up process is very quick, and you don't need to enter an address or credit card until you actually buy something. Once you sign up, your Xbox profile will be linked to your Microsoft account, and you'll automatically be signed in whenever you open the Music and Video apps.

If you own an Xbox game console, you can use your Xbox LIVE account as your profile.

To Create an Xbox Profile:

1. Click the Music app on the Start screen.
2. In the upper-right corner, click the Sign In button.
3. Select your Country from the drop-down list. If you would prefer not to receive emails, uncheck the box. When you are done, click I Accept.
4. You will receive a random name (called a "gamertag"). Note: You will not use this name to sign in, so it's not important to remember it. It will appear to other gamers if you play online games.
5. Click Ok. Your profile will be created, and you'll automatically be signed in.

Using the Music App

The Music app lets you listen to your Music library and browse for new music. Just like Apple's iTunes Store, you can buy individual songs or entire albums. You can also listen to up to 10 hours of music per month for free, although you'll need to watch an ad every few songs. If you buy an Xbox Music Pass, you can listen to unlimited music without ads.

Navigating the Music App

You have several different options when navigating the Music App:

1. Click on any tile to view an artist or album.
2. Click My Music to view your Music library.
3. Click All Music to browse for new songs (you may have to scroll to the right).
4. Hover the mouse in the lower-right corner to open the Charms bar, and then click Search to search for music.

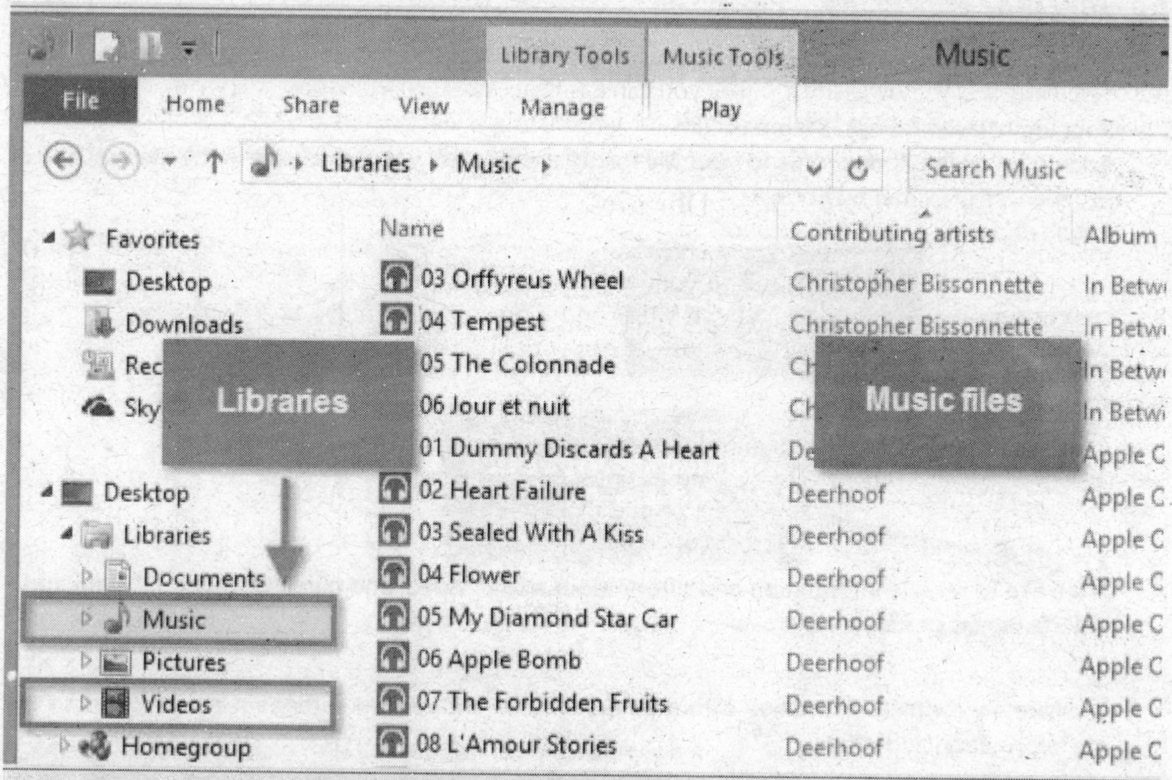

Managing files with libraries

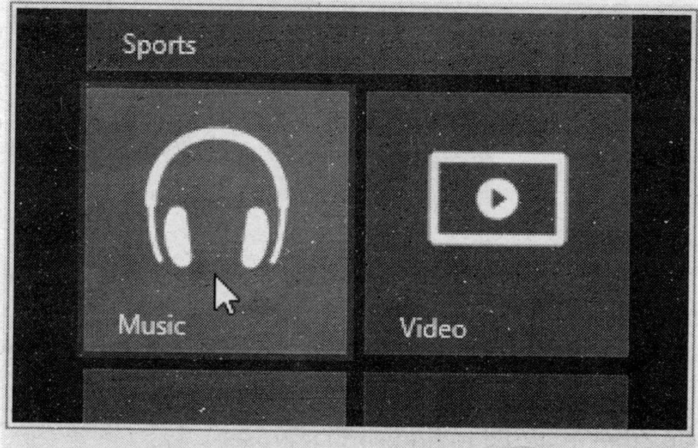

Opening the Music app

The Sign In button

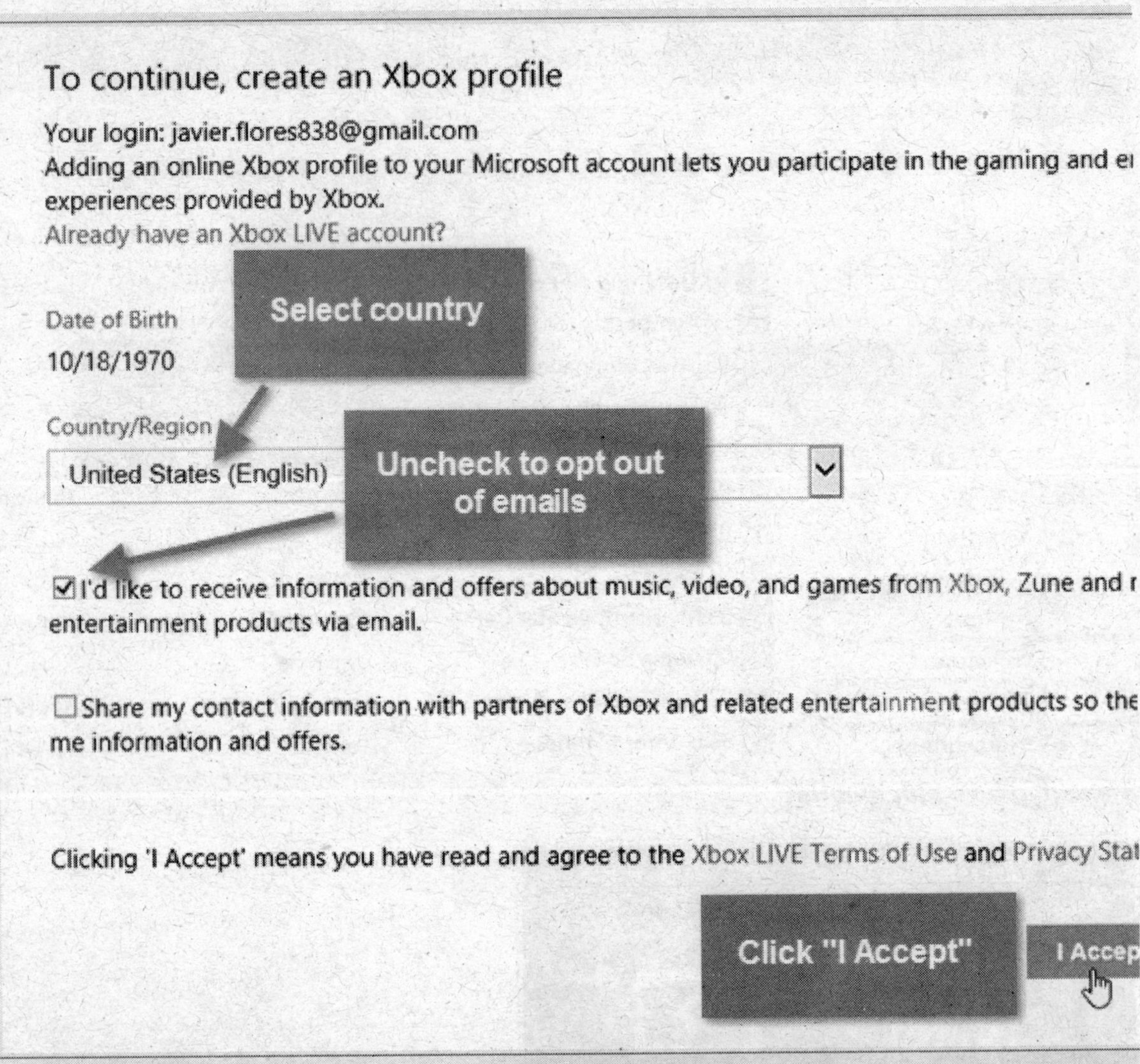

Entering profile information

Music Options

When you click on an artist's tile, you'll have several options, including playing songs, adding songs to your library, viewing the artist's albums, and using the Smart DJ to find similar artists.

Playback Controls

When you're listening to a song, you can right-click anywhere in the Music app to open a toolbar at the bottom of the screen. You can use the toolbar to pause the song or skip to a different song.

Buying Music

Although you can listen to music for free in the Music app (with ads), you may still want to buy songs or albums so that you can play them on other devices. You can also choose to buy an Xbox Music Pass, which lets you listen to unlimited music without ads.

Welcome to Xbox

We've given you the gamertag UncrownedHeart7. Your gamertag is your identity in the online wor can change it once for free at Xbox.com.

Your Xbox profile gives you access to Xbox Games, Video and Music on your Windows 8 device. Ac 360 console and an Xbox Gold membership opens up even more opportunities. Get the details he

Your current privacy settings

Gamertag

Click Ok to create profile

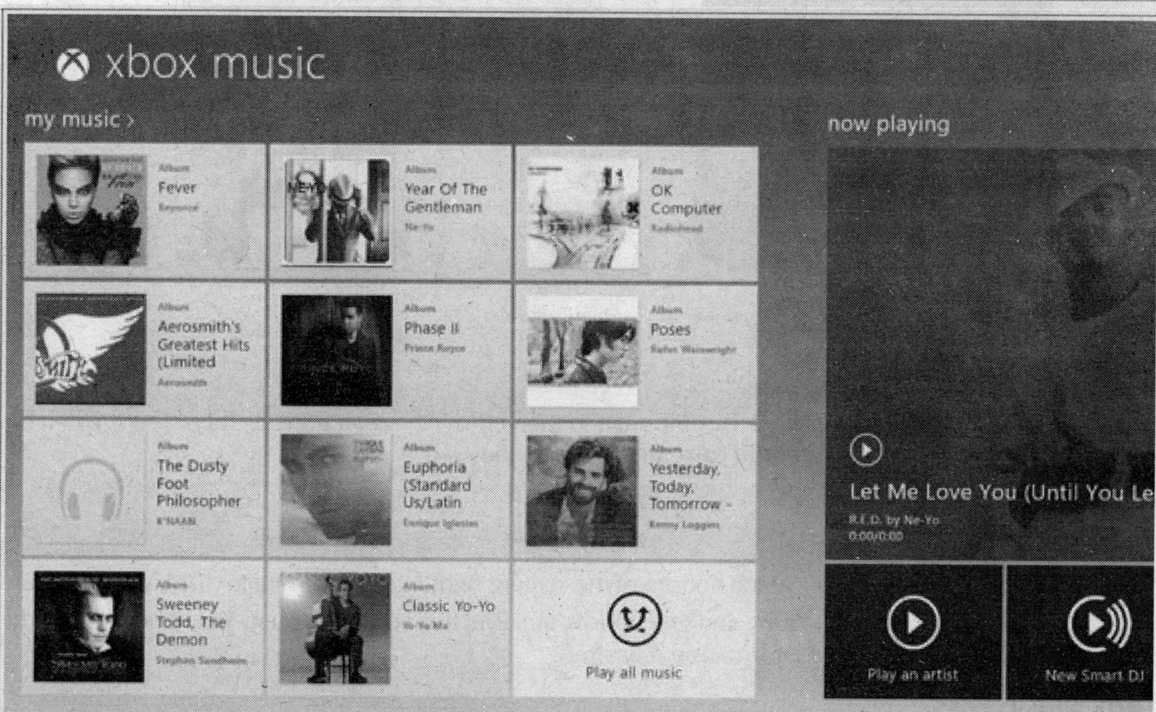

The Music app

Clicking on a tile

Viewing the Music library

To Buy an Album:

1. To buy an entire album, click Buy album and then follow the directions on the screen. You'll be able to add or edit your credit card information if desired.

To Buy an Individual Song:

1. Select the desired song.
2. If you don't see a toolbar at the bottom of the screen, right-click anywhere to display the toolbar.
3. In the toolbar, click Buy song and then follow the directions on the screen. You'll be able to add or edit your credit card information if desired.

Xbox Music Pass

If you want to listen to unlimited music without ads, you can buy an Xbox Music Pass for $9.99 a month.

Browsing for music

Searching for music

Music options

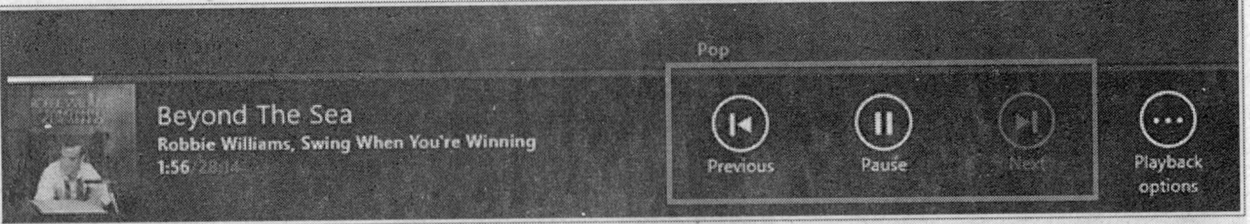

Playback controls

In addition to streaming music, you'll be able to download songs you like for no extra charge. Some songs may not be available through your Xbox Music Pass, so if you want to listen to those songs you'll need to buy them separately.

Using the Video App

The Video app lets you watch movies and TV shows from your Videos library. Your Videos library may include videos that you've purchased, as well as ones you've taken with your camera or phone. You can also use the Video app to buy or rent movies and buy TV shows.

Buying an album

Selecting a song

Buying a song

Navigating the Video App

You have several different options when navigating the Video App:

1. Click on any tile to view information about a movie or TV show.
2. Click My Videos to view your Videos library.
3. Click Movies Store or Television Store to browse for videos. You may have to scroll to the right to see these options.
4. Hover the mouse in the lower-right corner to open the Charms bar, and then click Search to search for videos.

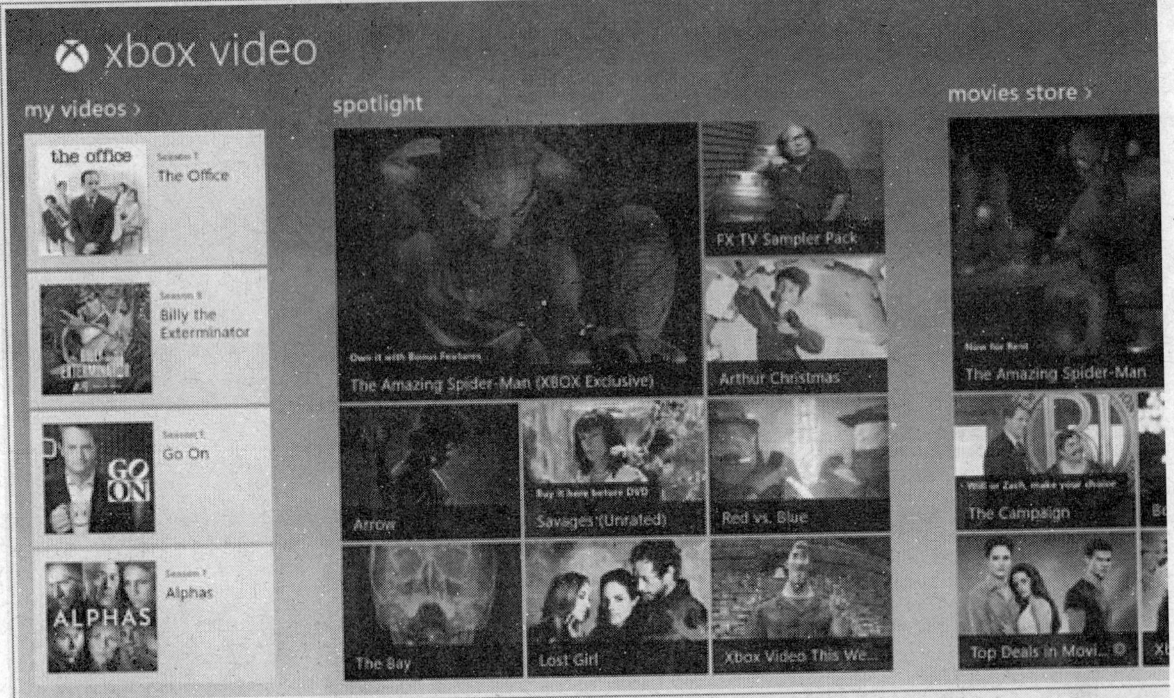

The Video app

Clicking on a tile

To Buy or Rent a Movie:

1. Click the desired movie.
2. Click Buy or Rent, and then follow the directions on the screen. You'll be able to add or edit your credit card information if desired. Note: Some movies may not be available to rent.

Viewing the Videos library

Browsing for movies

To Buy a TV Show:

1. Click the desired TV show.
2. Click View seasons.
3. Select the desired season on the right side of the screen. You may need to scroll to the right to see the seasons.
4. You can choose to buy the entire season or a single episode:
   - To buy the entire season, click Buy season.
   - To buy a single episode, select the desired episode and then click Buy episode.

Searching for vid

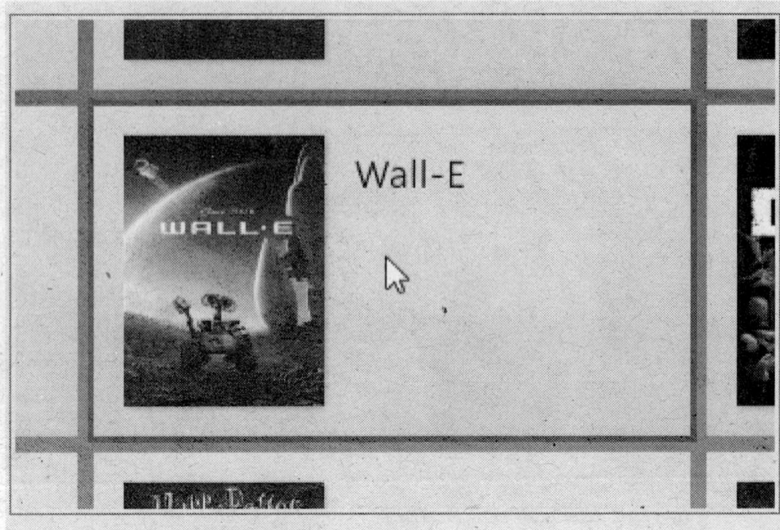

Clicking on a movie tile

Viewing seasons

Selecting a season

Buying an entire season

Buying a single episode

CHAPTER 10

Managing User Accounts and Parental Controls

In this chapter you will read about:

- Adding Users.
- Switching Users.
- Managing User Accounts.
- Using Parental Controls

Introduction

A user account allows you to sign in to Windows 8. By default, your computer already has one user account, which you were required to create when setting up Windows 8. If you plan to share your computer, you can create a separate user account for each member of your home or office.

You can also choose to associate any new user account with a Microsoft account. Signing in with a Microsoft account will bring all of your SkyDrive files, contacts, and more into the Start screen. You can even sign in to a different computer that has Windows 8, and all of your important files will be there.

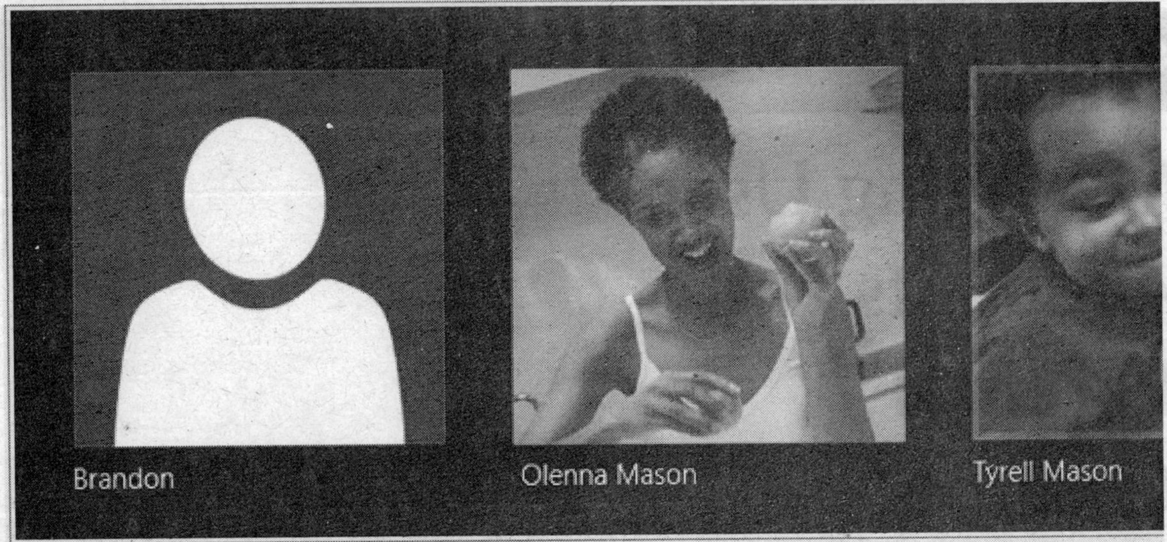

Choosing a user from the sign-in screen

Adding Users

It's easy to add new user accounts to your computer. Connecting users to a Microsoft account will help them get the most out of Windows 8, but you can also add a local user account that exists only on your computer if the user prefers not to create a Microsoft account.

You must be signed in as an Administrator (the first user account created on your computer) to add a new user.

To Add a New User (with a Microsoft Account):

1. From the Start screen, hover the mouse in the lower-right corner to access the Charms bar, then select Settings.
2. Locate and select Change PC Settings.

Accessing Settings from the Charms Bar

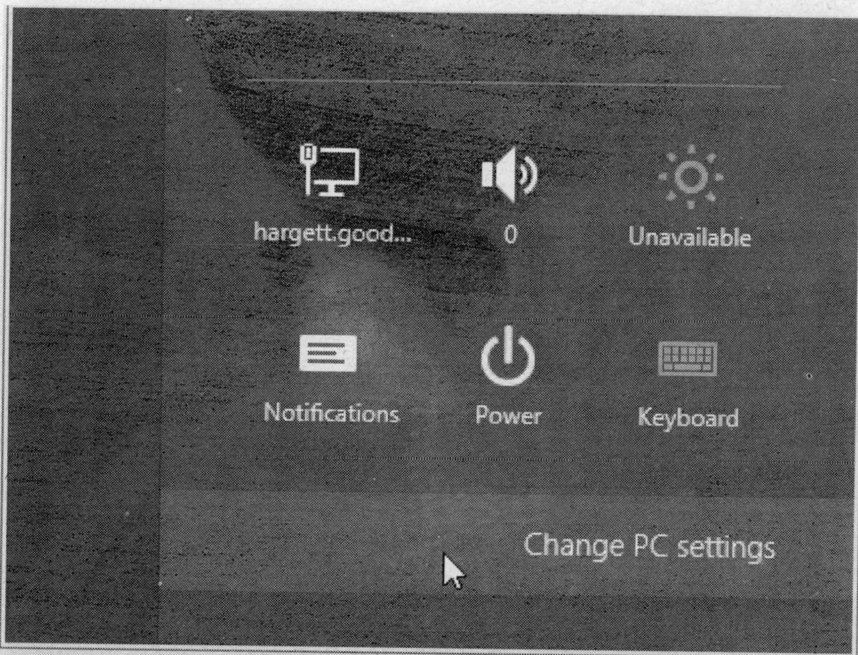

Clicking Change PC settings

3. PC Settings will appear. Select Users on the left.

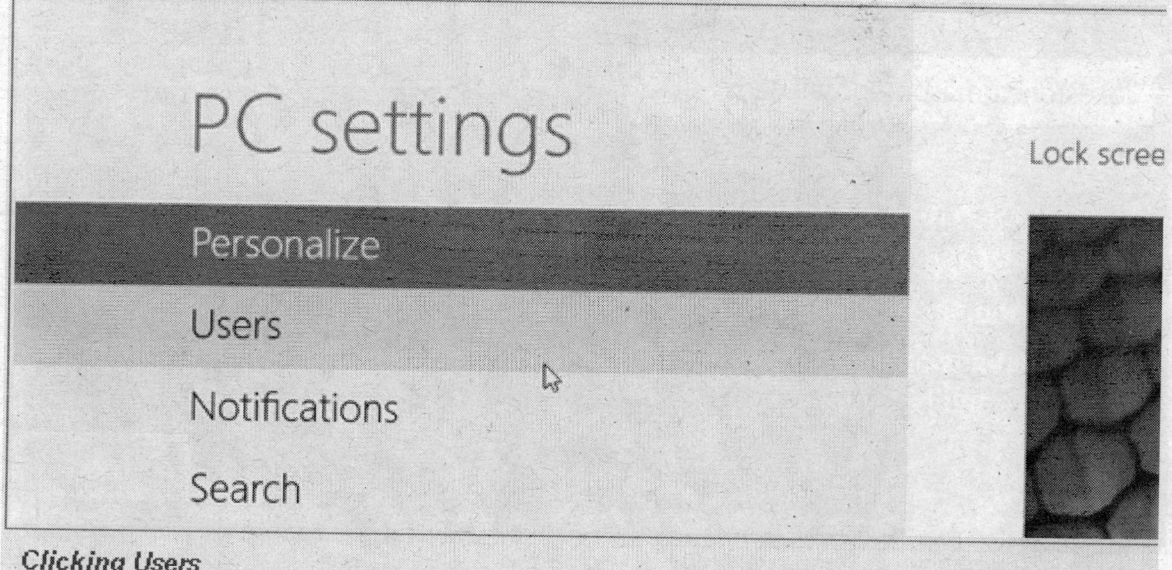

Clicking Users

4. The Users pane will appear on the right. Locate and select Add a user.
5. Enter the user's Microsoft account username, then click Next to continue.
6. Optional: If this user is a child, check the box to activate Family Safety, which will let you set parental controls. We'll talk more about parental controls later in this lesson.

Ease of Access

Sync your settings

HomeGroup

Windows Update

Other users

Add a user

Administrator
Local Account

Tyrell Mason
tyrellmason30@gmail.

Adding a new user

Add a user

What email address would this person like to use to sign in to Windows? (If you know address they use to sign in to Microsoft services, enter it here.)

lakestone.omason@gmail.com 

When you sign in to Windows with a Microsoft account, you can:

- Download apps from Windows Store.
- Get your online content in Microsoft apps automatically.
- Sync settings online to make PCs look and feel the same–this includes settings like favorites and history.

Next

Entering a Microsoft account username

7. Click Finish.
8. The user will be added.

It may take several minutes to configure a user's settings when logging in with a Microsoft account for the first time.

Clicking Finish

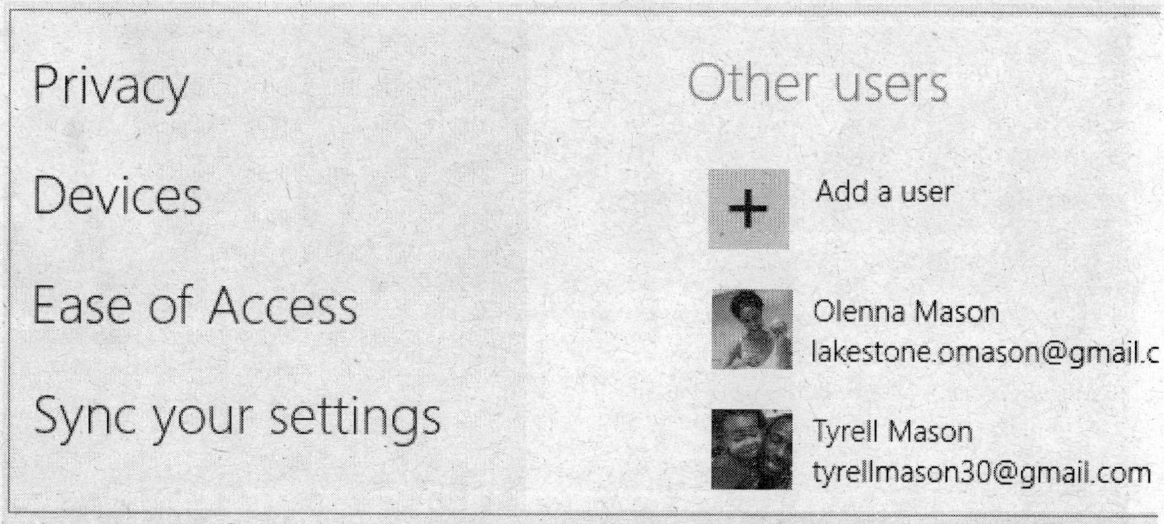

The added user

Add a user

What email address would this person like to use to sign in to Windows? (If you know
address they use to sign in to Microsoft services, enter it here.)

Email address

When you sign in to Windows with a Microsoft account, you can:

- Download apps from Windows Store.
- Get your online content in Microsoft apps automatically.

Privacy statement

Sign up for a new email address

Sign in without a Microsoft account

Next

Clicking Sign in without a Microsoft account

Add a user

There are two options for signing in:

Microsoft account

Signing in to PCs with your email address lets you:

- Your settings won't be synced across the PCs that you use.

Microsoft account | Local account | Cancel

Adding a Local user

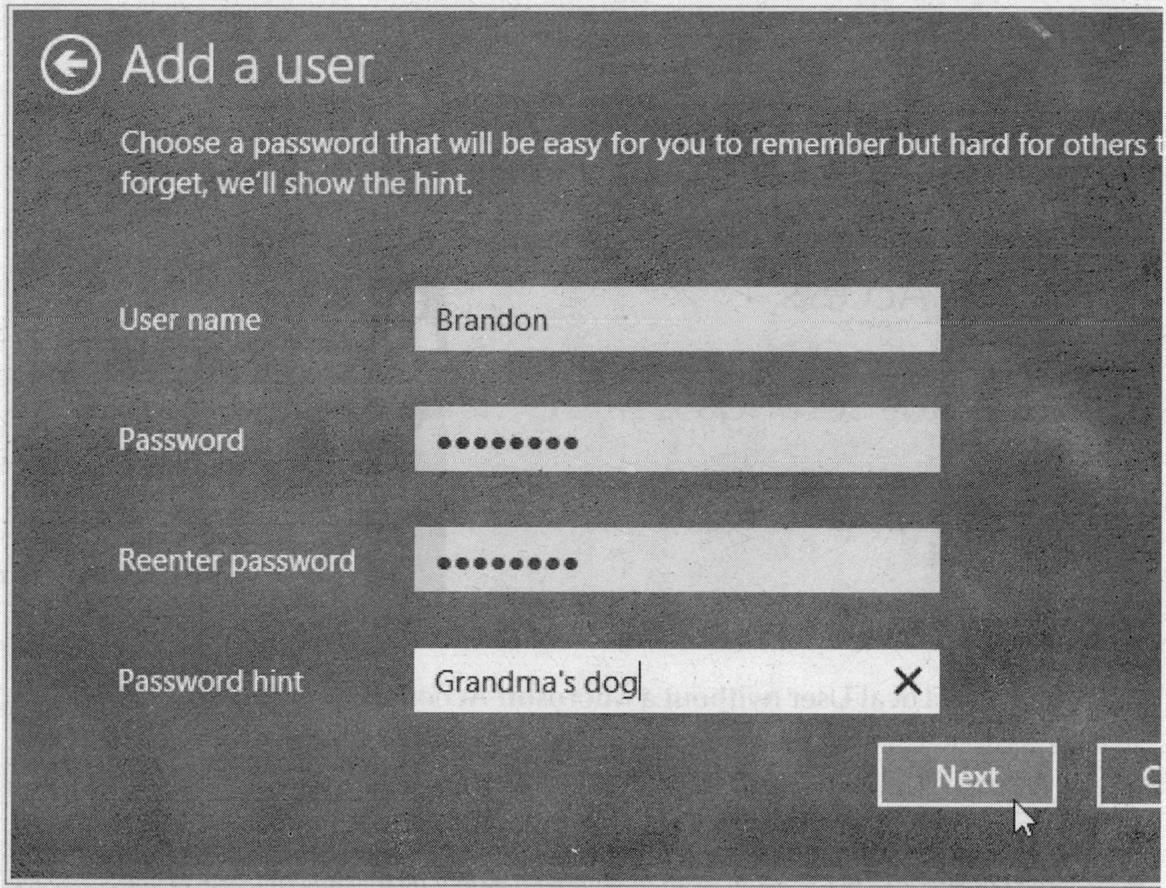

Choosing a password and adding account details

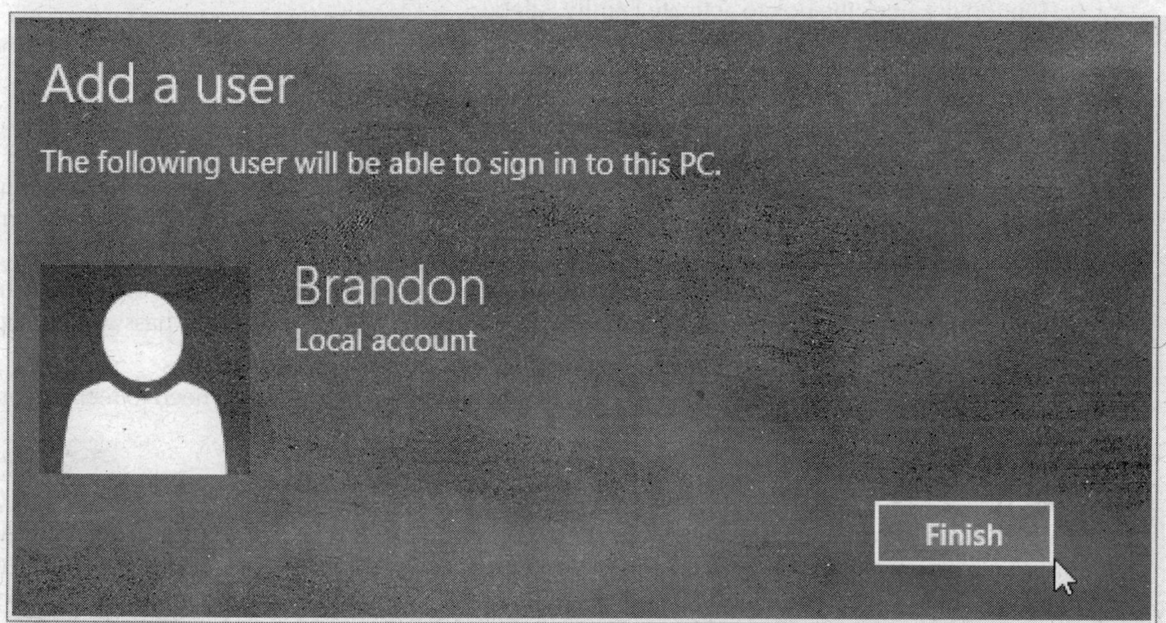

Clicking Finish

The added local user

To Add a New Local User (without a Microsoft Account):

1. Navigate to the Users pane from PC Settings. Click Add a user.
2. Locate and select Sign in without a Microsoft account.
3. Click Local account to continue.
4. Enter an account name and type the desired password. It's important to choose a strong password—in other words, one that is easy to remember but difficult for someone else to guess.
5. Reenter the password and include a hint, then click Next to continue.
6. Optional: Check the box to activate Family Safety.
7. Click Finish.
8. The user will be added.

Switching Users

If you have multiple user accounts on your computer, it's easy to switch between users without signing out or closing your current apps. Switching users will lock the current user, so you won't need to worry about someone else accessing your account.

- To switch users, click the current user in the upper-right of the Start screen and then select the desired user from the drop-down menu. The user will then need to enter their password to sign in.

You can switch back by selecting the desired user from the drop-down menu. You'll need to reenter your password to unlock the account.

Managing User Accounts

By default, the user account you created when setting up Windows 8 is an Administrator account. An Administrator account allows you to make top-level changes to the computer, like adding new users or modifying specific settings. Any users you add are automatically assigned to a Standard account, which

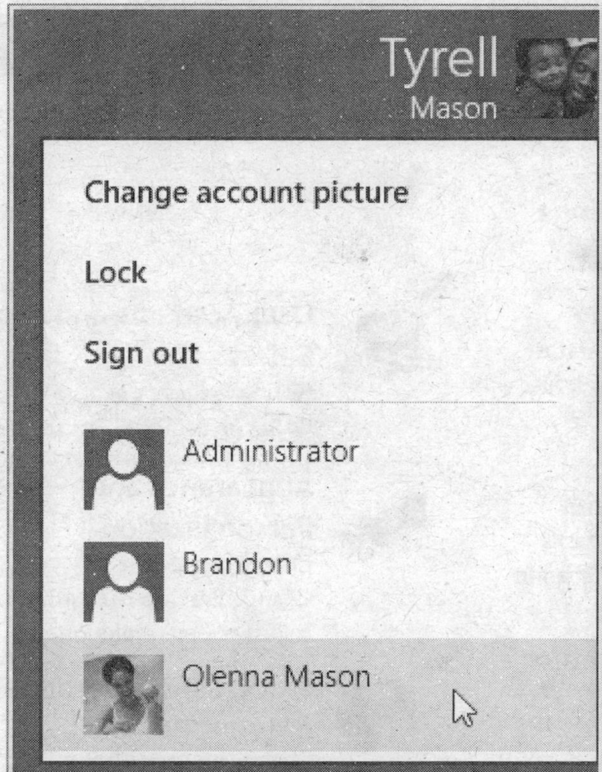

Switching user accounts from the Start screen

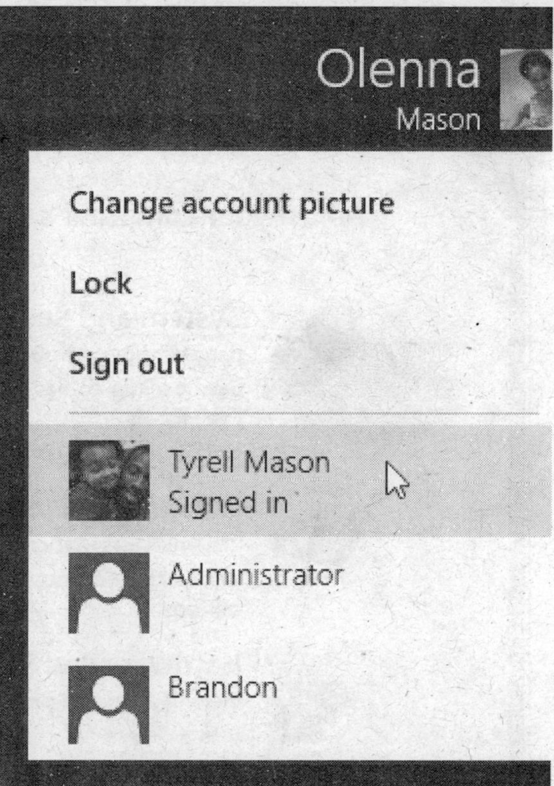

Switching back to the original user

Accessing Settings from the Desktop view

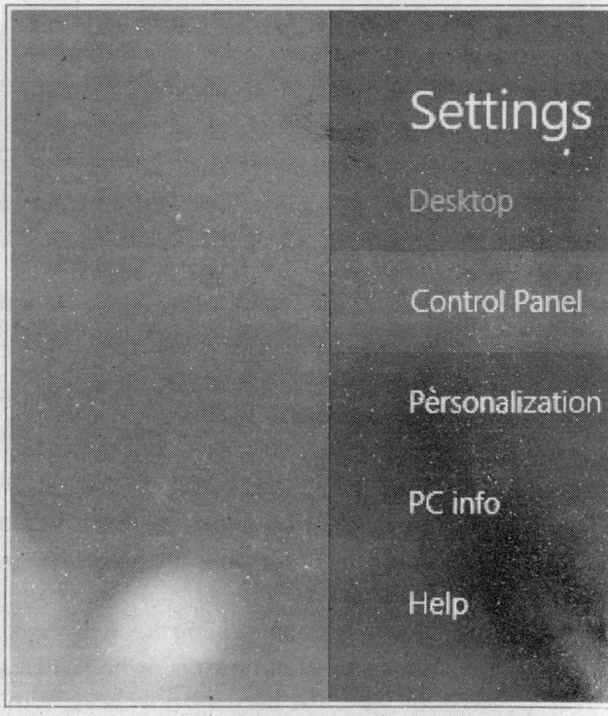

Clicking Control Panel

Clicking Change account type

should meet the everyday needs of most users. You will probably only need one Administrator account on a shared computer, but you do have the option to promote any user to an Administrator account should you choose.

To Change the Account Type:

1. From the Desktop view, hover the mouse in the lower-right corner to access the Charms bar, then select Settings.
2. Locate and select Control Panel from the Settings Pane.
3. The Control Panel will appear. Select Change account type below the User Accounts and Family Safety group.
4. The Manage Accounts dialog box will appear. Select the desired user account.
5. The Change Account Type dialog box will appear. Choose Administrator and then select Change Account Type. The user will now have Administrative privileges.

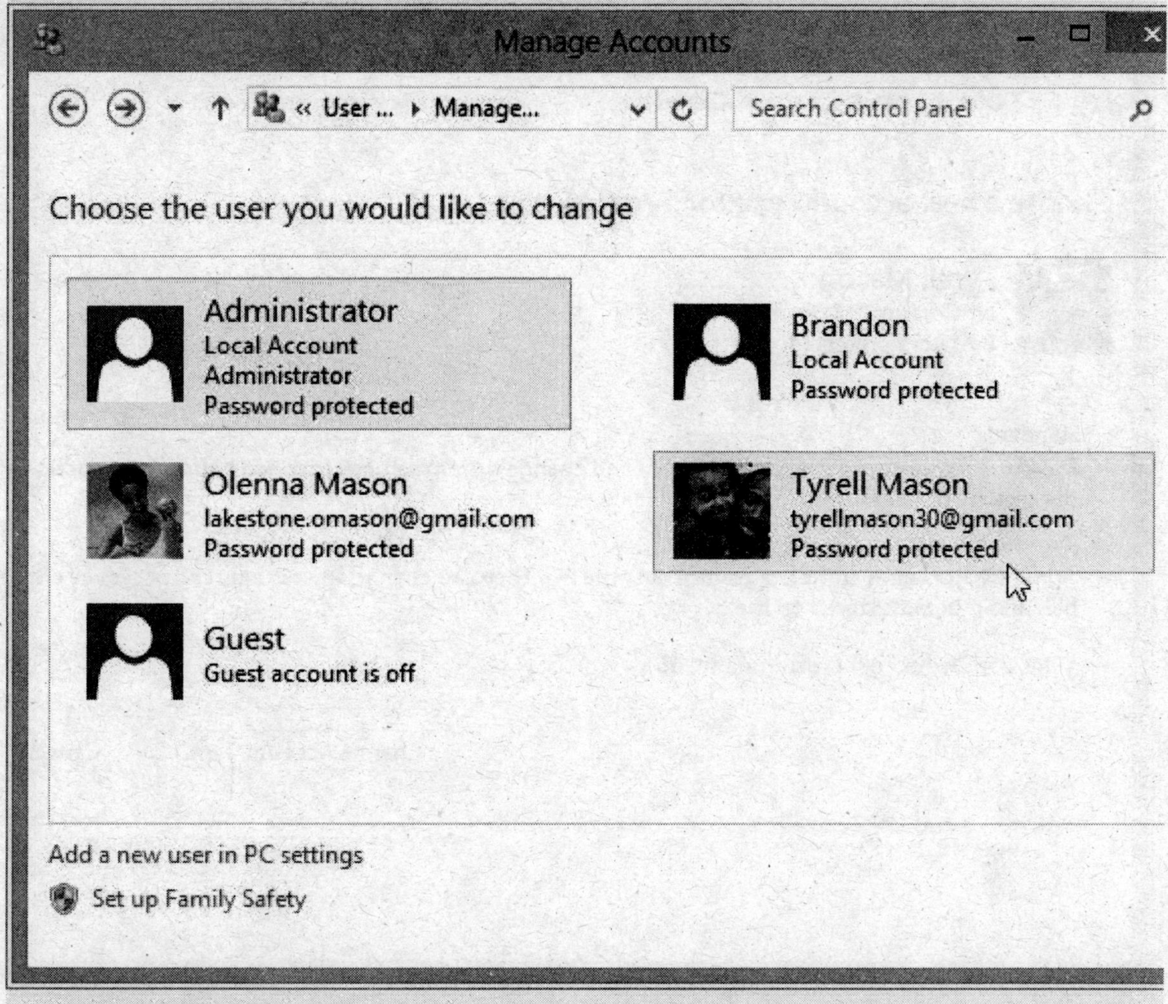

Selecting the desired user account

Parental Controls

Windows 8 offers a variety of parental controls that can help you monitor your child's activity and protect them from inappropriate content. For example, you can restrict certain apps and websites or limit the amount of time a user can spend on the computer. You'll need to add an account for each user you wish to monitor.

To Set Parental Controls:

1. From the Control Panel, locate and select Set up Family Safety for any user below the User Accounts and Family Safety group.
2. The Family Safety dialog box will appear. Select the desired user.
3. The Family Safety settings pane will appear. Make sure Family Safety is turned On. You'll then be able to set parental controls for the selected user.
4. Click the buttons in the interactive below to learn more about setting the parental controls from the Family Safety settings pane.

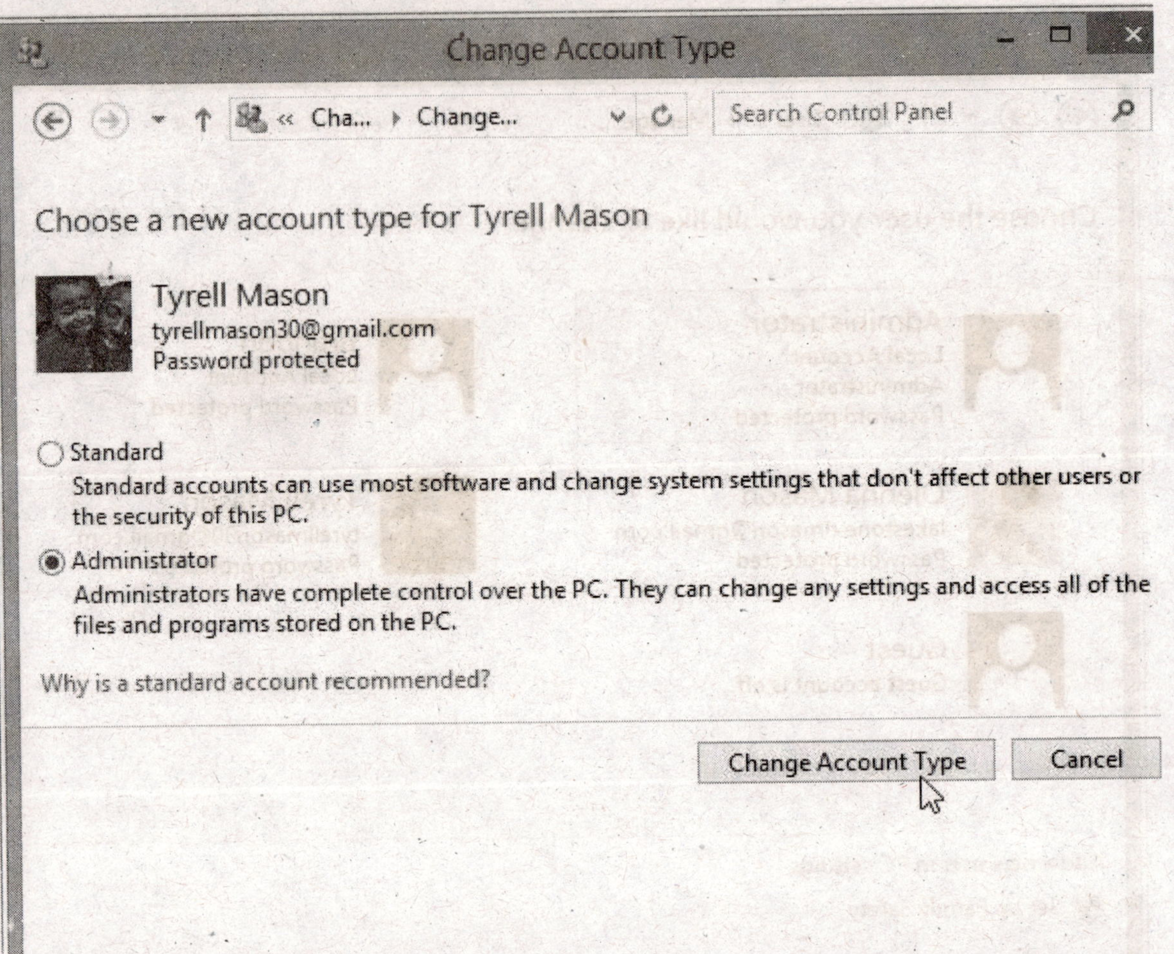

Granting Administrative privileges

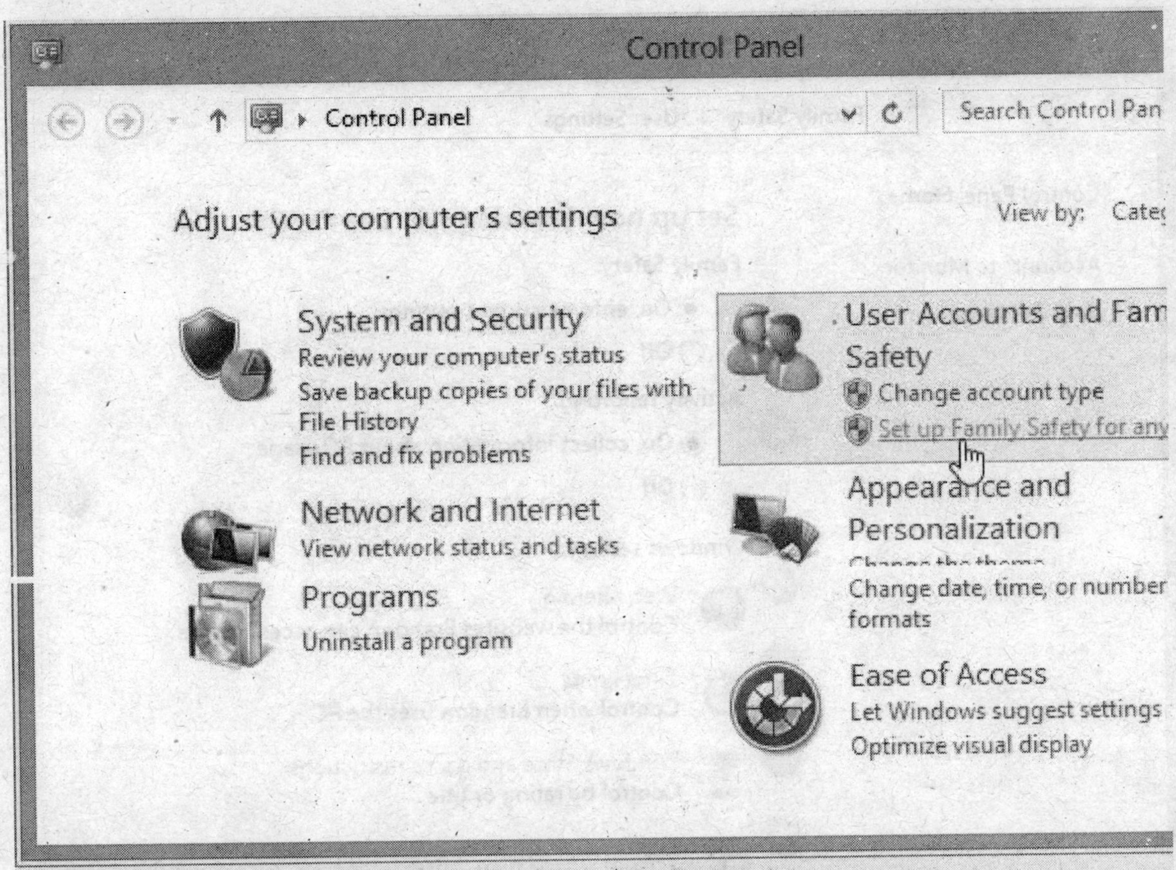

Opening parental controls

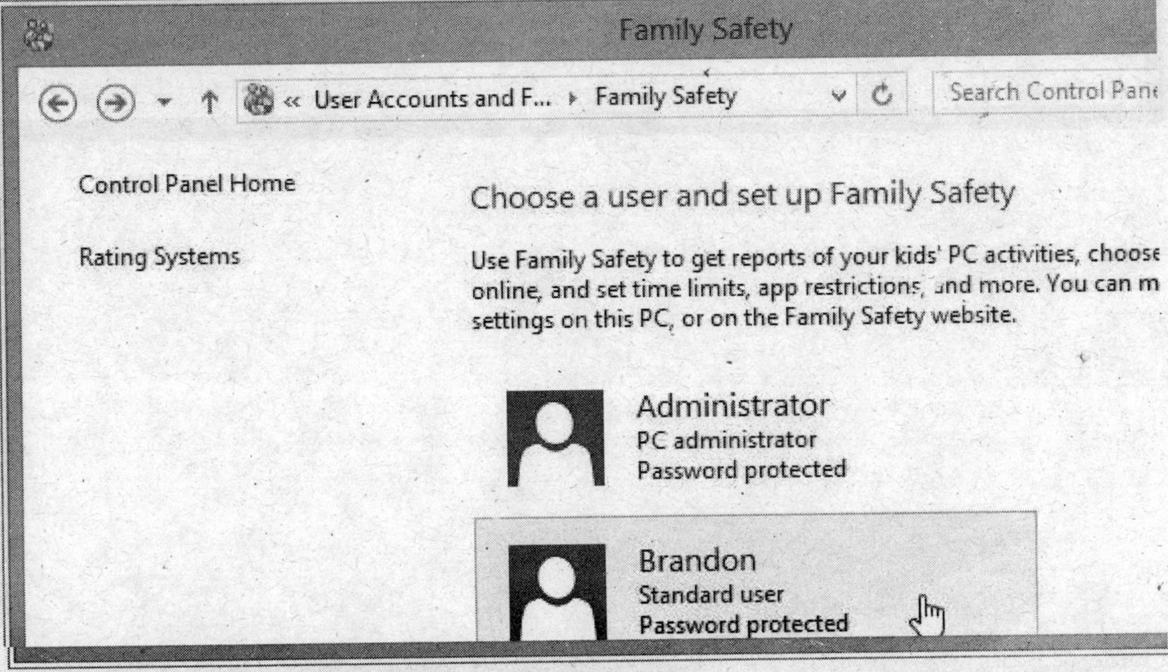

Choosing a user for parental controls

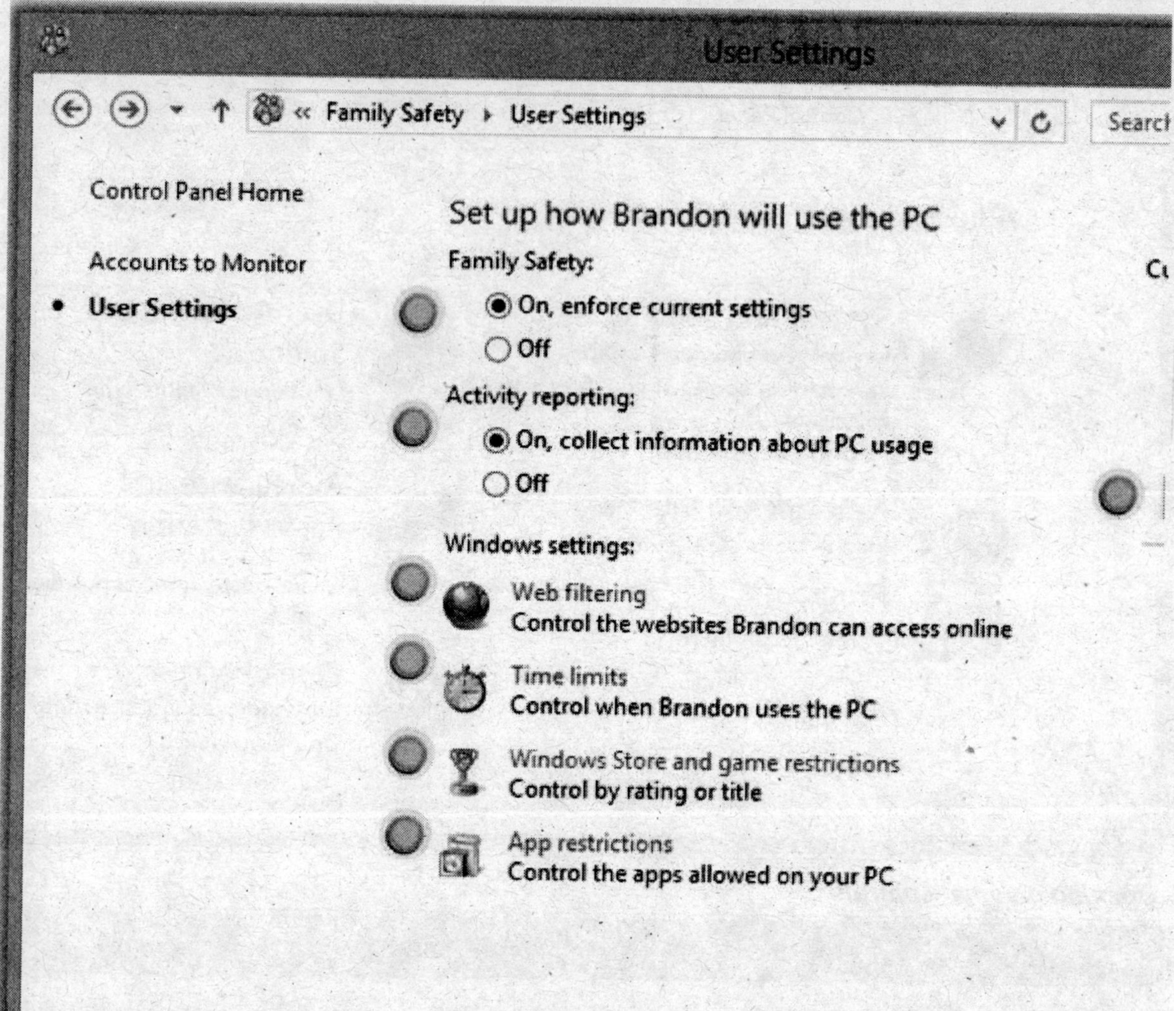
User Settings
« Family Safety › User Settings
Search
Control Panel Home
Accounts to Monitor
User Settings
Set up how Brandon will use the PC
Family Safety:
On, enforce current settings
Off
Activity reporting:
On, collect information about PC usage
Off
Windows settings:
Web filtering
Control the websites Brandon can access online
Time limits
Control when Brandon uses the PC
Windows Store and game restrictions
Control by rating or title
App restrictions
Control the apps allowed on your PC

CHAPTER 11

Security and Maintenance

In this chapter you will read about:

- Security and Maintenance.
- The Action Center.
- Troubleshooting.
- Using System Restore.
- Opening File with Different Applications

Security and Maintenance

In many ways, Windows 8 is the safest version of Windows ever released. There's substantially less risk of downloading harmful software because the apps you'll use from the Start screen are either designed or approved by Microsoft. Windows 8 also includes a number of security features to keep you safe.

Security Features in Windows 8

Windows 8 uses a wide variety of tools to protect you from viruses, malware, and other malicious applications that could harm your computer. Many of these services run in the background, so you may not even notice that they're constantly working to keep you safe.

User Account Control

User Account Control warns you when a program or user attempts to change your computer's settings. Your screen will be temporarily locked until an Administrator can confirm the changes. This helps to protect your computer against malicious software and accidental changes. User Account Control also allows you to decide how often you'll receive these warnings.

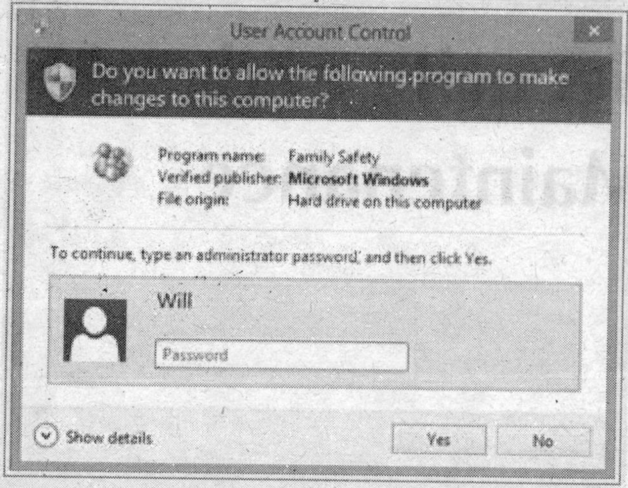

User Account Control

Windows Defender

Windows Defender provides anti-virus and malware protection for your computer. In addition to scanning your computer for potentially harmful applications, Windows Defender also provides real-time protection, double-checking each file or application you open without slowing down your computer.

Windows SmartScreen

Whenever your computer detects a security threat from a file or application, Windows SmartScreen will

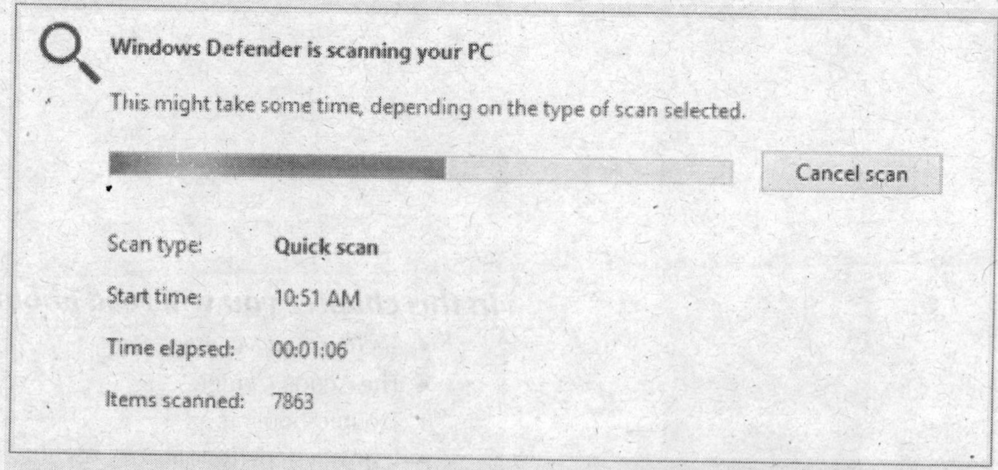

Windows Defender

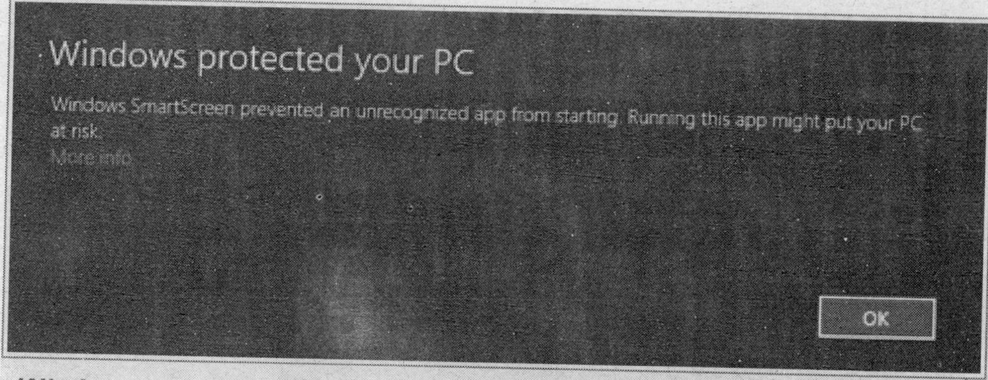

Windows SmartScreen

notify you with a full-screen warning. Whenever you see this warning screen, you should choose not to open the file or application unless you can verify that it will not damage your computer.

Windows Firewall

By default, Windows 8 will protect your internet connection with Windows Firewall. A firewall prevents unauthorized access from external connections and helps protect your network from threats that could harm your computer.

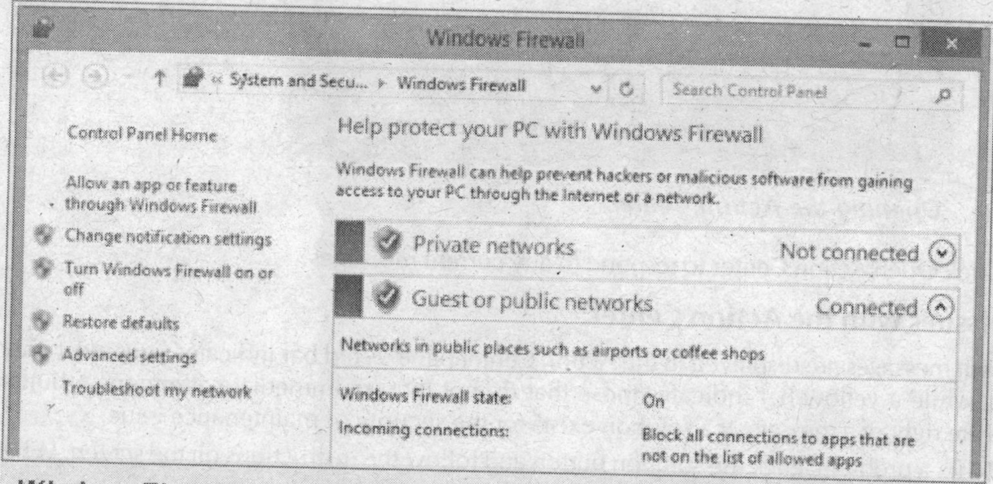

Windows Firewall

The Action Center

The Action Center is a centralized place to view security and maintenance messages, making it easier to identify and solve problems with your computer. The Action Center can be accessed from Deskop view.

To Open the Action Center:

If you have any important messages, the flag icon on the taskbar will display a red X symbol recflag icon.

1. To open the Action Center, click the flag icon on the taskbar.
2. Any current messages will appear.

Clicking the Action Center icon in the taskbar

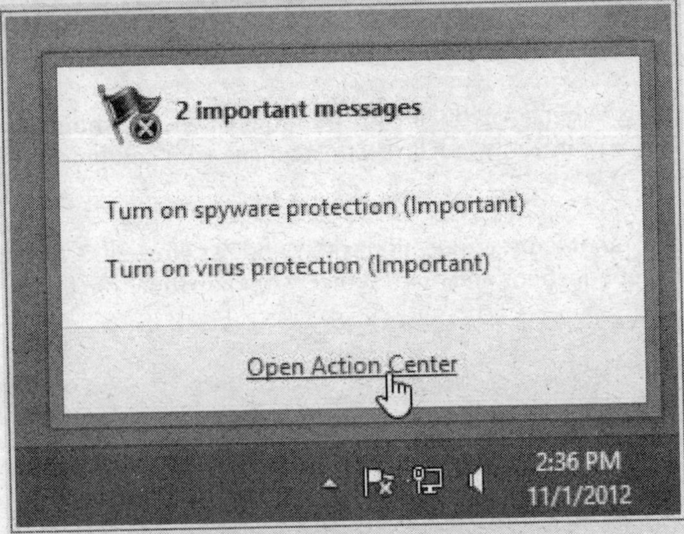

Opening the Action Center

3. Click Open Action Center to respond to any current messages.

Solving Issues with the Action Center:

Your current messages are displayed in the Action Center pane. A red bar indicates your most important messages, while a yellow bar indicates those that do not require immediate attention. A button will appear to the right of a message if a solution exists for the security or maintenance issue.

- To fix a problem, click the solution button and follow the instructions on the screen. When you are done, the message will disappear from the Action Center.

Some messages are just notifications and do not indicate a problem with your computer. These messages will not include a solution button, but they may still have important information or instructions.

Troubleshooting

Not all computer problems will be shown in the Action Center. For example, you may have trouble with a particular program or device or connecting to the internet. For these types of problems, you will want to open the Troubleshooting pane.

- To access the Troubleshooting pane, click Troubleshooting at the bottom of the Action Center. You will see several different options that will help you identify and fix problems with your software and hardware.

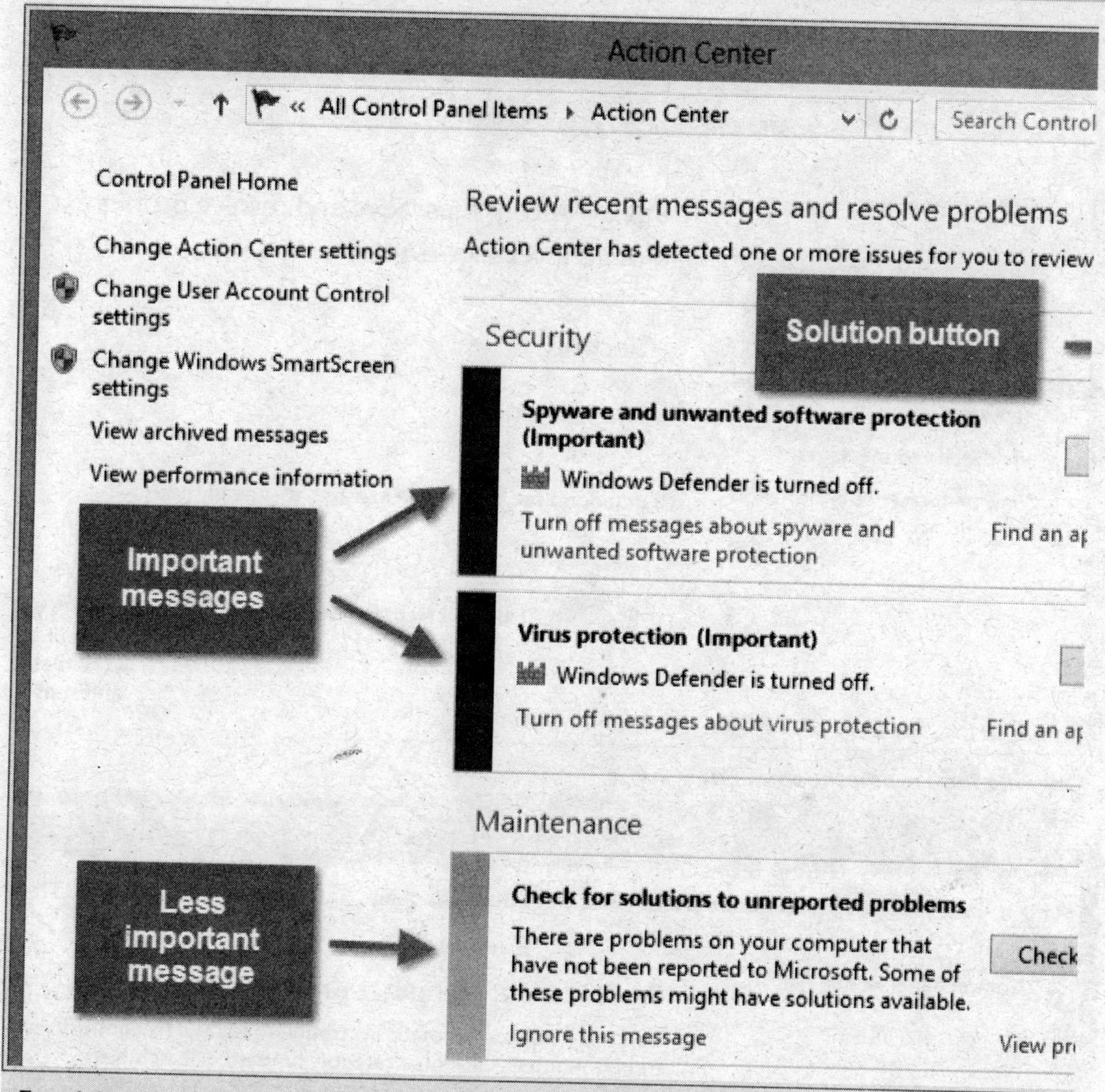

Resolving issues with the Action Center

Click the buttons in the interactive below to learn more about using the Troubleshooting pane. Note that your computer may have a slightly different list of options.

Using System Restore

You may occasionally experience problems with your computer after opening certain files or applications from the internet, which can affect your system settings. System Restore is often the easiest way to fix these kinds of issues. System Restore allows you to "rewind" your system settings to an earlier point in time, called a restore point. Keep in mind that a system restore will not erase your recently created files, nor can it be used to recover lost documents or other files. However, it may uninstall recently added applications and drivers.

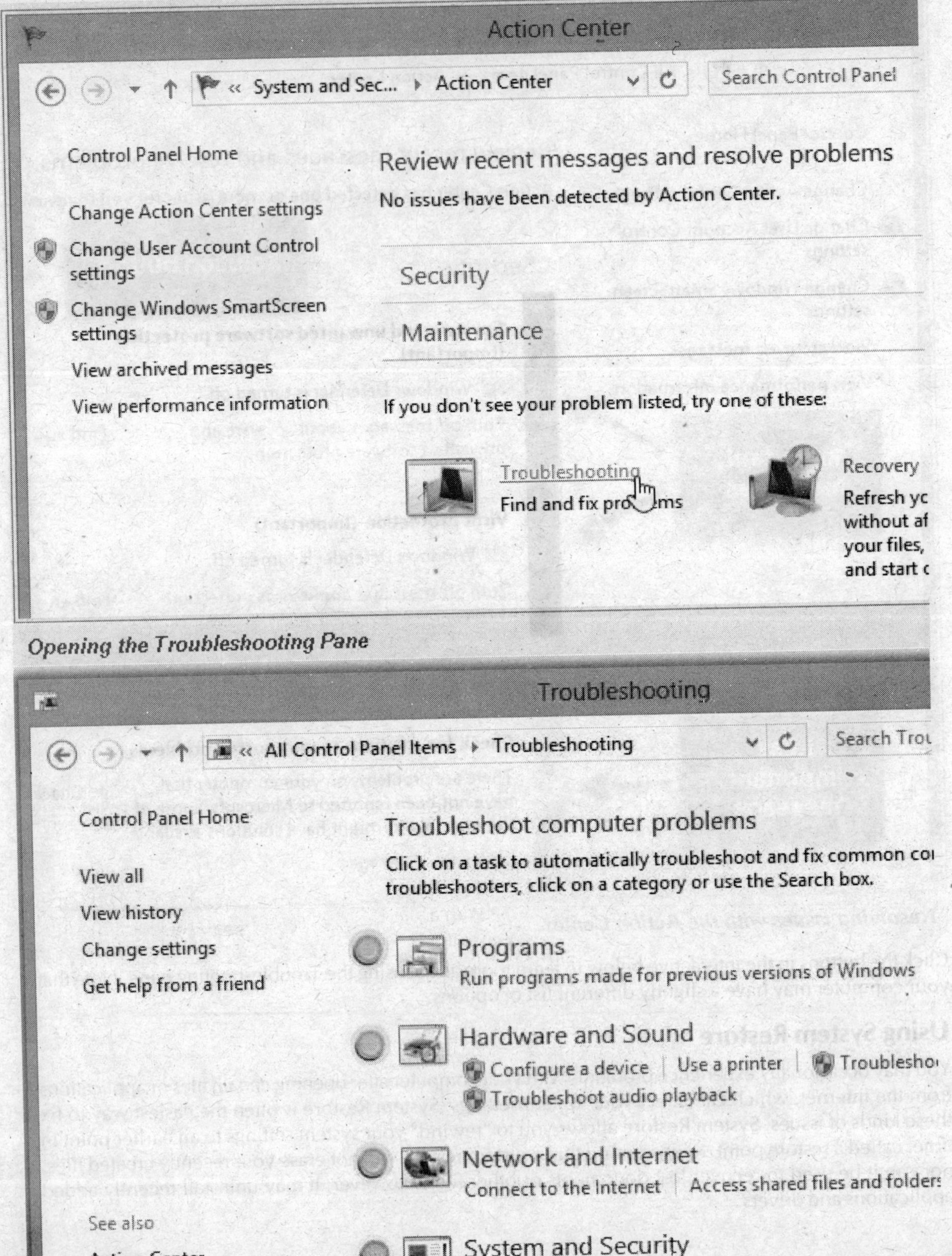

Opening the Troubleshooting Pane

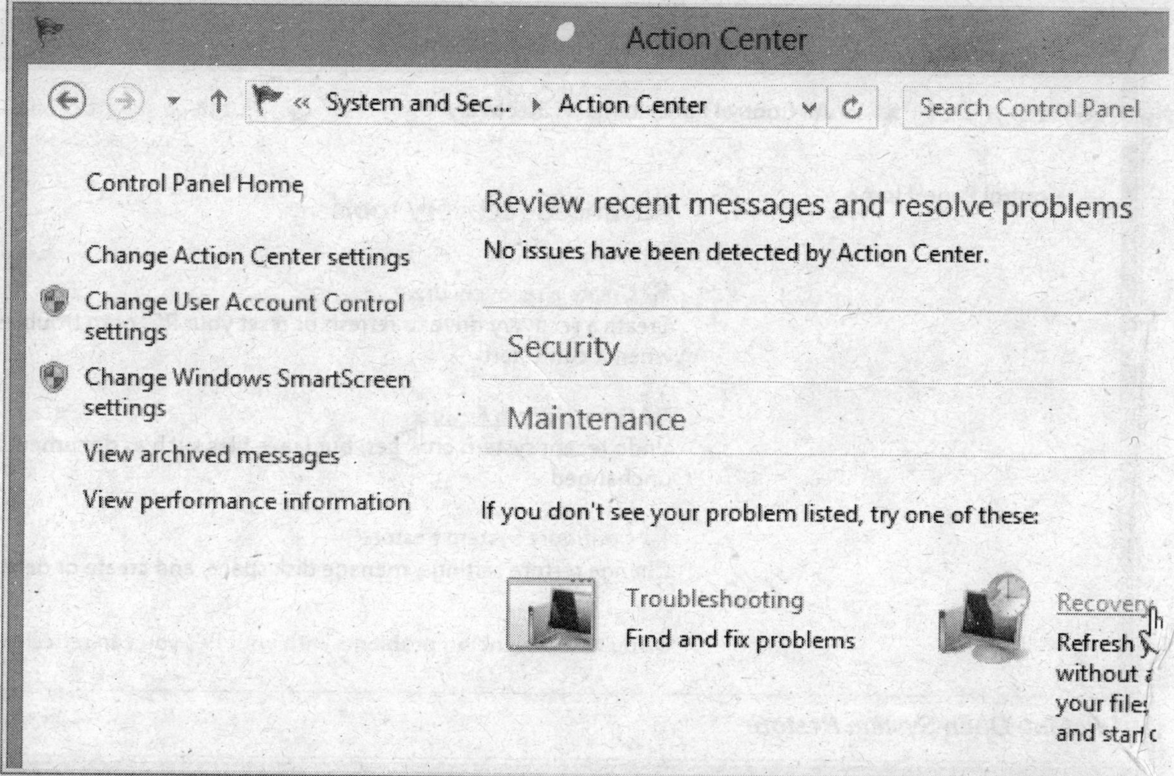

Accessing Recovery tools

To Perform a System Restore:

1. Locate and select Recovery at the bottom of the Action Center pane.
2. Click Open System Restore.
3. The System Restore dialog box will appear. Follow the instructions on the screen to return your system settings to an earlier restore point.

Opening Your Files with Different Apps

When you open a file in Windows 8, it will usually open with a Start screen app — even if you opened it from the Desktop. But you may not always want this. If you prefer to work in the Desktop, you can choose to open the file with a Desktop app. For example, a jpeg picture opens in the Photos app by default, but you can open it in Windows Photo Viewer instead.

To Open a File in the Default App:

1. In Desktop view, double-click the desired file.
2. The file will open in the default app. In this example, it opened in the Photos app.

To Open a File in a Different App:

Sometimes, you may want to open a file in a different app without changing the default. For example, you may want to open a photo with the Paint app to crop or resize it.

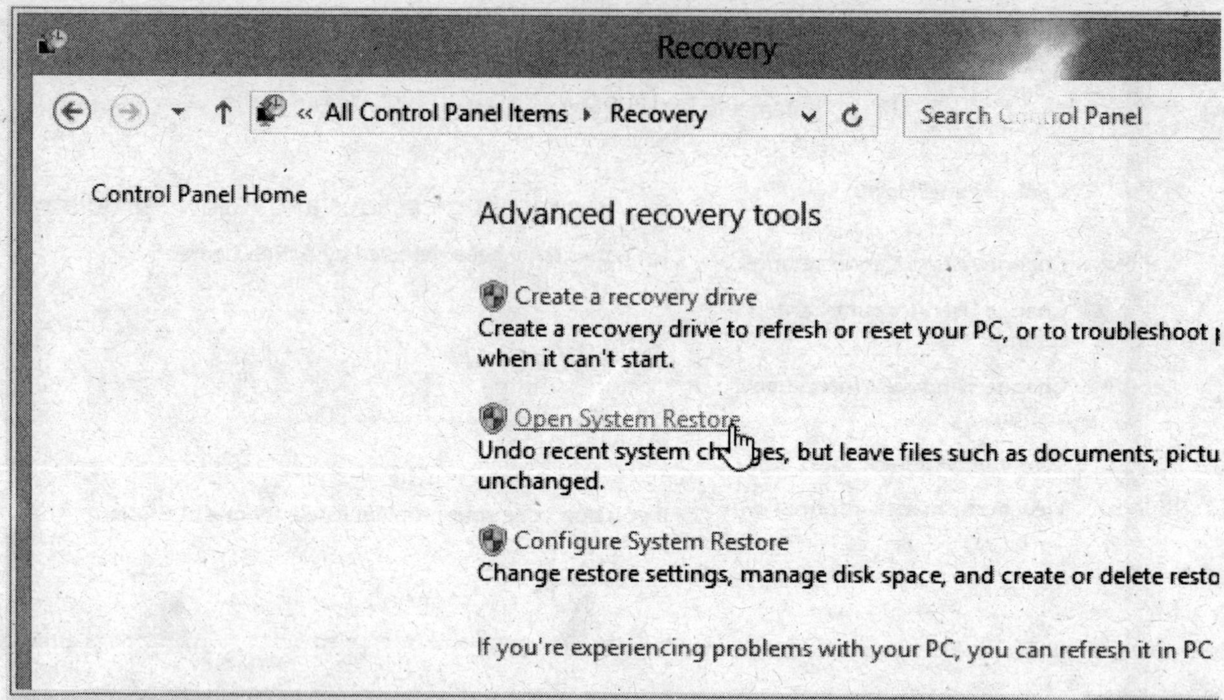

Recovery

« All Control Panel Items ▸ Recovery

Search Control Panel

Control Panel Home

Advanced recovery tools

Create a recovery drive

Create a recovery drive to refresh or reset your PC, or to troubleshoot
when it can't start.

Open System Restore

Undo recent system changes, but leave files such as documents, pictu
unchanged.

Configure System Restore

Change restore settings, manage disk space, and create or delete resto

If you're experiencing problems with your PC, you can refresh it in PC

Clicking Open System Restore

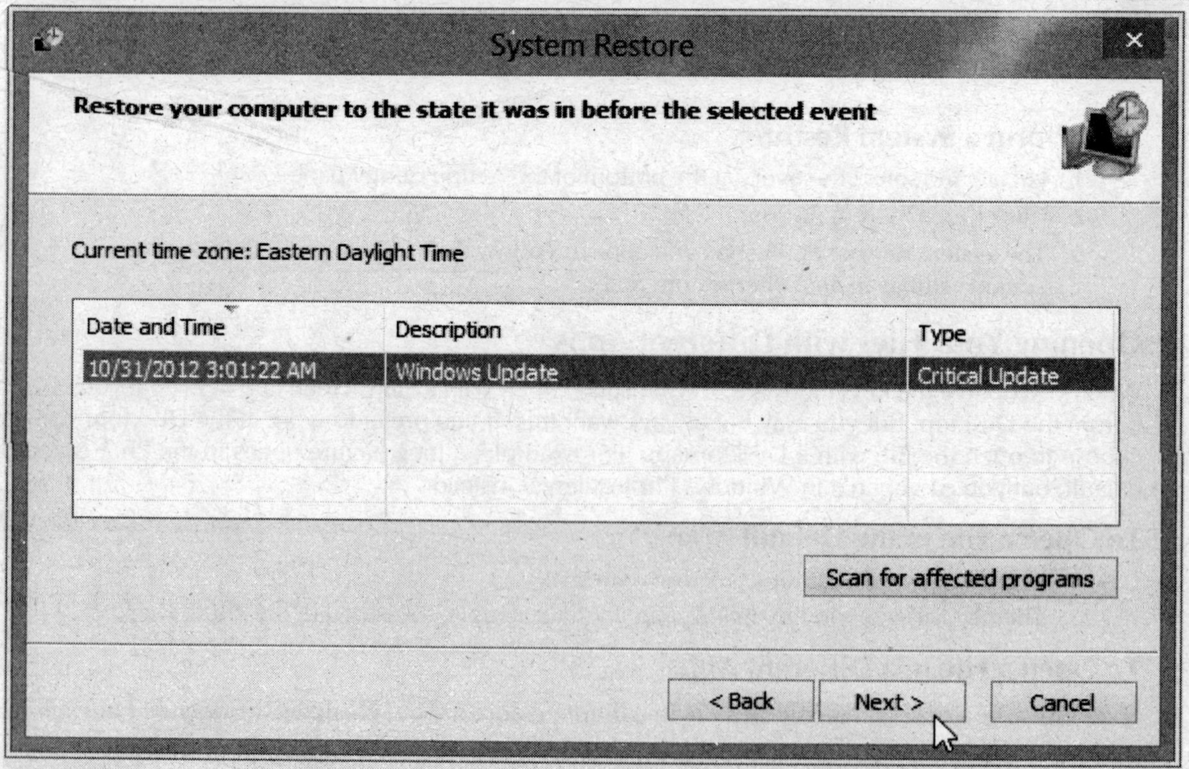

System Restore

Restore your computer to the state it was in before the selected event

Current time zone: Eastern Daylight Time

Date and Time	Description	Type
10/31/2012 3:01:22 AM	Windows Update	Critical Update

Scan for affected programs

< Back Next > Cancel

Choosing a restore point

1. In Desktop view, right-click the desired file.
2. From the drop-down menu, click Open with and select the desired app.
3. The file will open in the app you selected.

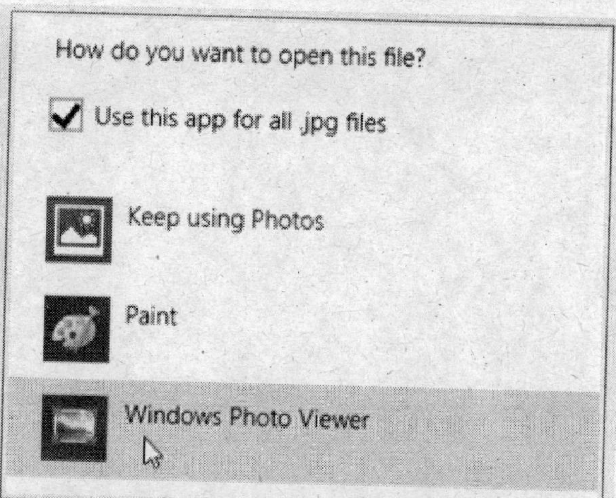

Selecting an app

To Change the Default App:

You may prefer to change the default app for certain types of files, so that they'll always open in the new app when you double-click them. For example, you may want your photos to always open in Windows Photo Viewer instead of the Photos app.

Double-clicking a file

1. In Desktop view, right-click the desired file.
2. From the drop-down menu, click Open with and select Choose default program....

The Photos app

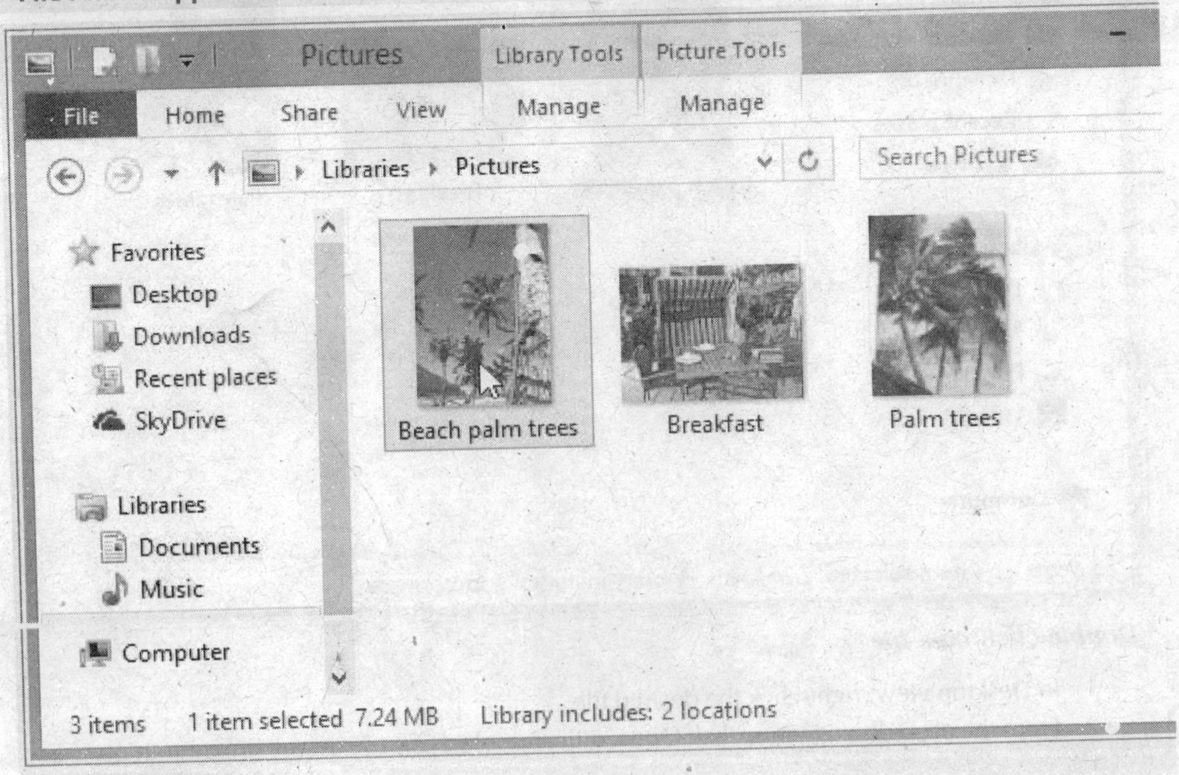

Pictures
Library Tools
Picture Tools
File
Home
Share
View
Manage
Manage
Libraries ▸ Pictures
Search Pictures
Favorites
Desktop
Downloads
Recent places
SkyDrive
Libraries
Documents
Music
Computer
Beach palm trees
Breakfast
Palm trees
3 items 1 item selected 7.24 MB Library includes: 2 locations

Right-clicking a file

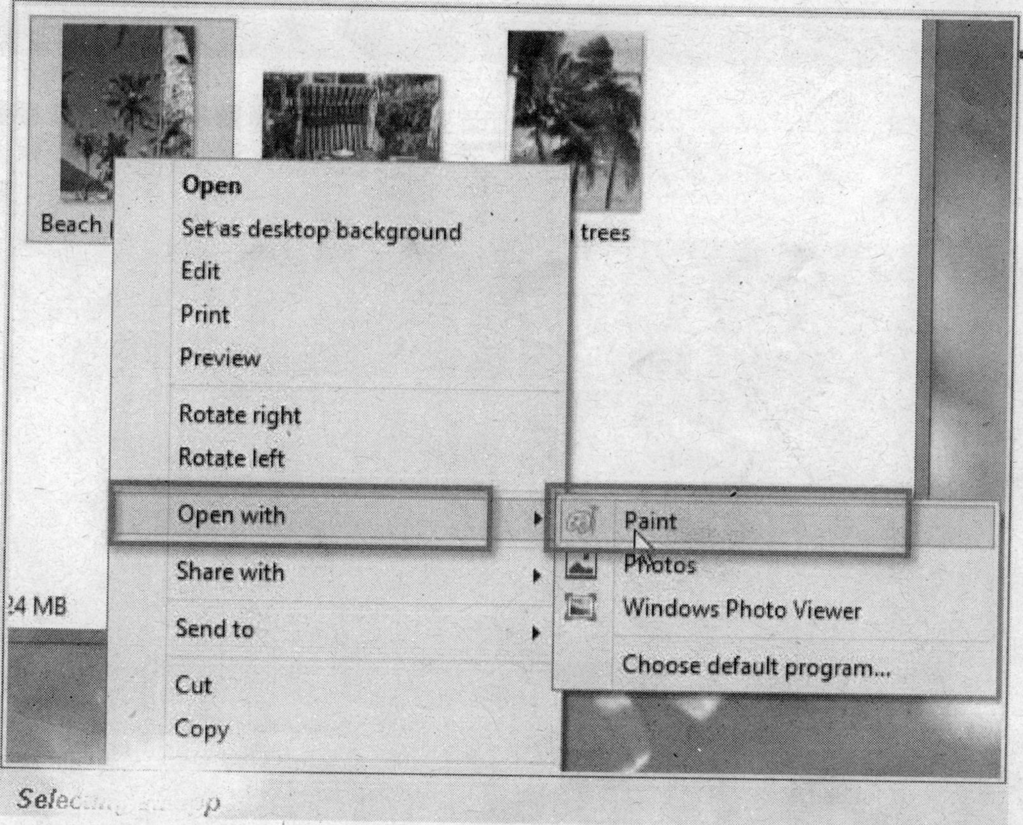

Selec[illegible]p

3. Select the desired app. If you don't see the app you want, click More options. In this example, we want to open the file in Windows Photo Viewer.
4. The file will open in the new app. The next time you double-click a file of that type, it will open in the new default app.

The Paint app

Right-clicking a file

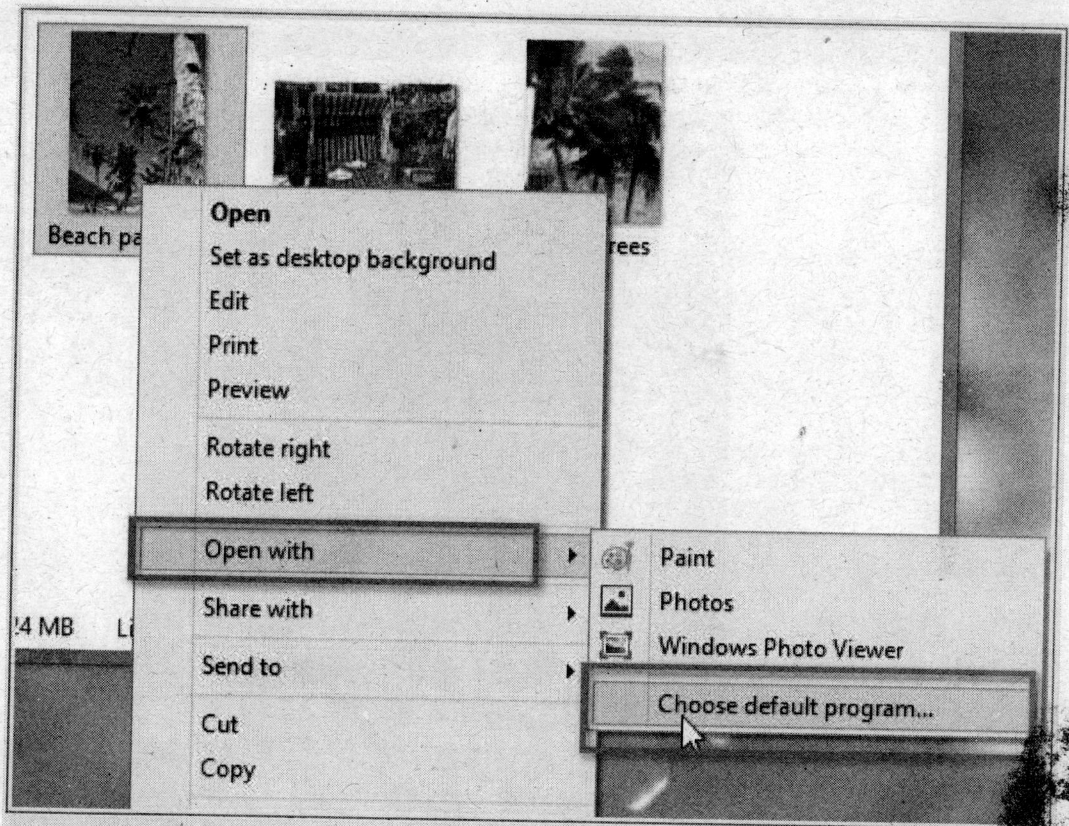

Choosing a default app

Selecting an app

Windows Photo Viewer

CHAPTER 12

Keyboard Shortcuts of Windows 8

In this chapter you will read about:

- Various keyboard shortcuts for working with Windows 8

New keyboard shortcuts

The following table contains new keyboard shortcuts that you can use to navigate around Windows.

Press this key	To do this
Windows logo key + start typing	Search your PC
Ctrl + plus (+) or Ctrl + minus (-)	Zoom in or out of a large number of items, like apps pinned to the Start screen
Ctrl + scroll wheel	Zoom in or out of a large number of items, like apps pinned to the Start screen
Windows logo key + C	Open the charms. In an app, open the commands for the app
Windows logo key + F	Open the Search charm to search files
Windows logo key + H	Open the Share charm
Windows logo key + I	Open the Settings charm
Windows logo key + J	Switch the main app and snapped app
Windows logo key + K	Open the Devices charm
Windows logo key + O	Lock the screen orientation (portrait or landscape)
Windows logo key + Q	Open the Search charm to search apps
Windows logo key + W	Open the Search charm to search settings
Windows logo key + Z	Show the commands available in the app
Windows logo key + spacebar	Switch input language and keyboard layout
Windows logo key + Ctrl + spacebar	Change to a previously selected input
Windows logo key + Tab	Cycle through open apps (except desktop apps)
Windows logo key + Ctrl + Tab	Cycle through open apps (except desktop apps) and snaps them as they are cycled
Windows logo key + Shift + Tab	Cycle through open apps (except desktop apps) in reverse order
Windows logo key + PgUp	Move the Start screen and apps to the monitor on the left (Apps in the desktop won't change monitors)
Windows logo key + PgDown	Move the Start screen and apps to the monitor on the right (Apps in the desktop won't change monitors)
Windows logo key + Shift + period (.)	Snaps an app to the left
Windows logo key + period (.)	Snaps an app to the right
Esc	Stop or exit the current task

General keyboard shortcuts

The following table contains general keyboard shortcuts that you can use to navigate around Windows.

Press this key	To do this
F1	Display Help
F2	Rename the selected item
F3	Search for a file or folder
F4	Display the address bar list in File Explorer
F5	Refresh the active window
F6	Cycle through screen elements in a window or on the desktop
F10	Activate the menu bar in the active app
Alt + F4	Close the active item, or exit the active app

Alt+Esc	Cycle through items in the order in which they were opened
Alt+underlined letter	Perform the command for that letter
Alt+Enter	Display properties for the selected item
Alt+Spacebar	Open the shortcut menu for the active window
Alt+Left arrow	Back
Alt+Right arrow	Forward
Alt+Page Up	Move up one screen
Alt+Page Dow	Move down one screen
Alt+Tab	Switch between open apps (except desktop apps)
Ctrl+F4	Close the active document (in apps that allow you to have multiple documents open simultaneously)
Ctrl+A	Select all items in a document or window
Ctrl+C (or Ctrl+Insert)	Copy the selected item
Ctrl+D (or Delete)	Delete the selected item and move it to the Recycle Bin
Ctrl+R (or F5)	Refresh the active window
Ctrl+V (or Shift+Insert)	Paste the selected item
Ctrl+X	Cut the selected item
Ctrl+Y	Redo an action
Ctrl+Z	Undo an action
Ctrl+plus (+) or Ctrl+minus (-)	Zoom in or out of a large number of items, like apps pinned to the Start screen
Ctrl+ mouse scroll wheel	Change the size of desktop icons or zoom in or out of a large number of items, like apps pinned to the Start screen
Ctrl+Right arrow	Move the cursor to the beginning of the next word
Ctrl+Left arrow	Move the cursor to the beginning of the previous word
Ctrl+Down arrow	Move the cursor to the beginning of the next paragraph
Ctrl+Up arrow	Move the cursor to the beginning of the previous paragraph
Ctrl+Alt+Tab	Use the arrow keys to switch between all open apps
Ctrl+arrow key (to move to an item)+Spacebar	Select multiple individual items in a window or on the desktop
Ctrl+Shift with an arrow key	Select a block of text
Ctrl+Esc	Open the Start screen
Ctrl+Shift+Esc	Open Task Manager
Ctrl+Shift	Switch the keyboard layout when multiple keyboard layouts are available
Ctrl+Spacebar	Turn the Chinese input method editor (IME) on or off
Shift+F10	Display the shortcut menu for the selected item
Shift with any arrow key	Select more than one item in a window or on the desktop, or select text within a document
Shift+Delete	Delete the selected item without moving it to the Recycle Bin first
Right arrow	Open the next menu to the right, or open a submenu

Left arrow	Open the next menu to the left, or close a submenu
Esc	Stop or leave the current task

Windows logo key keyboard shortcuts

The following table contains keyboard shortcuts that use the Windows logo key Windows logo key.

Press this key	To do this
Windows logo key + F1	Open Windows Help and Support
Windows logo key	Display or hide the Start screen
Windows logo key + B	Set focus in the notification area
Windows logo key + C	Open the Charms
Windows logo key + D	Display and hide the desktop
Windows logo key + E	Open Computer
Windows logo key + F	Open the Search charm and search for files
Windows logo key + G	Cycle through Gadgets on the desktop
Windows logo key + H	Open the Share charm
Windows logo key + I	Open the Settings charm
Windows logo key + J	Switch the main app and snapped app
Windows logo key + K	Open the Devices charm
Windows logo key + L	Lock your PC or switch users
Windows logo key + M	Minimize all windows
Windows logo key + O	Lock device orientation
Windows logo key + P	Choose a presentation display mode
Windows logo key + Q	Open the Search charm and search for apps
Windows logo key + R	Open the Run dialog box
Windows logo key + T	Cycle through apps on the taskbar
Windows logo key + U	Open Ease of Access Center
Windows logo key + V	Cycle through notifications
Windows logo key + Shift + V	Cycle through notifications in reverse order
Windows logo key + W	Open the Search charm and search for settings
Windows logo key + X	Open the Quick Link menu
Windows logo key + Z	Show the commands available in the app
Windows logo key + ,	Temporarily peek at the desktop
Windows logo key + Pause	Display the System Properties dialog box
Windows logo key + Ctrl + F	Search for PCs (if you're on a network)
Windows logo key + Shift + M	Restore minimized windows on the desktop
Windows logo key + number	Start the desktop app pinned to the taskbar in the position indicated by the number. If the app is already running, switch to that app.
Windows logo key + Shift + number	Start a new instance of the desktop app pinned to the taskbar in the position indicated by the number
Windows logo key + Ctrl + number	Switch to the last active window of the desktop app pinned to the taskbar in the position indicated by the number

Windows logo key + Alt + number	Open the Jump List for the desktop app pinned to the taskbar in the position indicated by the number
Windows logo key + Ctrl + Shift + number	Open a new instance of the desktop app located at the given position on the taskbar as an administrator
Windows logo key + Tab	Cycle through open apps (except desktop apps)
Windows logo key + Ctrl + Tab	Cycle through open apps (except desktop apps) and snap them as they are cycled
Windows logo key + Shift + Tab	Cycle through open apps (except desktop apps) in reverse order
Windows logo key + Ctrl + B	Switch to the app that displayed a message in the notification area
Windows logo key + Up arrow	Maximize the desktop window
Windows logo key + Down arrow	Minimize the desktop window
Windows logo key + Left arrow	Maximize the desktop window to the left side of the screen
Windows logo key + Right arrow	Maximize the desktop window to the right side of the screen
Windows logo key + Home	Minimize all but the active desktop window (restores all windows on second stroke)
Windows logo key + Shift + Up arrow	Stretch the desktop window to the top and bottom of the screen
Windows logo key + Shift + Down arrow	Restore/minimize active desktop windows vertically, maintaining width
Windows logo key + Shift + Left arrow or Right arrow	Move a window in the desktop from one monitor to another
Windows logo key + Spacebar	Switch input language and keyboard layout
Windows logo key + Ctrl + Spacebar	Change to a previously selected input
Windows logo key + Enter	Open Narrator
Windows logo key + Page Up	Move the Start screen and apps to the monitor on the left (apps in the desktop won't change monitors)
Windows logo key + Page Down	Move the Start screen and apps to the monitor on the right (apps in the desktop won't change monitors)
Windows logo key + Shift + period (.)	Snap an app to the left
Windows logo key + period (.)	Snap an app to the right
Windows logo key + /	Initiate IME reconversion
Windows logo key + Alt + Enter	Open Windows Media Center
Windows logo key + plus (+) or minus (-)	Zoom in or out using Magnifier
Windows logo key + Esc	Exit Magnifier

Dialog box keyboard shortcuts

The following table contains keyboard shortcuts that you can use to navigate dialog boxes.

Press this key	To do this
F1	Display Help
F4	Display the items in the active list
Ctrl + Tab	Move forward through tabs
Ctrl + Shift + Tab	Move back through tabs
Ctrl + number (number 1-9)	Move to nth tab

Tab	Move forward through options
Shift + Tab	Move back through options
Alt + underlined letter	Perform the command (or select the option) that goes with that letter
Spacebar	Select or clear the check box if the active option is a check box
Backspace	Open a folder one level up if a folder is selected in the Save As or Open dialog box
Arrow keys	Select a button if the active option is a group of option buttons

File Explorer keyboard shortcuts

The following table contains keyboard shortcuts for working with File Explorer windows or folders.

Press this key	To do this
Alt + D	Select the address bar
Ctrl + E	Select the search box
Ctrl + F	Select the search box
Ctrl + N	Open a new window
Ctrl + W	Close the current window
Ctrl + mouse scroll wheel	Change the size and appearance of file and folder icons
Ctrl + Shift + E	Display all folders above the selected folder
Ctrl + Shift + N	Create a new folder
Num Lock + asterisk (*)	Display all subfolders under the selected folder
Num Lock + plus (+)	Display the contents of the selected folder
Num Lock + minus (-)	Collapse the selected folder
Alt + P	Display the preview pane
Alt + Enter	Open the Properties dialog box for the selected item
Alt + Right arrow	View the next folder
Alt + Up arrow	View the folder that the folder was in
Alt + Left arrow	View the previous folder
Backspace	View the previous folder
Right arrow	Display the current selection (if it's collapsed), or select the first subfolder
Left arrow	Collapse the current selection (if it's expanded), or select the folder that the folder was in
End	Display the bottom of the active window
Home	Display the top of the active window
F11	Maximize or minimize the active window

Taskbar keyboard shortcuts

The following table contains keyboard shortcuts for working with items on the desktop taskbar.

Press this key	To do this
Shift + click a taskbar button	Open an app or quickly open another instance of an app
Ctrl + Shift + click a taskbar button	Open an app as an administrator
Shift + right-click a taskbar button	Show the window menu for the app

Shift + right-click a grouped taskbar button	Show the window menu for the group
Ctrl + click a grouped taskbar button	Cycle through the windows of the group

Ease of Access keyboard shortcuts

The following table contains keyboard shortcuts that can help make your PC easier to use.

Press this key	To do this
Right Shift for eight seconds	Turn Filter Keys on and off
Left Alt + left Shift + Print Screen	Turn High Contrast on or off
Left Alt + left Shift + Num Lock	Turn Mouse Keys on or off
Shift five times	Turn Sticky Keys on or off
Num Lock for five seconds	Turn Toggle Keys on or off
Windows logo key + U	Open the Ease of Access Center

Magnifier keyboard shortcuts

The following table contains keyboard shortcuts for working with Magnifier.

Press this key	To do this
Windows logo key + plus (+) or minus (-)	Zoom in or out
Ctrl + Alt + Spacebar	Preview the desktop in full-screen mode
Ctrl + Alt + D	Switch to docked mode
Ctrl + Alt + F	Switch to full-screen mode
Ctrl + Alt + I	Invert colors
Ctrl + Alt + L	Switch to lens mode
Ctrl + Alt + R	Resize the lens
Ctrl + Alt + arrow keys	Pan in the direction of the arrow keys
Windows logo key + Esc	Exit Magnifier

Narrator keyboard shortcuts

The following table contains keyboard shortcuts for working with Narrator.

Press this key	To do this
Spacebar or Enter	Activate current item
Tab and arrow keys	Move around on the screen
Ctrl	Stop reading
Caps Lock + D	Read item
Caps Lock + M	Start reading
Caps Lock + H	Read document
Caps Lock + V	Repeat phrase
Caps Lock + W	Read window
Caps Lock + Page Up or Page Down	Increase or decrease the volume of the voice
Caps Lock + plus (+) or minus (-)	Increase or decrease the speed of the voice
Caps Lock + Spacebar	Do default action
Caps Lock + Left or Right arrows	Move to previous/next item
Caps Lock + F2	Show commands for current item
Press Caps Lock twice in quick succession	Turn Caps Lock on or off
Caps + Esc	Exit Narrator

Narrator touch keyboard shortcuts

The following table contains keyboard shortcuts for working with Narrator on a four-point touch-enabled PC.

Press this key	To do this
Tap once with two fingers	Stop Narrator from reading
Tap three times with four fingers	Show all Narrator commands (including the ones not in this list)
Double-tap	Activate primary action
Triple-tap	Activate secondary action
Touch or drag a single finger	Read what's under your fingers
Flick left/right with one finger	Move to next or previous item
Swipe left/right/up/down with two fingers	Scroll
Swipe down with three fingers	Start reading on explorable text

Remote Desktop Connection on the desktop keyboard shortcuts

The following table contains keyboard shortcuts for working with Remote Desktop Connection on the desktop.

Press this key	To do this
Alt+Page Up	Move between apps from left to right
Alt+Page Down	Move between apps from right to left
Alt+Insert	Cycle through apps in the order that they were started
Alt+Home	Display the Start screen
Ctrl+Alt+Break	Switch between a window and full screen
Ctrl+Alt+End	Display the Windows Security dialog box
Ctrl+Alt+Home	In full-screen mode, activate the connection bar
Alt+Delete	Display the system menu
Ctrl+Alt+minus (-) on the numeric keypad	Place a copy of the active window, within the client, on the Terminal server clipboard (provides the same functionality as pressing Alt+Print Screen on a local PC)
Ctrl+Alt+plus (+) on the numeric keypad	Place a copy of the entire client window area on the Terminal server clipboard (provides the same functionality as pressing Print Screen on a local PC)
Ctrl+Alt+Right arrow	"Tab" out of the Remote Desktop controls to a control in the host app (for example, a button or a text box). Useful when the Remote Desktop controls are embedded in another (host) app.
Ctrl+Alt+Left arrow	"Tab" out of the Remote Desktop controls to a control in the host app (for example, a button or a text box). Useful when the Remote Desktop controls are embedded in another (host) app.

Windows Help viewer keyboard shortcuts

The following table contains keyboard shortcuts for working with the Help viewer.

Press this key	To do this
F3	Move the cursor to the search box
F10	Display the Options menu
Home	Move to the beginning of a topic

End	Move to the end of a topic
Alt + Left arrow	Move back to the previously viewed topic
Alt + Right arrow	Move forward to the next (previously viewed) topic
Alt + Home	Display the Help and Support home page
Alt + A	Display the customer support page
Alt + C	Display the Table of Contents
Alt + N	Display the Connection Settings menu
Ctrl + F	Search the current topic
Ctrl + P	Print a topic

Calculator keyboard shortcuts

The following table contains keyboard shortcuts for working with Calculator.

Press this key	To do this
F1	Open Calculator Help
F2	Edit the calculation history
Alt + 1	Switch to Standard mode
Alt + 2	Switch to Scientific mode
Alt + 3	Switch to Programmer mode
Alt + 4	Switch to Statistics mode
Alt + C	Calculate or solve date calculations and worksheets
Ctrl + E	Open date calculations
Ctrl + H	Turn calculation history on or off
Ctrl + L	Press the MC button
Ctrl + M	Press the MS button
Ctrl + P	Press the M + button
Ctrl + Q	Press the M- button
Ctrl + R	Press the MR button
Ctrl + U	Open unit conversion
Ctrl + Shift + D	Clear the calculation history
F9	Press the +/– button
R	Press the 1/× button
@	Press the square root button
Del	Press the CE button
Up arrow	Navigate up in the calculation history
Down arrow	Navigate down in the calculation history
Esc	Press the C button or stop editing the calculation history
Enter	Recalculate the calculation history after editing
F3	Select Degrees in Scientific mode
F4	Select Radians in Scientific mode
F5	Select Grads in Scientific mode
Ctrl + B	Press the 3?x button in Scientific mode
Ctrl + G	Press the 10x button in Scientific mode

Ctrl + O	Press the cosh button in Scientific mode
Ctrl + S	Press the sinh button in Scientific mode
Ctrl + T	Press the tanh button in Scientific mode
Ctrl + Y	Press the y?x button in Scientific mode
D	Press the Mod button in Scientific mode
I	Press the Inv button in Scientific mode
L	Press the log button in Scientific mode
M	Press the dms button in Scientific mode
N	Press the ln button in Scientific mode
O	Press the cos button in Scientific mode
P	Press the pi button in Scientific mode
Q	Press the x^2 button in Scientific mode
S	Press the sin button in Scientific mode
T	Press the tan button in Scientific mode
V	Press the F-E button in Scientific mode
X	Press the Exp button in Scientific mode
Y	Press the x^y button in Scientific mode
#	Press the x^3 button in Scientific mode
;	Press the Int button in Scientific mode
!	Press the n! button in Scientific mode
F2	Select Dword in Programmer mode
F3	Select Word in Programmer mode
F4	Select Byte in Programmer mode
F5	Select Hex in Programmer mode
F6	Select Dec in Programmer mode
F7	Select Oct in Programmer mode
F8	Select Bin in Programmer mode
F12	Select Qword in Programmer mode
A-F	Press the A-F buttons in Programmer mode
J	Press the RoL button in Programmer mode
K	Press the RoR button in Programmer mode
<	Press the Lsh button in Programmer mode
>	Press the Rsh button in Programmer mode
%	Press the Mod button in Programmer mode
|	Press the Or button in Programmer mode
^	Press the Xor button in Programmer mode
~	Press the Not button in Programmer mode
&	Press the And button in Programmer mode
Spacebar	Toggles the bit value in Programmer mode
A	Press the Average button in Statistics mode
Ctrl + A	Press the Average Sq button in Statistics mode

S	Press the Sum button in Statistics mode
Ctrl + S	Press the Sum Sq button in Statistics mode
T	Press the S.D. button in Statistics mode
Ctrl + T	Press the Inv S.D. button in Statistics mode
D	Press the CAD button in Statistics mode

Calendar keyboard shortcuts

The following table contains keyboard shortcuts for working with the Calendar app.

Press this key	To do this
Ctrl + 1	Show the day view
Ctrl + 2	Show the week view
Ctrl + 3	Show the month view
Ctrl + T	Go to today
Ctrl + N	Create a new event
Page up	In month view, go to the previous month
In week view, go to the previous week	In day view, go to the previous two days
Ctrl + H	In month view, go to the previous month
In week view, go to the previous week	In day view, go to the previous two days
Page down	In month view, go to the next month
In week view, go to the next week	In day view, go to the next two days
Ctrl + J	In month view, go to the next month
In week view, go to the next week	In day view, go to the next two days
Right arrow	In a view, go to the next day
Left arrow	In a view, go to the previous day
Down arrow	In a view, go to the next hour
Up arrow	In a view, go to the previous hour
Esc Go back	
Ctrl + S	Save or send the event
Ctrl + P, use up and down arrows to select Respond to an event	
Ctrl + D	Delete an event

Mail keyboard shortcuts

The following table contains keyboard shortcuts for working with the Mail app.

Press this key	To do this
Ctrl + R	Reply
Ctrl + Shift + R	Reply all
Ctrl + F	Forward
Ctrl + M	Move item to a different folder
Ctrl + Shift + F	Hide or show the Folder pane
Ctrl + Shift + A	Hide or show the Accounts pane
Ctrl + U	Mark as unread
Ctrl + Q	Mark as read

Ctrl + A	Select all messages
Ctrl + N	New Message
F5	Sync
Alt + B	Put focus on the bcc button
Alt + C	Put focus on the cc button
Alt + D	Decline
Alt + S	Send mail
Alt + T	Put focus on the To button
Alt + V	Open the invitation in Calendar
Ctrl + Enter	Send mail
Ctrl + Shift + F	Select a font
Ctrl + Spacebar	Clear formatting
Ctrl + Y	Redo
F4	Redo
Ctrl + [	Increase font size one point
Ctrl +]	Decrease font size one point
Ctrl + Shift + ,	Decrease font size
Ctrl + Shift + .	Increase font size
Ctrl + K	Add a link
Ctrl + E	Center
Ctrl + L	Left
Ctrl + R	Right
Ctrl + Shift + L	Bullets
Ctrl + M	Indent when text is selected
Ctrl + Shift + M	Outdent
Tab or Shift + Tab	Indent/outdent when text is selected or when focus is in a list
Ctrl + '	Acute accent
Ctrl + ,	Cedilla accent
Ctrl + Shift + 6	Circumflex accent
Ctrl + Shift + ;	Diaeresis accent
Ctrl + `	Grave accent
Ctrl + Shift + 7	Ligature accent
Ctrl + Shift + 2	Ring accent
Ctrl + /	Slash accent
Ctrl + Shift + `	Tilde accent
Alt + Ctrl + Shift + 1	Inverted exclamation mark
Alt + Ctrl + Shift + /	Inverted question mark

Messaging keyboard shortcuts

The following table contains keyboard shortcuts for working with the Messaging app.

Press this key	**To do this**
Ctrl + N	Start a new conversation

Ctrl + N	Open the people picker
Ctrl + E	Open or close the emoticon picker
Ctrl + >	Next conversation
Ctrl + <	Previous conversation

Paint keyboard shortcuts

The following table contains keyboard shortcuts for working with Paint.

Press this key	**To do this**
F1	Open Paint Help
F11	View a picture in full-screen mode
F12	Save the picture as a new file
Ctrl + A	Select the entire picture
Ctrl + B	Bold selected text
Ctrl + C	Copy a selection to the Clipboard
Ctrl + E	Open the Properties dialog box
Ctrl + G	Show or hide gridlines
Ctrl + I	Italicize selected text
Ctrl + N	Create a new picture
Ctrl + O	Open an existing picture
Ctrl + P	Print a picture
Ctrl + R	Show or hide the ruler
Ctrl + S	Save changes to a picture
Ctrl + U	Underline selected text
Ctrl + V	Paste a selection from the Clipboard
Ctrl + W	Open the Resize and Skew dialog box
Ctrl + X	Cut a selection
Ctrl + Y	Redo a change
Ctrl + Z	Undo a change
Ctrl + plus (+)	Increase the width of a brush, line, or shape outline by one pixel
Ctrl + minus (-)	Decrease the width of a brush, line, or shape outline by one pixel
Ctrl + Page Up	Zoom in
Ctrl + Page Down	Zoom out
Alt (or F10)	Display keytips
Alt + F4	Close a picture and its Paint window
Right arrow	Move the selection or active shape right by one pixel
Left arrow	Move the selection or active shape left by one pixel
Down arrow	Move the selection or active shape down by one pixel
Up arrow	Move the selection or active shape up by one pixel
Shift + F10	Show the current shortcut menu

People app keyboard shortcuts

The following table contains keyboard shortcuts for the People app.

Press this key	To do this
Ctrl + N	Add a contact
Ctrl + S	Save changes
Delete	Delete a contact
Ctrl + F	Make a contact a favorite
Ctrl + Shift + 1	Pin a contact to Start
Esc	Go back
Home	Go to beginning of contact list
Page down	Go forward in the contact list
Page up	Go backwards in the contact list
End	Go to end of the contact list

Reader keyboard shortcuts

The following table contains keyboard shortcuts for working with the Reader app.

Press this key	To do this
F8	Use two-page layout
Ctrl + R	Rotate the file 90 degrees clockwise
Ctrl + F	Find text in a file
F7	Use keyboard selection mode
Ctrl + P	Print a file
Ctrl + O	Open a file
Ctrl + W	Close a file
Ctrl + M	Reader app home

Remote Desktop Connection keyboard shortcuts

The following table contains keyboard shortcuts for working with Remote Desktop Connection.

Press this key	To do this
Ctrl + Alt + Home	Toggle appbars between the remote PC and the one in front of you
Ctrl + Alt + Left arrow	Switch your view to the previous session (when viewing a session)
Ctrl + Alt + Right arrow	Switch your view to the next session (when viewing a session)
Ctrl + Alt + Up arrow	Switch your view to the first session (when viewing a session)
Ctrl + Alt + Down arrow	Switch your view to the last session (when viewing a session)

SkyDrive keyboard shortcuts

The following table contains keyboard shortcuts for working with SkyDrive.

Press this key	To do this
Ctrl + A	Select all
Ctrl + Alt + 1	Change view (details/thumbnails)
Ctrl + U	Upload
Ctrl + Shift + N	New folder

Esc	Clear selection
Ctrl + O	Open with
Ctrl + Alt + O	View folder
Ctrl + Shift + V	Copy
Ctrl + Shift + Y	Move
Ctrl + S	Download
Alt + Up arrow	Go up
F2	Rename
F5	Refresh

Windows Journal keyboard shortcuts

The following table contains keyboard shortcuts for working with Windows Journal.

Press this key	To do this
F1	Open Journal Help
F5	Refresh the note list
F6	Toggle between a note list and a note
F11	View a note in full-screen mode
Ctrl + A	Select all items on a page
Ctrl + C	Copy a selection to the Clipboard
Ctrl + F	Find text in a file
Ctrl + G	Go to a page
Ctrl + N	Start a new note
Ctrl + O	Open a recently used note
Ctrl + P	Print a note
Ctrl + S	Save changes to a note
Ctrl + V	Paste a selection from the Clipboard
Ctrl + X	Cut a selection
Ctrl + Y	Redo a change
Ctrl + Z	Undo a change
Alt + F4	Close a note and its Journal window
Ctrl + Shift + C	Display a shortcut menu for column headings in a note list
Ctrl + Shift + V	Move a note to a specific folder

WordPad keyboard shortcuts

The following table contains keyboard shortcuts for working with WordPad.

Press this key	To do this
F1	Open WordPad Help
F3	Find the next instance of the text in the Find dialog box
F10	Display keytips
F12	Save the document as a new file
Ctrl + 1	Set single line spacing
Ctrl + 2	Set double line spacing

Ctrl + 5	Set line spacing to 1.5
Ctrl + A	Select the entire document
Ctrl + B	Make selected text bold
Ctrl + C	Copy a selection to the Clipboard
Ctrl + D	Insert a Microsoft Paint drawing
Ctrl + E	Align text center
Ctrl + F	Find text in a document
Ctrl + H	Replace text in a document
Ctrl + I	Italicize selected text
Ctrl + J	Justify text
Ctrl + L	Align text left
Ctrl + N	Create a new document
Ctrl + O	Open an existing document
Ctrl + P	Print a document
Ctrl + R	Align text right
Ctrl + S	Save changes to a document
Ctrl + U	Underline selected text
Ctrl + V	Paste a selection from the Clipboard
Ctrl + X	Cut a selection
Ctrl + Y	Redo a change
Ctrl + Z	Undo a change
Ctrl + =	Make selected text subscript
Ctrl + Shift + =	Make selected text superscript
Ctrl + Shift + >	Increase the font size
Ctrl + Shift + <	Decrease the font size
Ctrl + Shift + A	Change characters to all capitals
Ctrl + Shift + L	Change the bullet style
Ctrl + Left arrow	Move the cursor one word to the left
Ctrl + Right arrow	Move the cursor one word to the right
Ctrl + Up arrow	Move the cursor to the previous line
Ctrl + Down arrow	Move the cursor to the line below
Ctrl + Home	Move to the beginning of the document
Ctrl + End	Move to the end of the document
Ctrl + Page Up	Move up one page
Ctrl + Page Down	Move down one page
Ctrl + Delete	Delete the next word
Alt + F4	Close WordPad
Shift + F10	Show the current shortcut menu

CHAPTER 13

Questions

In this chapter you will read about:

- Various questions based on the topics read in the chapters of the book.

Chapter 1 — Exploring Windows 8

1. How is Windows 8 different from other Windows?
2. Describe the online features of Windows 8.
3. How will you upgrade to Windows 8?
4. What are the requirements of Windows 8?
5. How would you view the information about your computer?

Chapter 2 — Getting Started with Window 8

1. What are Hot corners?
2. What is Charms bar?
3. Describe the working with Screen Appl.
4. How would you open and close an application?
5. Describe the process of viewing two applications side by side.

Chapter 3 — Use SkyDrive with Windows 8

1. What is SkyDrive?
2. How would you upload files to SkyDrive?
3. How would you install the SkyDrive Desktop Application?

Chapter 4 — Using the Search Feature

1. How would you search from the Start button?
2. Describe the various search options.
3. How would you search from the Desktop?
4. How would you search on a tablet?

Chapter 5 — Personalizing Your Start Screen

1. How would you view your personalization settings?
2. How would you change your lock screen picture?
3. Describe the process of changing your start screen background.
4. Describe the process of changing your account picture.
5. How would you turn a Live Tile Off?
6. What do you understand by pinning and unpinning an application on the start screen?
7. How would you create an application group?
8, Describe the process of naming an application group.

Chapter 6 — Desktop and Managing Files

1. Describe the process of working with files.
2. How would you open File Explorer?
3. Describe the process of deleting files.
4. How would you pin applications to the Taskbar?

5. Describe the following desktop effects:

   Snap — Peek

   Shake — Flip

6. Describe the various taskbar features.
7. How would you manage your files using File Explorer?
8. How would you sort files in the directory?
9. What is Search bar?
10. What are Libraries?
11. How would you add Folders to Libraries?

Chapter 7 — Personalizing Your Windows

1. How would you change the font size and text display?
2. Describe the process of adding contacts.
3. How would you edit contacts?
4. Describe the process of finding a Contact.
5. How would you link a contact?
6. How would you pin a contact?
7. Describe the process of changing the Profile picture.
8. What is Mail Application?
9. Describe the process of reading and replying to messages.
10. How would you organize your mail?
11. Describe the process of deleting a message.
12. How would you add multiple accounts?
13. Describe the process of modifying account settings.

Chapter 8 — Using Internet Explorer

1. How would you start Internet Explorer?
2. What is a Address Bar?
3. What are Tabs?
4. How would you set Favorite websites?
5. Describe the process of pinning a website.
6. Describe the process of setting security for a web site.

Chapter 9 — The Music and Video Applications

1. Describe the process of accessing your Music and Video Library.
2. How would you create a Xbox profile?
3. Describe the process of using the Music Application.
4. How would you buy music?

5. Describe the process of using Video Application.
6. How would you rent a movie?

Chapter 10 — Managing Your Accounts and Parental Controls

1. Describe the process of adding New Users.
2. How would you switch between users?
3. What are Parental Controls?
4. Describe the process of setting Parental Controls.

Chapter 11 — Security and Maintenance

1. What are the security features of Window 8?
2. Describe Windows Firewall.
3. What is Action Center?
4. How would you restore the System profile?
5. How would you open a file in the Default application?